MANAGING BY VALUES

All readers of this book are invited to have a personal online Value Audit Assessment by using the following link: **www.mbvsuite.com**

MANAGING BY VALUES

A Corporate Guide to Living, Being Alive, and Making a Living in the 21st Century

Simon L. Dolan, Salvador Garcia
and Bonnie Richley

First published 2006 by
PALGRAVE MACMILLAN
Houndmills, Basingstoke, Hampshire RG21 6XS and
175 Fifth Avenue, New York, N.Y. 10010
Companies and representatives throughout the world

PALGRAVE MACMILLAN is the global academic imprint of the Palgrave
Macmillan division of St. Martin's Press, LLC and of Palgrave Macmillan Ltd.
Macmillan® is a registered trademark in the United States, United Kingdom
and other countries. Palgrave is a registered trademark in the European
Union and other countries.

ISBN-13: 978–0–230–00026–1
ISBN-10: 0–230–00026–6

This book is printed on paper suitable for recycling and made from fully
managed and sustained forest sources.

A catalogue record for this book is available from the British Library.

Library of Congress Cataloging-in-Publication Data
Dolan, Simon.
   Managing by values : a corporate guide to living, being alive, and making a living
in the 21st century / by Simon L. Dolan, Salvador Garcia and Bonnie Richley.
      p. cm.
   Includes bibliographical references and index.
   ISBN 0–230–00026–6 (cloth)
      1. Management—Moral and ethical aspects. 2. Business ethics. I. Garcia,
Salvador (Sanchez Garcia), 1955– II. Richley, Bonnie. III. Title.
HF5387.D646 2006
174'.4—dc22   2006046257

10   9   8   7   6   5   4   3   2   1
15   14   13   12   11   10   09   08   07   06

Printed and bound in Great Britain by
Creative Print & Design (Wales), Ebbw Vale

To **Adela**, who really taught me the art of blending 'living', 'being alive' and 'making a living' … *Simon L. Dolan*

To **Amparo**, who provided the tender, loving and care, facilitating the pursuit of my utopian thoughts … *Salvador Garcia*

To **Anthony**, for always making my dreams come true … *Bonnie Richley*

Contents

Foreword
by Belmiro de Azevedo

I was asked by Professor Dolan to write a preface for this book on *Managing by Values*. His request reached me at a particularly perplexing moment in my professional life where I am seriously reflecting on the company that I have been managing for over 40 years with a team of exceptional colleagues and staff.

While I do not wish to abuse the patience of you, the reader, I thought that I would share with you some of my reflections and career highlights, in order for you to grasp the links between my thoughts and experience, and the theme of this book.

On 2 January 1965 I was 26 years old, had recently graduated in chemical engineering and had two years' working experience in a large textile company. I reached the conclusion that this company was 'large in size' (i.e. number of employees), but 'small' in its strategic thinking and practices, and therefore decided to change my career path, moving from a big company to a very small one – Sonae (Sociedade Nacional de Estratificados SARL).

At that time, Sonae had between 60 and 70 employees; the company was poorly managed, was characterized by the lack of a good product, and it was experiencing financial difficulties. I decided to bring about change in this company: it was a bold move and very challenging, especially because of the lack of clear corporate vision and strategy. During the change process, I relied heavily on my own personal values as well as on those of my staff in the search for the definition of a clear vision for the company. Parameters such as education, training, transparency, and courage served as a core to the development of this vision.

Now (over 40 years later), I recall that I was plagued with doubt as to whether my determination to keep on fighting made sense. In retrospect, I am sure that this early experience significantly boosted my confidence, and helped me greatly to overcome other important challenges encountered later on in my professional life. In general, this early strategy turned out to be successful, and the same principles are still being used today.

Currently, I lead an excellent team of young professionals (most are half of my own age). We question ourselves on a daily basis as to how to respond to the new challenges of innovation and globalization that confront so many companies. Many of these challenges are well described in *Managing by Values,* specifically the challenge of creating an organizational culture that is governed by a blend of ethical, social, strategic, economic, and emotional-psychological values.

Today, as I write this foreword during a short vacation in Mallorca (27 February 2006), it has been made public that our group has decided to launch a takeover bid for a large communications company in Portugal. The market value of this company is three or four times greater than the parent company of the Sonae group (Sonae SGPS). It is obvious that by launching this bid we will face all the usual problems and obstacles typical of this type of initiative.

The fundamental idea underlying this huge project was easy to define by myself and the members of the project team. However, to put it into practice is a rather more complex issue: it required more psychological courage than any previous situation we have known, mainly because of the size and complexity of the deal under way.

Thus, my penchant for the decision-making process included elements such as 'de-learning', and 're-learning' from previous experiences, the experience of taking a zigzag course in professional career, and sharing my thoughts with all members of our work team. All in all, it can be summed up in the following formula:

Success = (New knowledge − Old obsolete knowledge)
            + Lifelong enriching experience
            + Permanent appetite for undertaking new projects
              and innovating

To see if this formula really works will be another enormous test for all of us. Additionally, it will also be a test for our country (Portugal), for our government, and for the sector's regulatory bodies.

In order to assess the probability of success, I apply my classic battery of tests that you cannot find in your traditional management literature. None the less, my experience proves that it works:

The consistency test   Is what we want to do consistent with what we have done throughout the life history of the company?

The coherence test   Is what we want to do coherent with everything we have said before, in similar or identical situations? For example, is this an operation that will create added value, and maximize profits for company employees and shareholders? Are the contingencies available to managers to foster team integration

	(while creating conditions for others to leave), good enough to motivate remaining employees to engage in a better project? To what extent is the project transparent to all stakeholders (i.e. government and public authorities, consumers, employees, shareholders and other stakeholders)
The CHC test	**CHC** stands for the abbreviation of **C**apacities, **H**onesty and **C**onfidence. The question becomes: (1) Do we have managers with intellectual **C**apacities and experience to undertake and succeed in the project? (2) Do we have **H**onest managers who have demonstrated their transparency in relationships to working with colleagues, in sharing information, and in other relevant aspects? (3) If this is so, then do we have **C**onfidence (trust) in a group of people who will 'positively contaminate' many others in the company in question, to lead the acquired company to a promising future?

This introduction is closely related to a line of thought expressed in *Managing by Values*. In particular, three groups of values are selected: ethical-social, economic-pragmatic, and emotional-developmental. These are seen as absolute requisites, guaranteeing a company's sustained development in the 21st century's global and competitive environment. The application of these core values will guarantee social cohesion within a broader systematic renovation of both technical assets and human resources.

Any such transformation must always bring in the 3 **Hs**:

Head	for thinking
Heart	for being generous, compassionate but demanding
Hands	for carrying out transactions in the shortest possible time

Managing by Values makes a fine contribution towards rethinking rational analysis to incorporate personal emotional assessment and practical advice. Action is the word, not stopping short at the rhetorical advice of Aristotle and his followers to employ the discourse of persuasion.

While I recognize the importance of persuasion and communication in organizational life, I should add that *no work is complete if it lacks quality and timeliness in performance.*

I end these notes by predicting the tremendous success of this book. I trust that readers will understand the lesson taught throughout the book – that privilege and power for the few is not compatible with material and professional dependence for the rest.

Belmiro de Azevedo is Chairman of the Board of SONAE SGPS (see below)

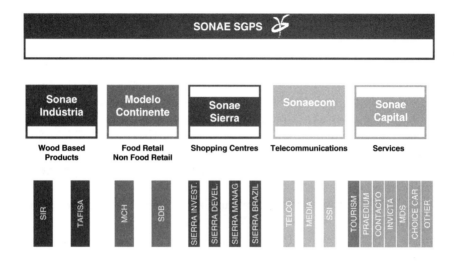

What is the significance of the Sonae symbol? The logo is made up of two germinating seeds, which signify the capacity for permanent growth and innovation in the Sonae Group. The seeds are surrounded by a ring of fire, the symbol of energy, movement and synergy between all of its business activities.

Foreword by John Abrams

In 1986 two long-time employees of my small design/build firm, South Mountain Company, came to talk to me. They told me they wished to continue their careers within the company, but that they felt they needed a stake – something more than a wage. I thought about this, and it became clear to me that this situation would arise over and over again if we did our job well and maintained a good place to work. So began a journey of exploration.

In 1987 I restructured the company into a worker-owned cooperative business loosely modeled on the Mondragon Cooperatives in the Basque region of Spain. It was a dramatic hinge point in our history that changed the company in many ways.

More than a decade later I spent four days in Mondragon learning first hand about the remarkable network of cooperatives that has thrived there since the 1950s, managing by values and transforming a community in the process. It was thrilling to experience the undertaking that had been the model for our business. In early 2006 Bonnie Richley contacted me to interview me about my Mondragon perspectives for her dissertation. We corresponded by e-mail; then we talked on the phone – she in Barcelona, me on Martha's Vineyard. She sent me some chapters from this book and asked me to write this foreword. I was pleased to have the opportunity.

We all know it at some level, but when we get down to business it is all too easy to forget: using money as the sole measure of prosperity fails to recognize that people have lives, families, and communities. Many people value the quality of their work environment as much as, or more than, the size of their paycheck. In addition to making a reasonably good living, we need to be satisfied by our work. We need the pleasure of good service, the joy of humor, the treasure of strong relationships, the fulfilment of collaboration, and the security of stability and longevity. Our enterprise must create sufficient profit to be able to serve all these worthy ends, but profit is simply the engine that drives a bottom line comprised of many parts.

Managing by Values. Is there any other way? We all manage by values, in some way, but our values diverge widely. This book is a lucid description of a set of values that is quite different from the norm, but that we may find is *becoming* the norm, and that will *be* the norm, I'm quite certain, in years to come. It makes too much sense for it not to be. Books like this one, and the good thinking found within, will pave the way.

The prescription put forth by the authors is the antidote to the traditional stifling command-and-control model: they describe a collaborative, people-centered, respectful form of leadership that unleashes creative potential. The book is a practical manual to help business leaders navigate the appropriate channels to substantive and successful company cultural change. Managing by Values is a tool that works in service to that goal. It makes the distinction between instructions (the tool of bosses), objectives (the tool of administrators) and values (the tool of leaders). It suggests that leaders who put values in front are more likely to be successful.

My experience suggests the same. The fifteen owners of South Mountain Company, and our non-owner employees who are on a path to ownership, practice our craft, run our business, and base our decisions primarily on values and only peripherally on profit. Profit is a tool to serve our expectation that we can, over time, be a restorative force, at least in some modest way. The essential values which guide us are shared ownership and workplace democracy, limited growth by intention rather than response to demand, commitment to place, and long-term thinking in the pursuit of craftsmanship and service of the highest quality. We hope that the company, and its service, will survive us, and, even, our children.

Since our restructuring, ownership has become available to all employees, enabling people to own and guide their workplace. The responsibility, the power, and the profits all belong to the group of owners. There are no outside investors and no non-employee owners. We decide what kind of business ours will be. The decisions are partly economic and partly philosophical, and the people making them have well-aligned interests.

Some people have a hard time believing that I gave up sole ownership and control, but they may not understand the tremendous rewards and benefits that derived from that decision, for me and for the company. I have the best job on the planet, and much of that is due to the colleagues who share ownership – and share the ride – with me.

A key element of our approach is hiring 'future owners' as opposed to employees. We envision people who enter the company staying and leading it forward. We don't know what they, as the perpetuators, will do or produce, but the essence of our collective enterprise will survive in them as they travel into a future we cannot even imagine. So we are not always looking for people with specific skill sets – often we can teach what we need to. We are looking for the kind of people we wish to share ownership with. This is, in a nutshell, Management by Values. And I am quite certain, although I can have no proof, that these values have been responsible for our minor successes. Corey Rosen, the director of the National Center for Employee Ownership, says, 'It's not about a *sense* of ownership. A sense of ownership is like a sense of dinner.'

In our case it's about the whole meal. This book is the whole meal, too.

It really is all about values. It doesn't matter if the organization is big or small. It only matters what drives us. And Managing by Values makes it clear that this is not about what we say, but about what we do. The authors say that 'the single most critical success factor for [Managing by Values] is congruence between what corporate leaders say they believe and what their actions and decisions communicate they believe, in both the short and long term.' This consistency is vital.

In the winters of 2002–3 and 2003–4, I took two six-month sabbaticals from work, to write a book, but also to be away from South Mountain Company and to give the company an opportunity to emerge from the shadow and constraints imposed by my leadership. Until December of 2002 never, for 28 years, had I been away from SMC for more than three weeks (and even that only once). So six months away, and then another six – it was very, very different.

Returning to South Mountain after the first six months, I found that things had gone well – no disasters at all – but the period had been marked by a bundle of stresses. Some felt they had shouldered unfair parts of the load. There was too little accountability. The management system we had put in place was ill-conceived. It felt slippery, like things were seeping through cracks. Between my return and my second departure, we worked on it, adjusted, tinkered, rerigged and realigned.

As I said, there were two parts to the sabbatical: to write a book and to give the company some space. As far as the second goes, the thrilling part – when I returned the second time – was to come back to a far better company than the one I left.

Managing the company in my absence gave people in the company a new sense of legacy. It brought visceral meaning to the idea that this company will endure far beyond my tenure, and the people truly stepped up, and took the reins, realized about themselves – especially the younger ones – that they are the people who will take on this task.

But we are still, quite clearly, a work-in-progress. In fact, we are only at the beginning of a long journey. There is so much room and need for improvement and growth that it is bound to fill lifetimes. A new company is under construction, and values are the blueprints. It was exciting to return and lend a hand.

One of the characteristics of the Managing by Values approach offered by the authors is Transformational Leadership that legitimizes change. That's what happened in our case – once change was legitimized, and deeply considered and worked on as well, the people in the company stepped up in remarkable ways.

I have hopes for this book. I hope it will be widely read by corporate leaders and I hope they will internalize the meaning of Managing by Values, begin to change their corporate cultures, and thereby change the way we think about business and the way we do business.

I recently saw an old friend with whom I had shared some powerful times in the late 1960s. We hadn't seen much of one another since the 1970s, but we had crossed paths now and then, at a conference or an event. Over the years he and his wife had five kids, a veritable tribe, but when I saw him he seemed mostly sad to me, unfulfilled, like someone whose life peaked too early and for whom the powerful momentum of a time could not be resurrected. But this time he seemed quietly joyous, satisfied, engaged, and comfortable. I said this to him: 'You seem different than when I've seen you in years past. What's changed?'

He looked at me and thought for a moment, and said, 'You know John, I have five kids. They're all in the area and I've come to realize that each of them is a kind person. Could I ask for anything more?' He didn't say they are successful. He didn't say they are powerful. He didn't say that they are intellectual giants, or that they are visibly changing the world. He said they are kind, and that he could ask for nothing more. I savored that moment. It was blissful in a way. At the same time there was a tension, because I felt envious that he could feel at once so peaceful and so clear about the source of his peace.

But then I realized that he had articulated, precisely, my penultimate goal for my company, and for the book you are about to read. I hope *Managing by Values* will encourage kindness, and the satisfaction that comes from it, in the often-unkind world of business.

John Abrams is co-founder and CEO of South Mountain Company, an employee-owned design-build company on Martha's Vineyard, Massachusetts. His 2005 book, *The Company We Keep: Reinventing Small Business for People, Community, and Place* (Chelsea Green), traces the history of South Mountain and explores the role of business as a potent force for cultural, social, and ecological progress.

The Authors

Born in Israel, and educated in Israel and the U.S., **Simon** (Shimon in Hebrew) **L. Dolan** is currently a full Professor of Work Psychology and Human Resource Management at ESADE, a world leading Business School in Barcelona (Spain). He obtained his doctorate (Ph.D.) at the Carlson Graduate School of Management, The University of Minnesota and taught over 25 years in Montreal (the Universities of Montreal and McGill). He is the former President and co-founder of the International Society for the Study of Work and Organizational Values (ISSWOV). He is co-author of more than 26 books in management and organizational psychology written in three languages, English, Spanish and French, and over 100 articles as well as book chapters in scholarly journals. Through his Montreal-based consulting firm, Gestion MDS Management Inc. (and more recently SPIRIT Consulting Group in Europe), he has consulted hundreds of organizations in N. America, Europe, Africa and the Middle East on subjects of human resource management, performance enhancement and management of change. Updated information on Prof. Dolan's activities can be obtained at his website at: www.mbvsuite.com/dolancv

Born in Spain and educated in Spain and the U.S., **Salvador Garcia** is currently an Associate Professor of Organizational Psychology at the University of Barcelona. He obtained his doctorate in Medicine (M.D.) in Spain and retrained as an organizational development specialist at Harvard Business School. He has been the President of the Spanish Organizational Development Society, and cofounder of the 'Utopia' movement (www.eutopia.es). Dr Garcia is the author (or coauthor) of four books related to the management of values and organizational stress. He had consulted numerous Spanish and Latin American organizations in the field of values, creativity and change management.

Born and educated in the U.S., **Bonnie Richley** is currently a Visiting Professor of Organizational Behavior in the Department of Human Resources at ESADE Business School in Barcelona. She recently completed her Ph.D. in Organizational Behavior from Weatherhead School of Management at Case Western Reserve University. She obtained her Masters of Science in Organizational Development (MSODA) from Weatherhead School of Management. She has consulted with organizations using Appreciative Inquiry methodology, experiential learning, leadership and development, and leading teams. She is also a certified executive coach in Emotional Intelligence competencies. Her research interests include the diffusion of values in social innovations, women in science and academia, change management and the creative process in organizing. She can be contacted at: b.richley@esade.edu

Acknowledgements

Simon L. Dolan wishes to thank three individuals, university professors in Minnesota and Israel, who, of all of his mentors, unknowingly had a formidable impact on his values and career: Prof. Arie Shirom, Tel Aviv University; Prof. Richard Hall, formerly of the University of Minnesota, currently at SUNY, Albany; and Prof. John Campbell, University of Minnesota. He also wishes to express gratitude to the members of the executive board and other active participants who acted along with him as founding members of the International Society for the Study of Work and Organizational Values (ISSWOV) back in the early 1980s; they helped him tremendously shape his values before, during and after the term of his presidency of ISSWOV (1994 to 1996); they include: from Israel – Dov Elizur, Meny Koslowsky and Rami Sagie (RIP); from the U.S. – Bill England, Luis Gomez-Mejia, David Balkin, Randall Schuler, Susan Jackson and Alison Conard; from Germany – Ingwer Borg; from Canada – Rabi Kanungo, W. Baba, Adnane Belout and Alan Auerbach; from Brazil – Fany Tchikovsky; from Japan – T. Yamauchi; from the U.K. – Susan Richbell and Cary Cooper; and from Spain – Ramon Valle Cabrera. He also wishes to thank ESADE Business School leadership (namely Carlos Losada, Xavier Mendoza and Ceferi Soler) for the support and the confidence trusted upon him by letting him lead the Institute for Labor Studies (IEL); for the past few years, he feels that he is not working anymore, but rather playing, and this 'feeling of playfulness' creates emotion and blends synergy amongst his peers; the end result translates into high 'MBV dividends' to all of ESADE stakeholders. Finally, Simon L. Dolan also wishes to thank his partners and associates in Spirit Consulting Group and Octrium BV for sharing the vision that MBV and the associated HR tools can and should become the flagship service to its corporate clients.

Salvador Garcia wishes to thank several people who have impacted upon his life and career. He is greatful to Dr Juan Wulff, psychoanalyst in San Pablo Hospital in Barcelona; Doctors Bayés de Luna and Manuel Wilke, cardiologists and founders of the coronary club 'Acard' that is presently presided over by Dr Jordi Rius; Dr Tom Thinkham, Professor of Organizational Behavior at Harvard; and Dr Simon Dolan, co-author of this book and its Spanish version whose scientific rigor and enthusiasm coupled with a good dosage of pragmatism has helped bring this project to a happy closure. His colleague at the University of Barcelona, Prof Santiago Quijano, has shown real camaraderie and support and his advice has been constructive in the shaping of his organizational behaviour knowledge. He also wishes to thank many of his patients, students and corporate clients that have helped him refine the concept of managing by values and made his own life philosophy richer and more fulfilling.

Bonnie Richley would like to thank her co-authors, Simon Dolan and Salvador Garcia, for inviting her to join them in such a rewarding endeavor as *Managing by Values*. She had learned from their experiences and perspectives in ways that have enriched her both professionally and personally. It is wonderful to be able to incorporate her research and interests on organizational values within the framework of MBV. MBV offers a way to move conversations about values from the margins and into the mainstream of organizational life that is desperately needed in today's challenging environment. She wishes to offer special thanks to Tony Lingham for his ongoing support and invaluable insight throughout the writing of this book. His belief in her and her work has given her the courage to do things she would have only dreamed about, and his wisdom and caring are never ending. Because this work is about values, specifically those central to our existence, it is important to thank her family for giving her a lifetime of learning about the value of unconditional love. A special thank you goes to Uncle Fred who reminded her to never give up no matter how long the journey or how tough the struggle; his brilliance is only outshone by his kindness. Also special thanks to David Cooperrider, from Weatherhead School of Management, who has been her anchor and guide throughout her educational journey, and other faculty members, in particular David Kolb, Eric Neilsen, Ron Fry, Richard Boyatzis, Melvin Smith, Sandy Piderit, Susan Case and Diana Bilimoria all of whom have positively impacted upon her life. Last, but certainly not least, she would like to thank her colleagues at ESADE for providing such wonderful opportunities to learn firsthand how values are very much a part of the life of a successful business school.

Finally, all three authors wish to acknowledge the great support and enthusiasm displayed by Palgrave Macmillan personnel involved in this project: Stephen Rutt, Global Publishing Director, believed in us, and in the project, and Alexandra Dawe has shown real professionalism and resourcefulness in mediating between us and the production department.

Barcelona, February 2006   SIMON L. DOLAN
                                                    SALVADOR GARCIA
                                                    BONNIE RICHLEY

Introduction

'Everything that can be counted does not necessarily count: everything that counts cannot necessarily be counted.'

(Albert Einstein, Physicist)

'It's not hard to make decisions when you know what your values are.'

(Roy Disney, Film Writer, Producer)

An overview

Recognizing the individual and collective value of employees to the success of any corporation has graduated from option to obligation. Seldom have the risks been higher for executives misguided enough to neglect the influence of both people and the corporate culture in which they work. Emerging labor shortages and changes in workforce demographics have created a seller's market in the North American work world. A growing trend toward knowledge workers and more highly educated employees has made effective human resource management a key metric separating the corporate wheat from the chaff.

Studies confirm that the way people are managed and developed delivers a higher return on investment than new technology, R&D, competitive strategy or quality initiatives,[1] and gives recruitment and retention advantages to those organizations demonstrating flexibility and innovation in their people policies. Other research linking employee effectiveness to shareholder returns[2] has helped crystallize through quantified bottom-line outcomes the imperative for recruitment excellence, clear reward policies and accountability, a collegial and flexible workplace culture, effective communication plans and prudent use of resources.

The broader implications of this reality are obvious for corporate contenders striving to enhance value through quality and customer-centricity in an increasingly complex, professionally demanding, and continuously changing global market. The system of beliefs and values that shaped the North American management and organizational model at the beginning of the 20th century is important in the new business paradigm. Traditional command and control management practices stifle the sparks of creativity critical to innovation and adaptation to a diverse environment and the ability to successfully compete. The changes of the 21st century have fuelled the drive for a fundamental rethinking of organizational structure and operating philosophy, toward a renewal of corporate culture.

Rigid management models based on hierarchical control of employees under conditions of relative stability externally and internally, are providing a shaky foundation for today's organizations existing amidst the turmoil of global and technological change. Stability must be created from within an organization and be embedded in a culture that preserves the best of its past and simultaneously fosters new ways of thinking and doing. The challenge is to retain effective mechanisms for monitoring results while stimulating the potential of each and every organizational member.

While just about everyone agrees with this proposition in theory, putting it into practice is another matter. Determining which values and beliefs to change, how and when to initiate the change process, how far to take it, and, most importantly, how to lead and steer cultural re-engineering without complete collapse, presents at the very least, major stumbling blocks. How can leaders and managers of change ensure that the opportunity for revitalizing a stagnant culture is both understood and leveraged?

Failing to fully grasp what is involved with instilling and nurturing new beliefs and values among employees at all levels destines to failure the successive fashions of such initiatives as Total Quality Management, Continuous Improvement, Just-In-Time Scheduling, Lean Management, and Business Process Re-Engineering. By neglecting an organization's foundation, namely its culture, all are fated to become mere management fads.

Countless analyses confirm the fallibility of such an approach. For instance, a recent study of the unremarkable performance reported by almost half of the companies that had implemented formal Value-Based Management (VBM) systems found that success was contingent on changes in corporate culture. Under VBM, companies use an economic profit measure to gauge performance and tie compensation to agreed-upon objectives in that metric. Survey results from 117 large VBM practitioners in North America, Europe and Asia led INSEAD researchers to conclude: 'VBM is about cultural, rather than financial, change. ... And therein lies the reason for most of the failures: Transforming beliefs in a large organization is, arguably, the most difficult of all managerial challenges ... seduced by the theoretical simplicity of VBM, companies may expect too much too soon and give up too early in the process' (Haspeslagh, Noda and Boulos, 2001, p. 66).[3]

In this book, we contend that the broader management models of Management by Instructions (MBI) and Management by Objectives (MBO) fail to position organizations for competitive success for the same reasons

VBM has failed. What is needed is a strategic leadership tool whose practical application will mine market potential through its relevance to individual organizational members. Management by Values (MBV) is just such a tool.

More than either MBI or MBO, MBV absorbs the complexity not easily realized in day-to-day work. MBV responds to the growing needs for quality and customer orientation, agile organizational structures, bosses as facilitators of their collaborators' success, and responsible autonomy and commitment by internal corporate stakeholders. By giving meaning to people's objectives and actions at work, MBV builds a culture that helps to channel daily professional efforts toward a company's strategic vision.

MBV may be considered neo-humanism. It proposes a cultural redesign consonant with the ideas that the humanistic focus of Organization Development has been successfully postulating since the mid-20th century. MBV facilitates inclusion of ethical and ecological principles into corporate strategic leadership and activities. This is vital for not only the long-term survival, but the prosperity of our world. It accommodates business ethics by regarding corporate beliefs and values as an opportunity for competitive differentiation, not as a threatening restriction on freedom of action.

Our approach

This book uses a two-pronged approach to present MBV. The logic of MBV precedes a discussion of its practical application, and the conceptual fundamentals of MBV are considered in the first four chapters.

Chapter 1 defines and explains MBV as an evolution of earlier management philosophies focused on, first, instructions, then objectives. Chapter 2 delves further into the essence of MBV and the general concept of company or corporate culture. Here, the power of values to transform behavior is considered. Chapter 3 discusses the need for organizations to be open to cultural change and reflects on the depth of change implicit in cultural redirection. Chapter 4 explores in more depth the logical differences between a culture oriented towards control and one focused on developing people. Understanding these differences is essential to the process of reformulating values, a precursor to cultural conversion.

We then focus on how to put MBV into practice. Chapter 5 presents the fundamentals of implementing change and how to overcome resistance inherent in every culture shift. While different strategies are considered, the level of communication skills necessary is emphasized. Chapter 6 describes the different roles played by protagonists in the cultural change process. Particular attention is paid to the critical role of leaders in such an initiative. Chapter 7 proposes a sequence of stages or phases of action for the process and intervention tools for initiating, consolidating and maintaining MBV. The focus on culture change and MBV is then addressed in Chapter 8 through a discussion of most frequently asked questions followed by suggestions for practitioners.

Lastly, in the postscript, we suggest that corporations can strive to achieve their potential by applying the concepts of MBV to its fullest. We try to present this approach not as utopian but rather as a very practical and yet challenging method to create better workplaces that enhance human capacity and exceptionality through value alignment and integration. We conclude by strongly reinforcing our message that MBV, when cultivated as central to an organization's culture, invariably generates corporate success in the present and for the future.

Intended audience

This book is written for leaders, managers and innovative business people. It is also relevant for students of management and organizational development. We hope that from the outset you are already convinced of three essential prerequisites:

- That you are paid, first and foremost, to *think and to learn*;
- That you have the responsibility to lead, drive, and to support and/or facilitate the cultural changes strategically necessary for your organization's success and its survival in an increasingly volatile and internationally competitive market; and
- That you are a 'valuable' member in a global society that depends on everyone to create a better tomorrow than we have today.

This book intends to help you discover the potential for creating added value by being a leader of change by means of values. It aims to help both present and future managers acquire theoretical perspectives that directly address the key practical issues and concerns in today's business world. Or to understand, as the late social psychologist Kurt Lewin so powerfully yet simply stated, 'There is nothing so practical as a good theory.'

Lastly – among our target readers, since, here, we assume we are preaching to the converted – we hope to provide at least a few ideas of use in the professional pursuits of fellow teachers, trainers and consultants.

Special features

The bid by most management books to be all-inclusive often results in them being complex, daunting, confusing and outdated. The form and content here is designed to blend the classic with the current, just a bit of theory and a large serving of the practical. The chapters are integrated and sequenced to flow naturally, yet each is sufficiently self-contained to permit reflection and assessment. Although we would like readers to contemplate the ideas presented, **Core Concepts** have been highlighted to capture the essentials and enable the busy person to skim and grasp the principal messages.

> **Core concepts have been highlighted to capture the essentials**

Throughout the book we pose key questions denoted by the following captions: **Action/Reflection** and **Reality Check**. These inquiries are designed to provoke interaction between reader and text and to encourage focused thinking and action planning to support the change process. Brief assessments are included at significant junctures to further understand central concepts of MBV. In addition, we offer examples from leading North American, Japanese and European corporations to illustrate various concepts.

We also present information about the Management by Values website: www.mbvsuite.com. The **MBVsuite**™ is an online software system designed to give an instant assessment of your own personal values compared to the values of your organization, team or other work units. An **access code** is included at the end of the book to provide you with a free trial of the MBV software online. Please login to the web link provided and use the access code for free diagnosis. We believe that by experiencing MBV personally you will begin to realize why it is an essential tool to help move both you and your organization successfully into the 21st century.

It should be noted that although every attempt has been made to cut redundancies, reference is made repeatedly to a few fundamental concepts. This reflects a belief that 'repetition is the key to new learning and change.' Hopefully, the fine line between useful and tedious repetition has not been transgressed.

We hope that you will find reading this book an experience as pleasant and intriguing as its writing has been for us. Additional information about Management by Values may be found at the MBV websites: (1) www.managementbyvalues.com and (2) www.mbvsuite.com. Any comments you wish to make towards the development of MBV will be gratefully received by email at any one of the following addresses: simon.dolan@esade.edu; sgarcia@psi.ub.es; or bar2@case.edu.

Notes

1.   For instance, a UK study, reported in *Management Today*, provides quantified results to support the effect that human resources has on bottom-line

performance. In a seven-year effort, the Institute of Personnel and Development measured the balance sheet results of 100 medium-sized manufacturing companies. It found that human resource management accounted for 19 per cent of the variation in productivity between companies and 18 per cent of the difference in profitability, more than double the outcome produced by research and development. Moreover, researchers determined that initiatives in quality improvement, new technology and competitive strategy contributed barely more than a 1 per cent gain in income. J. Oliver (1998, March), 'Invest in People and Improve Profitability and Productivity', *Management Today*. tsupport@bellhowell. inforlearning.com

2. A study by Watson Wyatt Consulting determined that the Human Capital Index, which uses a formula to assess the impact of various human resource practices on corporate performance and presents it in a summarized index, proves a clear relationship exists between the effectiveness of a company's human capital and superior shareholder returns. Further, investigators using a simple set of measures to quantify which human resource practices and policies have the most influence on shareholder value concluded that recruitment excellence, clear reward policies and accountability, a collegial and flexible workplace culture, effective communication plans, and prudent use of resources significantly enhance shareholder values. I. Kay and R. Luss (1999), *Creating Superior Returns to Shareholders through Effective Human Capital Management, The Watson Wyatt Human Capital Index*. See also: *Human Capital Index: Linking Human Capital and Shareholder Value.* http://www.watsonwyatt.com/homepage/Human_Capital_Index/index.htm

3. Haspeslagh, P., Noda, T., and Boulos, F. (2001, July–August), 'Managing for Value: It's Not Just About the Numbers', *Harvard Business Review*, 79, pp. 65–73.

Part I
Management by Values: Logic and Content

1 Managing by Values: Its Foundation and Evolution

'Mutual trust is a critically important lubricant for the working of social systems.'

(Kenneth J. Arrow, Winner of Nobel Prize for Economics, 1972)

'Greed is good!'

(Gordon Gecko, Movie, *Wall Street*, 1985)

The world is seeing a marked shift in management focus. Managers are being held to higher standards of performance as a result of society's increased demands concerning professional responsibility, quality and customer service. Managers must be able to lead and to facilitate necessary change in order to respond to these expectations. The world has also become a more uncertain and complex place. Managers must also possess the abilities needed to confront continuous and increasing levels of complexity both internal and external to the organization.

In the past, the progress of any entity (i.e., person, organization, society), was primarily determined by its ability to become bigger, richer or faster. In the 21st century's global arena, and in the wake of corporate scandals, wars and natural disasters, progress and success is moving toward being measured also by that which is core to our humanness – our values. Leaders and managers are perhaps facing the biggest challenge in history, | Shaping, developing and adequately rewarding the achievement of shared values is one of the most important tasks of a leader.

how to create and maintain successful organizations based on what is equally good for business, people and society. Indeed, shaping, developing and adequately rewarding the achievement of this tripartite mission is fast becoming the most important task of a leader who wishes to promote behavior directed towards corporate success.

Harmonizing the beliefs and values of the owners of a company and employees is a vital source of competitive advantage. What can better

3

motivate performance, or strengthen an organization, even a small team, than genuinely shared – and lived – values? Yet, as widely accepted as this truth is, how many companies can actually articulate the principles of action or essential values that guide day-to-day working activity and behavior? The most important information for organisational leaders and managers of the 21st century may well be to learn how to put values into practice.

It is no surprise then that Management by Values (MBV) is fast becoming the principal driver for the 'how to' toward developing a sustainable, competitive and more humane culture. MBV can be defined as both a managerial philosophy and practice whereby focus is concurrently maintained on an organisation's core values *and* aligned with its strategic objectives. This approach focuses on three value-based domains: (1) Economical–Pragmatic; (2) Ethical–Social; and (3) Emotional-Developmental.

MBV acknowledges that the essence of true leadership has always been marked by human values. A leader's job is to compel the organization to move in alignment with its strategic direction and its core values. This is done by creating a shared culture of value creation that implicitly and explicitly guides the daily activities of employees at all levels and in all functions. By 'humanizing' its basic strategic vision, a firm can nurture its own survival and growth, maximizing economic returns by establishing buy-in among both internal and external stakeholders.

> The essence of true leadership has always been marked by human values.

A generic definition of MBV can be divided into two elements: *MBV is a 'new' strategic leadership tool.* More than a new way of managing a company, MBV is a new way of understanding and applying knowledge. It stems from an approach developed by social psychologists and other behavioral scientists in the mid-20th century. Variations of MBV exist worldwide, a result of managerial response to the imperatives of corporate survival and differentiation. MBV is the practical outcome of the theoretical implementation of the now classic techniques found in the field of organizational development. This application is aimed at the basic goal of introducing the human or personal dimension into management thinking, not only theoretically, but also in daily work activity.

> MBV is a flexible framework for ongoing renewal of corporate culture, critical for inspiring the collective commitment to creativity of which innovation is borne.

MBV is also a flexible framework for ongoing renewal of corporate culture, critical for inspiring the collective commitment to creativity of which innovation is born (Dolan and

Garcia, 2002). For instance, if a firm's performance priority is professional quality, then qualitative factors, or values, such as trust, creativity or honesty, are as or more important than traditional economic measures, like efficiency or return on investment.

Accustomed to considering themselves 'rational' professionals, managers customarily disregard their firm's system of established values, underestimating the substantial worth and potential contributions of this very real asset. They fail to properly manage, and mine, their organization's values system, opting to focus on more tangible pursuits, like budgets, taxes or technology. Proof of the financial power inherent in managing by values is demonstrated by Siebel Systems, Inc. Founded in 1993, Siebel Systems has grown to become the world's leading provider of eBusiness application software. Specializing in Customer Relationship Management, the company's revenue exceeded $2 billion during the four quarters ending 30 June 2001, and net income topped $263 million for the same period. Its three-year annual rate of revenue growth reached 106 per cent and its three-year annual rate of growth in earnings per share 155 per cent.[1]

That performance secured Siebel Systems top place among Fortune's 100 fastest-growing companies in 1999, third place in 2000 and second in 2001. *Business Week* named CEO Thomas Siebel as one of the world's top 25 managers in January 2001 and tagged the company the second leading information technology firm globally in July 2000.[2]

The firm's impressive financial performance is not a result of an approach aimed at growing revenue, market share or stock price. Rather, it is the outcome of integrating the values implicit in its line of business into a corporate philosophy dedicated to customers.

> We are in business to make our customers successful. This is our fundamental philosophy. We regard it as a privilege to serve our customers and are committed to doing *whatever it takes* to ensure our customers are 100 per cent satisfied. All of us at Siebel Systems gauge our success by our customers' success … We judge ourselves individually and collectively based on how our customers are fulfilling *their* business objectives. Based on this commitment, we have achieved the highest levels of customer satisfaction in the software industry.[3]

MBV's usefulness as a leadership tool may be considered at various levels, but its basic purpose is threefold: to simplify; to guide; and to secure commitment.

> MBV has a threefold purpose: to simplify; to guide; and to secure commitment.

- Simplifying involves cutting through the organizational complexity created by the ever-increasing need to adapt to change at all levels in a company.
- Guiding means channeling strategic vision towards the future.
- Securing commitment involves translating the goals of strategic management into people policies designed to nurture employees' commitment to quality professional performance in their day-to-day work.

The evolution of MBV: from MBI, through MBO, to MBV

The increasing complexity, uncertainty and rapidity of change that emerged in the 20th century work world have fuelled an evolution in organizational management. The traditional approach of Management by Instructions (MBI), prevalent at the beginning of the century, gave way in the 1960s to the still popular Management by Objectives (MBO). Now, a new approach is surfacing: Management by Values (MBV).

  Figure 1.1 presents a schematic view of the evolution from MBI to MBO resulting in MBV. This evolution is a consequence of the emergence in recent decades of four organizational trends that have forced organizations to adapt to remain competitive in increasingly demanding and unpredictable markets.

MBI = Management by Instructions; MBO = Management by Objectives; MBV = Management by Values

Figure 1.1 **Evolution of three ways of managing companies: by instructions, by objectives and by values[4]**

These four interconnected trends, in turn, heighten organizational complexity and uncertainty. They are:

1. The need for quality and customer orientation;
2. The need for professional autonomy and responsibility;
3. The need for 'bosses' to evolve into leaders/facilitators; and
4. The need for 'flatter' and more agile organizational structures.

THE NEED FOR QUALITY AND CUSTOMER ORIENTATION

> Competition today requires that value be continuously added to productive processes to ensure complete customer satisfaction.

Companies that want to survive and compete in an increasingly demanding market must recognize the inappropriateness of the industrial management models from the beginning of the 20th century. Designed to enable production of huge quantities of standardized products, they are now antiquated and ineffective. Competition today requires that value be continuously added to productive processes to ensure complete customer satisfaction with the relationship between product price and quality/performance. A key competitive dynamic of The New Economy, personalization, epitomizes this trend. One company, JetBlue Airways provides an example of how values are translated into their corporate culture of customer service.

THE COLOR OF SUCCESS: JETBLUE

JetBlue Airways is an example of how one organization created a values-centered approach that led to a culture of success. Guided by a desire to serve, David Neeleman, CEO and founder of JetBlue Airways has channeled this energy into building a thriving company while much of the industry struggles to survive. As Gareth Edmondson-Jones, VP of Corporate Communications, says,

> We wanted to bring the humanity back to airline travel. It's not enough just to launch a low-fare airline that can be undersold by the big carriers.

To achieve this, they instill an attitude of friendly, compassionate, caring service in the air and on the ground. After safety, customer service is the main feature of training for JetBlue staff. And there's no dead wood on board. Crewmembers whose attitudes don't soar are deplaned altogether (which means they are looking for jobs on all those *other* airlines … you've been warned). This attention to internal brand management is boosting JetBlue's external brand – on flights where the big carriers match JetBlue's prices, passengers still choose to fly JetBlue. That can only mean the leather seats, extra legroom, and kindly service is having an impact on a sore group of fed-up flight victims.

When asked what the greatest offense of the large carriers is, Edmondson-Jones hit the nail on the head by saying,

> Indifference. Indifference directed at the passenger. It's easy to feel that you've lost your dignity flying the big guys. You are a number and a boarding pass. It's like a cattle call.... Everyone's trying to shave three or four cents off a passenger. Passenger expectations are so low that when you help them with their baggage, it's a real shock from what they're used to.[5]

As for serving others, CEO David Neeleman believes in living his values:

> This week I'm flying to Florida for work, and on the way down and back I'll serve drinks and snacks along the with the crew and take out the garbage when we're done. It's a chance to serve the customer directly. On a much larger scale, we run what we call the JetBlue Crewmember Crisis Fund: everyone gives money to it, and it's used to help employees in crisis.
>
> When employees know they're coming to a great job where they get full benefits – and that if something terrible happens to them the other employees will help them out – they do their best work, and they serve their customers well.[6]

THE NEED FOR PROFESSIONAL AUTONOMY AND RESPONSIBILITY

Technology, from robotics and process automation to data telecommunication and state-of-the-art management information systems, has heightened the demand for quality and customized service. As a result, the level of professional knowledge and skills required of employees has ballooned.

Accompanying the need for enhanced employee professionalism and creativity are higher expectations from capable recruits that they will be treated as mature individuals with their own performance criteria. Professionals can articulate their own values and translate them into initiatives, into creative behavior at work. They are autonomous, flexible and committed employees. A professional without autonomy is not a real professional, only an operative or dependent worker. Autonomy is essential to accepting responsibility.

Named America's No. 2 computer and office equipment company by Fortune 500 in April 2000, Hewlett-Packard Company recognized the power of an autonomous workforce when it drafted its corporate objectives more than four decades ago. Combined with a management style built on mutual trust and understanding and an agile organizational structure, HP and its subsidiaries now have 88,500 employees in 120 countries[7,8] and realized more than $48.7 in net revenue in fiscal 2000.

HP sees 'the individual, the personal dignity of each and the recognition of personal contributions' as critical to its success. 'In the final analysis, people at all levels determine the character and strength of our company.'[9] It expresses those beliefs by valuing autonomy:

> Autonomy fosters individual motivation, initiative and creativity, and gives employees the opportunity to work with a wide latitude of freedom in achieving common goals and objectives.[10]

THE NEED FOR 'BOSSES' TO EVOLVE INTO LEADERS/FACILITATORS

Employee autonomy, in turn, drives the need for facilitating leaders who ensure the right things happen. A facilitative management style eliminates the reactive tendency typical of administrators always on the defensive, an approach bred by the hierarchical control structures of the early and middle 20th century. The contemporary approach is that 'a boss should be the facilitator of the success of his or her colleagues.'

Instructions are the management tools of bosses, and objectives are those of administrators. Leaders use values. While few

> **Instructions are the management tools of 'bosses' and objectives are those of administrators. Leaders use values.**

REALITY CHECK

HAVE YOU DONE ANYTHING **WORTHWHILE** LATELY?

WORTHWHILE MAGAZINE – Pursuing work with purpose, passion and profit!

'WORTHWHILE was created by Anita Sharpe and Kevin Salwen, veterans of The Wall Street Journal, with four decades of financial journalism experience and a Pulitzer Prize between them. The editorial mission of WORTHWHILE is to put purpose and passion on the same plane as profit. WORTHWHILE offers a roadmap for business success that is more personally fulfilling and socially responsible. We live by the motto that it is impossible to have a meaningful life without meaningful work.'

What do you value, and maybe more importantly, where are your values leading you?

Source: WORTHWHILE Online Magazine
http://www.worthwhilemag.com

concepts are as extensively discussed as leadership, there is agreement on its essential characteristic: to inspire, channel the efforts and hold together teams of professionals. No matter how effective leadership is defined, it is fundamentally something much more complex than traditional command and control management.

THE NEED FOR 'FLATTER' AND MORE AGILE ORGANIZATION STRUCTURES

Bureaucratic structures, with their hierarchical levels and watertight compartments, are too rigid for effective competitiveness in open market environments. Reducing the number of levels in a hierarchy has been proven to enhance organizational efficiency. Today, few would dispute the need for flatter corporate structures and efficient work teams. However, these needs are more easily articulated than achieved. Those who have actually attempted such a task best understand its challenges.

A traditional culture oriented towards hierarchical control typically groups employees into three categories:

1. Those who direct and think (or are supposed to);
2. Those who control those who produce; and
3. Those who produce.

Figure 1.2 suggests that the mistrust or lack of confidence felt by 'those who direct and think' about the capacity for responsible autonomy by 'those who produce' drives the need for a substantial number of people dedicated to controlling and supervising work. Under such a framework, those who work and succeed in satisfying customers' needs usually do so in spite, not because of the control exercised by middle managers.

Some 'bosses', but only a few first-class ones, continue to be necessary, but not as controllers of irresponsible operatives. Rather, their role should be to transmit values, facilitate work processes, and allocate and co-ordinate resources. Otherwise, that vital quality sought of employees, initiative, will be squelched.

> Some 'bosses', but only a few first-class ones, continue to be necessary, but not as controllers of irresponsible operatives. Rather, their role should be to transmit values, facilitate work processes, and allocate and co-ordinate resources.

Emergence of a global market economy has fueled the need for new organizational structures that can react to changes with greater agility; are based on networks, project

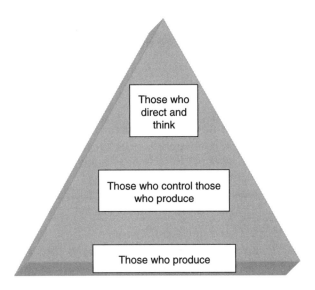

Figure 1.2 **The three levels of the vertical company oriented towards hierarchical control: 'top-down management'**

- **Those who direct and think** (and lack confidence in the capacity for responsible autonomy by those who produce)
- **Those who control those who produce** (inspired by the lack of confidence of those who direct and think in those who produce)
- **Those who produce** (in spite of control by those in the middle and the lack of confidence of those at the top)

teams and 'mini-businesses' or strategic business units; and go beyond the standard decentralization models. Such structures are replacing the hierarchical bureaucratic models that date back to the beginning of industrial development.

As compelling as the arguments are for more flexible and horizontal organizational charts, effecting such a transformation is challenging. Further, a flattened corporate framework generates much more ambiguity and uncertainty than the raked or pyramid schematics of bureaucratic hierarchies. Nevertheless, horizontal organizations remain the structure of choice.

Dana Corporation, a leading supplier of components, modules and complete systems to global vehicle manufacturers and their related aftermarkets, began the exercise of organizational flattening in the 1980s. Founded in 1904 in Toledo, Ohio, Dana has more than 300 major facilities in 34 countries and employs over 78,000 people. Winner of the prestigious Malcolm Baldrige National Quality Award in 2000, its second such award, Dana reported sales of $12.3 billion in 2000.[11]

Dana's bid to eliminate as many middle management and supervisory positions as possible started, for instance, by reducing to eight from 12 the number of levels between Dana's president and front-line workers in its Ohio head office. Accompanying this initiative was the establishment of autonomous strategic business units. By the end of the decade, the resulting rise in employee and customer satisfaction, coupled with markedly higher profits, led to a commitment to organizational flattening that continues today.

Dana's operations are now conducted through seven strategic business units focused on the company's primary markets in the automotive, commercial vehicle and off-highway sectors, which 'allows Dana people in each of these areas to leverage their resources to best serve Dana's global customers.'[12] Moreover, the firm's efforts to flatten its organizational structure has resulted in there now being only five layers of management to its World Operating Committee.[13]

In Figure 1.1, another important factor, tied to the increasing challenge generated by the four adaptive trends, can be seen. The complexity, represented by the rising curved arrow, is not linear; it starts to fall again in the top right-hand area of the graph, indicating that MBV serves to absorb – thus reduce – the effects of growing complexity. In other words, an organization that has genuinely clear, accepted and shared values will become much more efficient in accommodating creativity and exploiting complexity and uncertainty. It will outdistance competitors operating solely on specific objectives or, even more so, simply obeying instructions or observing a procedural manual.

Why? As much as objectives and instructions reduce complexity, and may even succeed in eliminating it or nullifying its effects on employees, they stifle the innovation possible when professionals are able to be truly creative. Employees, who become accustomed to complexity, not only tolerating it, but also absorbing it, are able to mine it. A truly competitive company cannot allow itself the luxury that its employees do not know how to tolerate, or be unwilling or incapable of tolerating, complexity and uncertainty.

Nowadays, being capable of tolerating ambiguity is a prerequisite for engaging in organizational life (Soto et al., 2005). One might even go so far as to say that the ability to tolerate ambiguity is a key competency for both personal and professional development. A person who only wishes to know which button to press when a certain light flashes is not tolerating any ambiguity or complexity. The likelihood is that he will remain pressing the same button in response to the same light. Such people, are, in effect, automatons. This does not mean that values eliminate the need for objectives, nor even for instructions. What values do is make both objectives and instructions more meaningful, more sensible and more acceptable.

Because the environment has changed so dramatically, managers have found it necessary to alter their practice to meet the needs of the times. In

HENRY MINTZBERG ON THE FLATTENING TRUTH

Henry Mintzberg is a leading management scholar. His view about the complexities of theory and practice in management is reflected in the following excerpt:

I am a great believer in the flat earth theory. We thought we discovered TRUTH several hundred years ago: the earth is not flat, it is round. Out with the old, in with the new.

Well, I flew into Schiphol Airport in Amsterdam recently, and, looking out the window, I thought: can anyone really believe they corrected for the curvature of the earth in building that runway? In other words, for certain very practical purposes, the flat earth theory remains perfectly acceptable. Of course, I hope the pilot didn't use it on his flight in from Gothenburg. For flying airplanes, the round earth theory isn't bad. But it is no more truth than the flat earth theory, or else airplanes coming into Geneva from Italy would smash into the Alps (i.e. the earth is not perfectly round either; it is bumpy. Moreover, it is not really round at all, since it bulges at the center).

The point is that it is arrogant to consider any theory true, new or old. All theories are false – they are just words and/or notations and/or exhibits on pieces of paper. Theories are more or less useful, that is all, depending on the circumstances, which means old theories can sometimes be as useful as new theories.

Excerpt from Mintzberg (1988)

the early 20th century, management by instruction (MBI) was considered to be an appropriate and adequate way to run an organization. Change happened at a slower pace and therefore the way things were done in the past worked well enough to pass on to others. By the 1960s, change was accelerating to the point where more flexibility of action was required by managers. Thus, the introduction of management by objectives (MBO) enabled managers to agree on a direction and to choose their own strategy. As changes in the environment began to intensify (e.g., global competition, impact of technology), however, MBO proved to be an insufficient strategy for managing in an interconnected and fast-paced world.

In fact, organizations still relying on MBO often discover that their managers fail to meet their objectives. Frustration also increases when, in spite of their best efforts, they are unable to determine what went wrong. Many times it is not that the goals were lofty or unrealistic, simply, many unforeseen changes occurred that were not and could not be predicted. As a result of this growing complexity, scholars began to draw upon chaos and systems theories as a way to better understand organizational behavior. During this period organizations came to be seen as complex and dynamic systems existing in a state of flux and interaction with their environment.

Years of research has confirmed that the key to understanding the behavior of such systems is to understand the corresponding values of these living systems. Values systems are the motivators that drive the behavior of individuals, organizations and society, leading to the emergence of management by values (MBV) today.

The three management approaches represented by MBI, MBO and MBV may be distinguished from one another on the basis of 14 metrics, summarized in Table 1.1.

Triaxial model and key factors of MBV

We propose a method to understand MBV as managing three facets (or dimensions) of an organization's value system that affects general human behavior: (1) economic-pragmatic values; (2) ethical-social values and (3) emotional-developmental values. The MBV taxonomy of values can be observed and applied to most organizations, and can be described as follows:

- **Economic-pragmatic values** are necessary to maintain and bring together various organizational sub-systems. They include values relating to efficiency, performance standards and discipline. These values guide such activities as planning, quality assurance and accounting.
- **Ethical-social values** of individuals guide the ways they behave in a group setting. Ethical-social values emerge from beliefs held about how people should conduct themselves in public, at work and in relationships. They are associated with social values such as honesty, congruence, respect and loyalty. A person's ethical-social values will influence how they behave when living their personal economic-pragmatic values and their emotional-developmental values.
- **Emotional-developmental values** are essential to create new opportunities for action. They are values related to trust, freedom and happiness. Examples of such values are creativity/ideation, life/self actualization, self-assertion/directedness, and adaptability/flexibility.

The instrumentality of such classifications have been demonstrated in understanding the tendencies of values (and behavior) of future executives as revealed in a recent study of mature MBA students enrolled in 28 leading business schools throughout the globe.[14]

MBV offers a triaxial model of values-based management centered on identifying the 'corporate core' (key organizational values) and building a culture in alignment with these values and the organization's strategic objectives (Figure 1.3).

Table 1.1 **Primary characteristics of MBI, MBO and MBV**

	MBI	MBO	MBV
Preferred situation for application	™Routine work or emergencies	™Moderately complex ™Relatively standardized production	™Need for creativity to solve complex problems
Average level of professionalism of organization's members	™Management of operatives	™Management of employees	™Management OF professionals
Leadership type	™Traditional	™Focused on resource allocation	™Transformational (Legitimizes transformations)
Image of customer	™User buyer	™User customer	™Discriminating customer with freedom of choice
Product market type	™Monopolistic, standardized	™Segmented	™Highly diversified, dynamic
Type of organizational structure	™Multi-tiered pyramid	™Pyramid with few levels	™Networks, functional alliances, project teams
Need for tolerance of ambuguity	™Low	™Medium	™High
Need for autonomy, responsibility	™Low	™Medium	™High
Type of Market	™Stable	™Moderately variable	™Unpredictable, dynamic
Social organization	™Capitalistic industrial	™Capitalistic post-industrial	™Post-capitalistic
Philosophy of control	™Top-down control, supervision	™Control and stimulation of professional performance	™Self-supervision encouraged
Organizational purpose	™Maintain production	™Optimize results	™Continually improve processes
Reach of strategic vision	™Short term	™Medium term	™Long term
Core cultural values	™Quantitative production ™Loyalty, conformity, discipline	™Measuring results ™Rationalization, motivation, efficiency	™Developing participation, continuous learning. ™Creativity, mutual trust, commitment

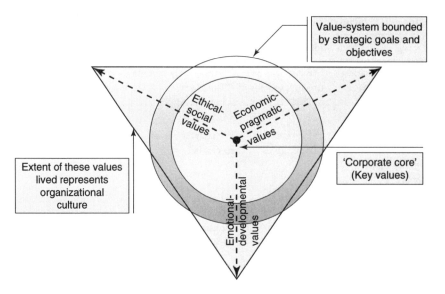

Figure 1.3 **MBV triaxial model**

As shown in the MBV triaxial model, we first present that organizations have these three value dimensions at their core. The organizational culture reflects the extent to which each of these dimensions are lived. MBV is the bounding and expansion or adapting to these three dimensions to align it with the organization's goals and objectives. Two particular organizations that represent the shift to focusing on the importance of values are General Electric (GE) and Mondragon Corporacion Cooperativa (MCC).

GE's shared values take on greater importance when imprinted on a small, wallet-size card that GE employees now carry with them. GE's values are so important to the company, that Jack Welch, Former CEO and chairman, had them inscribed and distributed to all GE employees at every level of the company. But before the cards were furnished to the staff, GE had undergone a process by which a consensus was reached on which core values it wanted to cultivate in its employees. Many hours were spent at GE's Leadership Institute and elsewhere deciding on exactly what those values should be. 'It became a badge of honor not only to carry the card but also to uphold the values.' As Jack Welch notes: 'There isn't a human being in GE that wouldn't have the Values Guide with them. In their wallet, in their purse. It means everything and we live it. And we remove people who don't have those values, even when they post great results.'

Mondragon Corporacion Cooperativa (MCC) is another example of a values-centered organization. The cooperative was created in 1956 as a way to address the debilitating job shortage in the local community and the resultant departure of people leaving the area in search of work following the Spanish Civil War. What began as a single cooperative with only a handful of people is today a for-profit organization with approximately 70,000 worker-owners. MCC is comprised of 168 enterprises including MCC Worldwide (i.e., 7 corporate offices and 38 plants). Founded on Catholic Social Thought (CST), MCC remains committed to its original values (i.e., CST) and the creation of greater social wealth by focusing on 'people and production.' MCC's recognition as a world leader in co-operativism led to the creation of Otalora in 1987, the Co-operative and Business Training Centre. The Centre's purpose is to provide information and educational programs about MCC and co-operativism to people and organizations around the world. 'In 2003 over 1,200 people visited Otalora to find out about the Mondragon Co-operative movement in situ'.[15] The cooperative's influence via Otalara has been global across diverse organizations and groups. The strange attractor of MCC is the values-based innovation and vision that brings together business and society. Not only is MCC growing globally but numerous organizations have also adopted or adapted elements of this values-based innovation.

MBV as the means for integrating strategic management with 'people' policies and building commitment

Besides guiding strategic redirection, MBV is invaluable for navigating the reefs that hinder us every day from making the best use of what we have. MBV is ideal for integrating two often disconnected areas within organizations: strategic direction/management and human resource management.

Ensuring people deliver a high caliber of daily performance is a key task of every leader-manager. This is true, regardless of corporate size or sector. Among the skills vital for this task is knowing how to manage values, not just in the 'constitutional' sense, or during major events, but in day-to-day work.

> A leader-manager has to know how to manage values, not just in the 'constitutional' sense, or during major events, but in day-to-day work.

MANAGERS' RESPONSIBILITY FOR CONSISTENCY BETWEEN WHAT IS THOUGHT/BELIEVED AND WHAT IS DONE

The curious and common inconsistency between theory and practice in organizational behavior has long been noted. An example is the discrepancy that emerges between 'formally declared values' and 'values in action'.

> The conflict between what is done in theory and what is observed in practice generates confusion, lack of commitment and 'psychological absenteeism' among employees.

Argyris (1971) coined this phenomenon as 'espoused values,' which can be interpreted as values people publicly avow that they hold. Espoused literally means married to and clearly conveys the idea of a moral, if not religious, commitment, affirmed publicly, even ceremoniously. As with marriage, the 'theoretical' commitment, 'till death do us part,' becomes, in practice, something quite different in determining people's behavior in daily life.

The conflict between what is done in theory and what is observed in practice generates confusion, lack of commitment and 'psychological absenteeism' among employees. Senior executives typically pronounce that 'our people are our greatest asset,' yet often opt to drastically reduce the number of employees as their less than imaginative response to corporate crisis.

Acknowledging that credible leadership and mutual trust are essential for effective functioning of any organization, MBV provides a framework for greater consistency between what is said and what is done. It can eliminate the gap between strategic intentions related to essential corporate values and the day-to-day activities of everyone in the organization, from the president and CEO to the most recently hired junior recruit.

For all true leadership and cultural change, the values underlying every decision and activity must be understood. Despite this reality, values usually receive only superficial attention and are often regarded as frivolous. Seldom are they properly formulated, monitored or evaluated. How many companies actually consider, much less develop, operating values during their strategic planning process, or attempt any kind of assessment to gauge the degree to which core values are observed within the organization?

> How many companies actually consider, much less develop, operating values during their strategic planning process, or attempt any kind of assessment to gauge the degree to which core values are observed within the organization?

A serious consequence of the inconsistency between what management says publicly and what it actually does creates a detrimental impact on employees' commitment. So significant is this factor that it can determine whether an employee continues working for a firm, although actual departure is subject to other constraints.

A well-known economist labeled this phenomenon Exit-Voice (Hirschman, 1970). Hirschman suggested that exiting is real not only when an employee departs for a better alternative, but also when he voices dissatisfaction and resigns psychologically. Companies where such situations occur have come to be termed 'hypocritical organizations'. The single most critical success factor for MBV is congruence between what corporate leaders say they believe and what their actions and decisions communicate they believe, in both the short and long term.

> **The single most critical success factor for MBV is congruence between what corporate leaders say they believe and what their actions and decisions communicate they believe, in both the short and long term.**

THE IMPORTANCE OF MORALE AND JUSTIFYING THE EFFORT OF DOING A PROFESSIONAL JOB WELL

What do we really mean when we say that employees are demoralized, dispirited, fed up? We are saying that they have no morale or spirit, that they lack the collective drive to give their best, to be fully involved and fully productive. Morale is vital for healthy social functioning. The word morale is derived from the Latin word mores, or customs. A society's customs usually reflect its basic values. To say employees are demoralized is to suggest they lack customs or values. Customs represent a 'good' life, the ethics of social systems. Understanding how essential they are makes the importance of addressing them obvious.

This point appears to have eluded most organizations. A preoccupation with technical matter typifies the ideas and documents of most companies. Inefficiency and lack of competitiveness are evidence of organizational cultures devoid of spirit and lacking ideas to fuel morale and give meaning to the drive to work hard and perform well, to deliver optimum results. Even as elementary a practice for employee commitment to excellence as relating the two interdependent variables of employee effort and employee pay is foreign to many companies.

United Parcel Service is among those exceptional companies that put their money where their mouth is. The world's largest package distribution company, UPS transported more than 3.5 billion parcels and documents in 2000[16] and generated US$2.9 billion in net income from US$29.8 billion in total revenue.[17] With a service area including every address in the US and more than 200 countries and territories globally, its 359,000 employees used 1,748 operating facilities, more than 600 aircraft, and a delivery fleet of 152,500 to serve an average of 7.9 million customers daily in 2000.[18] Employee commitment is among four core corporate values found in The UPS Charter:

> We believe that people do their best when they feel pride in their contribution, when they are treated with dignity, and when their talents are encouraged to flourish in an environment that embraces diversity.[19]

Two of the five components of its mission statement relate to people:

> We strive to be a responsible and well-regarded employer by providing our people with an impartial, rewarding, and co-operative environment with the opportunity for advancement.

> We build on our legacy as a caring and responsible corporate citizen through the conduct of our people and company in the communities we serve.[20]

UPS maintains that 'our people are our brand, and it is through their incredible achievements that the company continues to grow.'[21] Beyond an extensive compensation and benefits program designed to attract, retain, and motivate talent, the company invests millions in training to secure employees' commitment and keep them on the industry's cutting edge.

> We know the bottom line of our success is our employees. That's why we reward dedication, performance, and personal growth through three long-standing company initiatives and guiding principles: employee ownership, an award-winning career development program, and continuous learning and training. And it shows. The UPS team has a solid commitment to improving the business and realizing the rewards and recognition that come with achievement.

> We keep each employee on top of changing trends with job training unparalleled in the industry. And, in an environment where value is placed on personal and organizational growth, our employees are motivated to prepare themselves for advancement.[22]

The triad that conditions efforts towards a job well-done – capability, know-how and desire – is shown in Figure 1.4. Synergy between an individual's beliefs and values of those of his employer determines both his desire to work well and pride in belonging to a successful organization. Such values may include pride in being the best or creativity in process improvement.

Aligning individual and corporate beliefs and values is crucial to understanding and facilitating how work is done. It fosters the perception that this work makes sense and is worth the effort of doing it professionally and to the best of one's ability, regardless of any minimum acceptable standards. Obligation enters the equation only in the individual's obligation to his or her own principles. Ideally, these are shared with colleagues and the corporate entity. The schematic diagram in Figure 1.5 further highlights this concept.

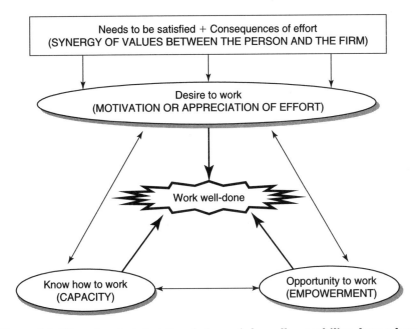

Figure 1.4 **The classic triad for doing a job well: capability, know-how and desire/will**

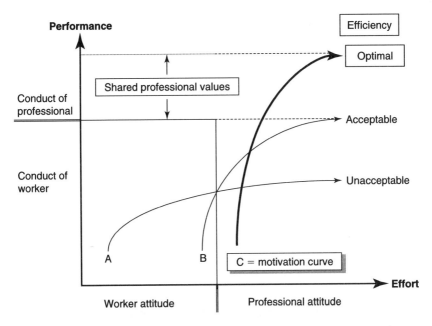

Figure 1.5 **Motivation to do one's work well (or why work beyond mere obligation)**

Optimum performance may be seen as the result of professional activity, while acceptable performance may be viewed as the outcome of activity by operatives. The former is driven by the presence of shared values that justify and give meaning to the idea of doing one's utmost at work. Among typical values people may share with

> MBV aims to achieve high performance in day-to-day work by making it more meaningful.

work colleagues are: pride in doing a superior job; the sense of achieving high standards of professionalism; and the belief that 'man (and woman) is worthy of his (or her) hire,' a Biblical reference to the expectation that the effort put into one's work should be directly reflected in financial reward. MBV seeks to not only provide financial reward but aims to achieve high performance in day-to-day work by making it more meaningful.

MBV and corporate ethics: two close, but disparate concepts

MBV differs from the emerging discipline of business ethics, but the two are linked.[23] For example, the value of creativity for enhancing innovation and competitiveness, a central concern of MBV, is not the same as talking about minorities' rights to work, a common subject in business ethics.

Business ethics tends to refer more to ethical, moral factors of individual decisions, usually made at the senior level. Its core involves four dimensions:

1. Making business decisions that present an ethical or moral dilemma, such as: 'Should we lie to the tax authority to save jobs?'; 'Can we dodge certain bureaucratic controls regulating the hygiene of food products so we can sell them for less?'; or 'Is it right to invest in a country whose government sanctions torture or violates other fundamental human rights?'
2. Establishing codes of conduct to prevent fraud, such as those formulated by many banks, which otherwise might have been subjected to stricter government regulation or not even survived.
3. The need to respect employees' basic human rights by not discriminating on the basis of race, sex or religion, treating them with dignity, respecting privacy; etc.
4. Embodying respect for the environment by incorporating explicit criteria affecting all corporate operations. Clearly, this ethical imperative is basic to the survival of the planet as a whole in the medium and long term.

An expression of such environmental ethic may be found in the mission statement of PepsiCo Inc. A world leader in convenient foods and beverages, PepsiCo employs more than 135,000 people in nearly 200 countries and territories. Its brands include Pepsi-Cola, Tropicana, Frito-Lay, and, as of late 2000, Quaker Oats. PepsiCo Inc. and its subsidiaries produced net income of US$2.2 billion on net sales of US$20.4 billion in 2000.[24]

PepsiCo's mission is to improve the value of shareholder investment 'through sales growth, costs controls, and wise investment of resources. We believe our commercial success depends upon offering quality and value to our consumers and customers; providing products that are safe, wholesome, economically efficient, and *environmentally sound*; and providing a fair return to our investors while adhering to the highest standards of integrity.'[25] The company honors the environment through principles contained within its code of conduct. An excerpt from the company's Environmental Commitment report reads:

> As a consumer products company, PepsiCo does not have the major environmental problems of heavy industry. Our biggest environmental challenge is packaging generated by our products. Packaging is important to public health and a critical component of the distribution system that delivers products to consumers and commercial establishments. To meet both consumer demand and safeguard the environment, we recycle, reuse, and reduce packaging wherever possible. Each business is also committed to responsible use of resources required in manufacturing our products.[26]

Some observers contend that ethical conduct and profit maximization are incompatible, that there is a point at which one or the other must take precedence. The reality is that the two are integral for sustained development, or 'good life' over time. The ethics of a business are expressed through what is deemed to be appropriate conduct and what the right rules of the game are for the life of the business. Occasionally businesses choose a course for survival and development, which may not in the short term at least, serve the interests of some, or all of the people who comprise the business or are affected by its activities. This raises a different kind of ethical dilemma, a conflict between different ethics or responsibilities. Such situations require a balance be struck among economic, workforce, and societal responsibilities to ensure long-term corporate prosperity. The key lies in a broad interpretation of what the business needs. What is required for the next profit and loss report is not the same as what is required for strategic business development in the medium to long term.

For example, choosing behavior that respects the environment may be reflected as a cost in the next accounting period. However, benefits must be weighed against costs, the cost of doing so compared to the cost of not doing so. Eventually environmental contamination will negatively affect profits, damaging the corporate image, alienating consumers, complicating operations through sanctions, or affecting cash flow by financial penalties for non-compliance.

An ethical notion is implicit within the word, benefit, which communicates reward, profit, earnings, pay, etc. It is derived from the Latin *bene-facere*, meaning to do well, to make or produce goods or good things. Even the concepts of debit and credit convey ethical notions. The thought that 'doing what is right is profitable for the company' expresses a morality, gives meaning to, and, in particular, motivates proactive employee behavior.

From an ethical perspective, companies striving to improve their results should incorporate principles of conduct that communicate respect for all its internal and external stakeholders – shareholders, employees, customers, suppliers, and citizens in general.

> There are many possible ways of living, but there are some ways that make living impossible.

This 'should' is profoundly consistent with strategic viability, as much at the level of senior management as at the overall corporate level. This justification should serve to overcome any initial discomfort managers may experience in dealing with business ethics.

As Fernando Savater (1991), a well-known Spanish philosopher, said to his son, Amador, about values:

> There are many possible ways of living, but there are some ways that make living impossible.[27]

Summary

- Whereas values were once considered by managers as 'too soft' to be included in any serious approach to management they have now become a central part of organizational strategy.
- MBV can be defined as both a managerial philosophy and practice whereby focus is concurrently maintained on an organization's core values and aligned with its strategic objectives.
- MBV centers on three value-based domains: (1) Economic-Pragmatic; (2) Ethical-Social and (3) Emotional-Developmental.

- MBV is a flexible framework for ongoing renewal of corporate culture, critical for inspiring a collective commitment
- Managers who are still operating from the belief that people hold the same values they held in the 20th century, will not be as effective at motivating a workforce; the world is in a state of flux and to function effectively in this turbulent environment, today's managers must be able to identify the value system of their organization, they must be able to communicate to their internal and external stakeholders the key role that values have in achieving their shared goals, and they must be able to match their organizational structure and processes to their value system.

NOTES

1   David, Grainger, Esposito, Fabiana and Watson, Noshua (2001 3 Sept.). Fortune's 100 Fastest-Growing Companies. *Fortune,* pp. 95–110.
2   http:/www.siebel.com/about/company_information/ceo_profile.shtm
3   http://www.siebel.com/about/siebel_difference.shtm (see emphasis)
4   This conceptualization is based on ideas put forward by Richard Norman in a seminar on organizational learning held in Stockholm in 1992.
5   Robin D. Rusch, *Blue Skies Ahead,* www.brandchannel.com
6   Daisy Wademan, 'Lessons from the Slums of Brazil,' *Harvard Business Review,* March 2005, p. 24.
7   http://www.hp.com/hpinfo/abouthp/main.htm
8   http://www.hp.com/hpinfo/abouthp/main.htm
9   http://www.hp.com/hpimfo/abouthp/corpobj.htm
10 http://www.hp.com/hpinfo/abouthp/hist_50s.htm
11 http://www.dana.com
12 http://www.dana.com
13 http://www.dana.com/corporate/style/pdf/DanaStyle
14 Dolan, S.L., 'Managing by Values', *ESADE MBA Review,* 2003; and Dolan, S.L., Garcia S. and Díez Piñol M., 'Validation of, "triaxial" Model of Values-Based Management: Towards New Perspectives to Manage Culture in Organizations,' Paper presented at ISSWOV 9th International Conference of Work Values and Behavior, New Orleáns, August 3–6 2004.
15 Mondragon Corporación Cooperativa, (2003). *Annual Report.* http://www.mcc.es
16 http://pressroom.ups.com/about/facts/0,1056,267,00.html
17 http://www.corporate-ir.net/media_files/NYS/UPS/reports/00ar.xls
18 http://pressroom.ups.com/about/facts/0,1056,267,00.html
19 http://pressroom.ups.com/about/facts/0,10556,128,00.html
20 *Ibid.*
21 http://ups.softshoe.com/cgi-bin/parse-file?TEMPLATE=/htdocs.works.html

22 http://www.upsjobs.com

23 The growth of interest in business ethics as an academic discipline is evident
    from the recent appearance of a clutch of specialist journals, such as *Business
    and Professional Ethics, Journal of Business Ethics,* and *Employee Rights and
    Responsibilities.*

24 http://www.pepsico.com/2000/financial_highlights.html

25 http://www.pepsico.com/corp/content.shtml

26 http://www.pepsico.com/corp/content.shtml

27 Translated into English from the original text in Spanish.

2 Values: But, What Actually Are They?

'You can live according to all kinds of systems, but there are some systems that don't let you live.'

(Fernando Savater)

'First, you've got to have a good time. Second, you've got to put your heart into everything you do. Third, you've got to go in the opposite direction to everyone else.'

(Anita Roddick, Body Shop)

If you go into any bookstore that specializes in management and enquire about books on values, chances are that you will be sent first to the section on stock markets or to the section on business ethics or ethical investment. However, the relationship between values and business results or share values brings in various interpretations of the word 'value.'

So far we have taken a general view of MBV in its generic functions of absorbing organizational complexity, orienting the strategic vision, and strengthening professional commitment. In this context we have used the word 'value' many times. But we have not defined what is really meant by this concept: this must be done before we can work effectively with 'values.'

The meaning of the word 'value'

Values are not only words. Values guide and direct our behavior and affect our daily experiences. We usually only notice our values however when we experience a 'values clash' meaning when we encounter a situation that conflicts with what we consider to be right or wrong. The words and definitions that we ascribe to identify our values are particularly powerful

> Values are not only words. Values guide and direct our behavior and affect our daily lived experiences.

for giving meaning to and channeling human efforts, both on the personal and organizational levels. The term *axiology* refers to the study of these powerful words known as values, and originates from the Greek *axios* meaning that which is valuable, estimable or worthy of being honored. It also means 'axis', the point around which the essential elements turn.

Professor Milton Rockwach of the University of Minnesota is one of the world authorities on the study of values. His definition of 'value' and 'value system' has become a classic:

> A value is an enduring belief that a specific mode of conduct or end-state of existence is personally or socially preferable to an opposite or converse mode of conduct or end-state of existence. A value system is an enduring organization of beliefs concerning preferable modes of conduct or end-states of existence along a continuum of relative importance.
>
> (Rockeach, 1973, p. 5)

In Spanish and other Latin languages, the word 'value' or 'valor' represents three different but mutually complementary meanings of the word that can be categorized into the following dimensions according to MBV: **ethical-social values** (one's beliefs about conduct), **economic-pragmatic** (orientation to efficiency, performance standards and discipline) and **emotional-developmental** (provide motivation for personal fulfillment). Together, these three dimensions form the basis for understanding what is essential in this book: *the importance of identifying core values* (i.e., yours and the organizations); *aligning core values with desired objectives;* and *illuminating your personal quest for why you want to manage by values.*

THE ETHICAL-SOCIAL DIMENSION: PREFERENTIAL CHOICES

Values are strategic lessons learned, maintained and relatively stable over time. These lessons teach us that one way of acting is better than its opposite in order to achieve our desired outcome. Meaning, our values and value systems guide our behavior toward that which will turn out well for us based on these beliefs.

Values form the nucleus of human liberty, to the extent that they constitute deliberate or preferentially strategic choices, in the medium to long term, for certain ways of behaving and against others, towards the survival or *good life* of a particular system. We shall look at this again when we discuss final or instrumental values. Under this concept, quality in one's work may be chosen in preference to its opposite, the botched, improvised or rushed job. Or genuine concern for people in the company might be preferable to feelings of contempt or indifference toward them. Other examples of values could be the creation of wealth, rather than ruin, or destroying it; autonomy, or healthy independence against unhealthy dependence; happiness instead of sadness; honesty as opposed to fraudulent behavior; a priority for team spirit and cooperation, versus privileging individualism. Our true, or core values, are revealed through our actions rather than what we merely state as being a value.

Values that are demonstrated through behavior are lived values, while espoused values are those that are expressed, either verbally or in writing, but may not be consistently enacted. An example of this might be the individual who adamantly states that health is their 'number one' value but then goes on to smoke cigarettes, take harmful drugs or never exercise. Similarly, an organization may have a company values statement that lists honesty as its highest value but then engages in questionable book-keeping practices or withholds criti-

> **Espoused values represent a mismatch between what we say and what we do. Values that are demonstrated through consistent and enduring behavior are lived values.**

cal information from employees or other stakeholders. Both cases reflect espoused values; they look good on paper or sound good in conversation but they fail the test of consistent and enduring lived behavior. In essence, espoused values represent a mismatch between what we say and what we do.

When there are no clearly formulated value options in a society, this is said to be an 'anomic' society (Allport, 1924). 'Organizational anomia' is an important explanatory element for the lack of vitality, collective coherence and morale, and the unwillingness to make an effort which can be observed in many companies today. Understanding the various types and definitions of values can help individuals and organizations to develop a common language and meaning about an often fuzzy, complex and critical aspect of personal and professional life. In this regard, values can either be a strong link between people and their organization or the weak link that breaks this all important bond.

THE ECONOMIC-PRAGMATIC DIMENSION: WORTH

From an economic perspective, *value* is also the measure of the significance or importance of something. In this sense, values are criteria used to evaluate things with respect to their relative merit, adequacy, scarcity, price or interest. By 'things' here we mean people, objects, ideas, actions, feelings or facts (Zander, 1965). For example, one may speak of the value of mutual confidence, of the value of creativity at work, or of the value that a particular process adds to the products the customer buys. Of course, one can also talk of the value of money, the value of a machine, or the value of a particular expert working for the firm.

From the point of view of the technique of 'value analysis' (European Commission No. 143, 1994), this term refers to making sure the product or service functions optimally in generating customer or user satisfaction, at the minimum possible cost. Of course, it is precisely the existence of

> From an economic perspective, *value* is also the measure of the significance or importance of something.

values like creativity, confidence in the company, commitment, etc., that contributes to behavior and actions that add value to a product. In fact, even the concept that became popular in the management jargon of the 1990s namely 'continuous improvement' is based on a particular set of values.[1]

VALUE ANALYSIS AT DEUTSCHE AIRBUS

Deutsche Airbus company based in Hamburg (Germany) has been using value analysis since 1971. Over the past 25 years, the production division has developed over 100 important projects with the objectives of reducing costs and improving quality. The results are astonishing.

Through means of stimulating open communications and group creativity processes across departments and functions, the various projects of value analysis generated over the years economic values exceeding 10 times the global costs. Fundamentally, this was done via improvements in the design of airplane sections with less components/parts, materials that were more economically viable, less waste of precious materials and fast reaction time to customers' feedback.

Another economic concept is that of the 'chain of value' (Porter, 1985) which refers to the linked set of activities (logistics, operations, marketing, etc.) that the company carries out, and that add or subtract value, leading to the total or final value of the product. According to Porter, the chain

> The *chain of value* of a company is a reflection of the shared values of the people that constitute the company.

of value of a company is a reflection of its history and strategy, and is a critical and differentiating element for achieving competitive advantage. But even more importantly, the chain of value of a company is a reflection of the shared values of the people that constitute the company. Without shared values a company's value chain is damaged. This brings to mind the old but appropriate adage; *a chain is only as strong as its weakest link.* Consider this: What constitutes the weak links in your company value chain? How does this impact the *value* of your organization?

THE EMOTIONAL-DEVELOPMENTAL DIMENSION: PERSONAL FULFILLMENT

The pursuit of individual happiness and fulfillment is a concept with different meanings throughout the world. In MBV, emotional-developmental values are those related to trust, freedom and happiness, or more broadly, personal fulfillment. Different ideations create a vast continuum along this dimension with the common theme being the notion of creating a life worth living.

In fact, this final definition can be interpreted as including the three criteria of MBV: the ethical dimension (one's beliefs about conduct), the economic-pragmatic (orientation to efficiency, performance standards and discipline) and the emotional-developmental (provide motivation for personal fulfillment). The story below illustrates how one man, David Batstone, created an alignment between these dimensions and his life.

CORE VALUES: A LIVING EXAMPLE

Living our core values can be tough. It is not as simple as stating, 'I know what I stand for, period.' Living one's values means making difficult choices among competing values and then being at peace with our decisions. David Batstone, in his book, *Saving the Corporate Soul*, explains one such pivotal point in his life. Batstone was once the CEO of a flourishing start-up IT company in the 1990's. He championed a team that put everything into their work to make the company a success. He writes:

> I worked with my executive team eighty or ninety hours a week to write a business plan...and to develop financial projections, sales strategies, technology platforms, and operational protocols. All the while, we were out courting potential customers and investors, making the rounds to blue-chip venture capitalists and corporate fund managers looking for the best partners to fuel our enterprise. (p. 240)[2]

It paid off when he was contacted by Michael Milken who offered to provide financing by way of 'tens of millions of dollars of financing' if they could agree that Milken's newly formed Knowledge Universe would be the single investor in Batstone's company.

> ...Michael gave me a call. We went over a few final details to our mutual satisfaction, and then he put to me his final test: 'David, I trust you realize that once we make this deal, this company will be your life.' I swallowed hard...his words thudded on top of me like a ton of bricks. (p. 241)[3]

Batstone, stunned by Milken's words, began to consider the implications of this statement on his life:

...I was forced to confront my motivation, that is, my purpose for being in this business. Down deep I knew the reason: I was hawking widgets, pieces of technology. I had no passion, none at all, to help corporations solve their operational dilemmas and become more efficient. To be completely honest, I was in it for the money.

This will be your life. Once off the telephone...I put together a mental inventory of the things that I deeply valued. I saw four small children who had not seen much of their dad for the previous year. I thought of my love for teaching at the university, my passion for writing, and the profound meaning I gained promoting human development in poverty-stricken countries. What was the price I could put on all that? Priceless, my inner voice replied. (pp. 241–2)[4]

Several days later Batstone resigned from the company he had put so much energy into creating. In the end, his core values became actionable through his decision to resign from the company he started and to pursue another career path. His is a brilliant illustration of how choosing to live by one's values is quite often never as easy as one might imagine. Living your values requires courage, honesty and sometimes, the risk to be different.

In today's ever changing and challenging work environment leaders, managers and employees must work toward a shared agreement about how work is accomplished. They must accept risks to innovate, adopt better practices, and to offer new products and services. It can also be stated that the orientation of efforts in accordance with shared values increases both the attainment of organizational objectives and individual fulfillment.

ETHICAL-SOCIAL VALUES: ARE THEY ENDS OR MERELY MEANS?

Often, values in general are confused with ethical values, which are not just appropriate means to secure our ends. When speaking of values it is important to differentiate between those that we can term final (e.g., often referred to as terminal or even absolute), meaning a desired end state, and those of an instrumental nature. Instrumental values are those forms of behavior that are sufficient or necessary to achieve our ends. For example, honesty may be considered an ethical-instrumental value for achieving one of the ends valued by most people: being happy and content with one's life.

There is not necessarily an exact correspondence between final and instrumental values. For example, respectful conduct towards others may be a form of behavior or 'custom' that may serve various ends, like social justice, happiness and even the accumulation of wealth. However, a specific set of instrumental values such as honesty, money and positive thinking, may be necessary in order to secure a particular final value, such as happiness.

> According to Rockeach (1973), while the number of final values that people habitually claim to hold are no more than about a dozen, the number of instrumental values is much greater, although never reaching one hundred.

Figure 2.1 demonstrates that **final values** can be sub-divided into two types: personal and ethical-social.

1. *Personal values:* those to which the individual aspires for him or herself, and are the response to the question: 'What are the most important things in your life?' They range from the generic 'being happy' to 'having prestige.'
2. *Ethical-social values:* constitute aspirations or purposes that benefit society at large, such as respect for the natural environment or for human rights. They are the response to the question: 'What do you want to do for the world?'

Figure 2.2 demonstrates that **instrumental values** can be sub-divided into two types: ethical-moral values and values of competition.

1. *Ethical-moral values:* These refer to forms of conduct that are necessary to reach our final values. In fact, the word 'moral' is derived from the Latin *mores,* meaning customs. For example, loyalty may be (or is) an instrumental value for maintaining friendship (a final value). Ethical-moral values answer the question: 'How do you think you should behave towards other people, those around you?' Moral

Personal values: What are the most important things in your life?	Living, happiness, health, salvation, family, personal success, recognition, status, material goods, friendship, success at work, love, etc.
Ethical-social values: What do you want to do for the world?	Peace, planet ecology, social justice, etc.

Figure 2.1 **Examples of final values (desired end state)**

Ethical-moral values: How do you think you should behave towards other people. Those around you?	Honesty, sincerity, responsibility, loyalty, solidarity, mutual confidence, respect for human rights, etc.
Values of competition: What do you believe is necessary to be able to compete in life?	Culture, money, imagination, logic, beauty, intelligence, positive thinking, flexibility, sympathy, capacity to work in teams, courage, etc.

Figure 2.2 **Examples of instrumental values (means for achieving ends)**

values are a type of instrumental value that have two very peculiar characteristics:[5]

(a)　they are put into practice in relation to other people; and

(b)　in emotionally balanced people, when such values are held and subscribed to but not translated into consequent or consistent behavior, they tend to generate feelings of guilt and shame, or at least of dissatisfaction with oneself.

2.　*Values of competition*: Other instrumental values, which may be called values required for competing, are more individual although they are also socially conditioned and are not directly related to morality and guilt. They answer the question: 'What do you believe is necessary to be able to compete in life?' Such values might include imagination, initiative and logic.

The degree of pressure felt by an individual to adopt a new value, and to change their conduct in order to comply with this new value, depends very closely on whether this value is truly shared by the other members of his or her reference group. For example, one might feel guilty, or somehow lacking in ability as a result of not acting creatively when one does not belong to a reference group that by consensus believes creativity is a critical element for its survival. Whereby an advertising team would value creativity in its members, a supply chain group may place a higher value on efficiency.

It is important to recognize that a person may experience conflict between two moral values (for example, behaving honestly with another person and at the same time not hurting them with bad news), or between two values of competition (for example, being imaginative and logical at the same time), or again, between a moral value and a competition value (for example, behaving respectfully yet giving constructive criticism).

ACTION/REFLECTION

IDENTIFYING YOUR INDIVIDUAL VALUES

PART I – FINAL VALUES:

Personal values:

What are the most important things in your life?

1. _____
2. _____
3. _____

Ethical-social values:

What do you want to do for the world?

1. _____
2. _____
3. _____

PART II – INSTRUMENTAL VALUES:

Ethical-moral values:

How do you think you should behave towards other people, toward those around you?

1. _____
2. _____
3. _____

Values of competition:

What do you believe is necessary to be able to compete in life?

1. _____
2. _____
3. _____

PART III – ALIGNMENT AMONG VALUES:

1. Which of the values stated above are the most incongruent with your actual behavior in life? What causes this incongruity?
2. How do you feel about this discrepancy? What are the consequences to you? To others in your life and to your work?

ARE ALL VALUES OF EQUAL WORTH?

Our system or *scale of values* results from ordering values according to their relative importance in our personal hierarchy and priorities. The importance we attribute to various different values is continually being changed throughout the course of our lives according to our experiences, our reflections and the social persuasions that have exerted influence on us. It is difficult to maintain that the values held by people according to their own scale of relative priorities are better or worse than others in absolute or universal terms. Neither does the classification between final and instrumental values allow such a differentiation to be drawn. Thus it is difficult to state that, say, imagination is a 'better' value than honesty, or peace in the world is better than health. What is the basis for such value judgments, other than purely subjective views and feelings?

Moving from beliefs to behavior, via values

There are three concepts taken from social psychology that are closely related to values; these must be understood and correctly sequenced before MBV can be fully understood and applied by management. These concepts are: *beliefs, norms* and *attitudes*.

WHAT ARE BELIEFS?

As we have stated, values may be generally understood as the strategic choices we make regarding what is required to achieve our goals. It is important to recognize that these choices, in turn, are derived from basic suppositions or beliefs about human nature and the world around us. In short, each person chooses to think and act in specific ways according to what they believe about people, things, events, ideas, and the world around them.

One very common assumption is that beliefs are the same as supposed 'truths.' However, generically, beliefs are structures of thought developed and deeply-rooted over the years from learning and experience, which serve to explain and make sense of our reality; these structures precede the for- mulation of our values. For example, being convinced that never having enough time is a sign that someone is successful in their life may contribute to sustaining the value that hard work is worthwhile. Another example might be the belief that what counts are immediate results, rather than the process of improvement which could support, in part, the value of immediate benefit, of speed in production or work, and even perhaps, of the usefulness of a quick botch job over a slower quality outcome. Similarly, the belief that 'poor quality involves a higher cost in the long run' leads to consolidating good quality as an accepted value.

The relationship between beliefs and values is extremely close. For this reason, throughout this book, 'changes in beliefs and values' is spoken of much more often than change in values alone. As illustrated in Figure 2.3 and as shall be noted later, when we deal with the practice of MBV, the 'unlearning' of some beliefs is essential in order to replace or renew values, change behavior and exert a positive influence for individuals and organizations.

WHAT ARE NORMS?

Values play a special role in the formation of norms or what can be more commonly referred to as the 'rules of the game.' Our values inform us about what we believe is ethical, good, valid, competitive, appropriate, beautiful or desirable; they are continually being generated and reinforced throughout our lives.

Values are held at the level of the individual but norms tend to emerge from group interactions. Norms are rules of conduct adopted by consensus, whereas values are criteria for evaluating, accepting or rejecting norms. Further, non-compliance with norms usually incurs external sanctions,

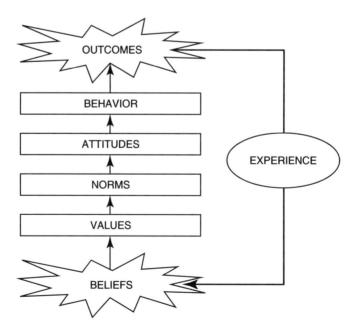

Figure 2.3 **Hierarchy or sequence of beliefs and outcomes**

'Emerging norms' and 'Hanging on to values'

In situations of confusion, novelty or ambiguity (such as in crisis situations), individuals tend to look for a guide or rule that will allow them to structure and understand the situation. In this way they will tend to interact more with other people and be more easily influenced by what others say and do. Their susceptibility to suggestion increases.

(Turner and Killian, 1987)

---

whereas non-compliance with values results in feelings of guilt or 'internal sanctions.'

Organizations need to reach a carefully considered consensus on their basic operating values, from which should emerge their system of standards and their objectives. This process is not usually done well, since it is very common to observe how conflicts between incompatible values translate into the existence of contradictory standards and conducts within an organization. Who of us in management have not needed to resolve, on almost a daily basis, such contradictions as *short-term benefits* vs *long-term viability*, *profitability* vs *market share*; *better quality* vs *lower cost*; and so on.

WHAT ARE ATTITUDES?

Often the concept of 'change of attitude' is used wrongly to refer to the change of something else, namely a change in values, conduct, beliefs or behaviors. Consider these examples: a change of values such as commitment; a change of conduct such as lack of punctuality; or a change of beliefs, such as 'it is dangerous to detect errors in others and then publicize them.' This is partly the result of the popularization of the concept of attitudes and trends of 'changes in attitude', for example through social surveys. Usually the confusion originates from those researchers in the field of social psychology, who find it easier to measure attitudes than values.

An attitude is a consequence of the values and norms that precede it, and is an evaluating tendency/factor, either positive or negative, towards other people, deeds, events, things, etc. Our attitudes reflect how we feel towards someone or something and predict our tendency to act in a certain way. For example, we can have a positive attitude towards a particular job or project and dedicate ourselves to it enthusiastically; such conduct would then represent the possibility of putting into practice a certain value (e.g., creativity), which in turn depends on certain beliefs (e.g., 'we must be creative in order to survive in our market'). In order to modify conduct, better than aiming to change directly a specific attitude, what we should do is modify our values and beliefs that underlie the conduct.

Beliefs and outcomes: the emergence of stress

Ideally everyone would be able to create an environment where their beliefs, values, norms, attitudes and behaviors are perfectly aligned and result in the optimal work/life fit. Rarely does reality manifest itself so neatly. Conversely, demands on our lives and work have continued to increase more rapidly than ever before. These dynamics converge to demonstrate the basic relationship between beliefs, values and behavior that can be clearly exemplified by a subject that is infrequently dealt with in a formal manner in the business world. Stress today represents a growing worry around the globe. Many people are increasingly aware that their quality of life depends largely on their conditions of work. Of course, one thing is to worry: being able to solve this problem is something else.

For an organization as a whole, if the managers and leaders suffer from a poor quality of life, it is often due to their stressful working environment (Dolan, 1995). And once the leaders of an organization are stressed, there is a spillover effect on the rest of the members of the firm which usually results in poor performance and general ineffectiveness. Additionally, it becomes very difficult to break the vicious cycle even when attempts are made to improve the psychological and physical conditions (Dolan, 2006).

In spite of the fact that thousands of articles on stress appear in professional and popular journals, the concept is still very poorly understood by the general public. For one, the phenomenon of stress has attracted the attention of researchers in several disciplines (e.g., medicine, psychology and management) each using respectively its own jargon, semantics, models and point of reference. The result is that there are various

> **Workplace stress is the entire process in which people perceive and interpret their work environment in relation to their capability to cope with it.**

definitions of stress. Today, most refer to workplace stress as *the entire process in which people perceive and interpret their work environment in relation to their capability to cope with it*. Under this definition, stress is present when the environment poses (or is perceived to be) a threat to the individual, either in the form of excessive demands or in the form of insufficient resources to meet the individual's needs (Dolan, 2006).

Although most of us are able to adequately respond to stressful situations most of the time, our bodies and minds *have a limited capacity to respond to stressors*. In other words, when a person is exposed to too many stressors over a long period of time, his or her ability to cope with these stressors may diminish. Simply put, constant activation of the stress response (i.e., and the corresponding hormonal secretion such as adrenalin and noradrenalin) takes a toll on our physical and mental resources. If this happens, a person suffers from what is known as strain. Strain is excess stress that is characterized by undesirable consequences to our health and/or work performance; it is a sign or symptom of our inability to deal with everyday problems. The problem is that some of the signs and symptoms of strain are not always obvious, and in many instances they are hidden. Only when the individual is exposed to a prolonged period of strain does an acute state manifest and result in a serious illness. It is for this reason that we need to make an effort to diagnose strains early in the process in order to intervene and prevent a debilitating state from occurring.

> **Workplace stress is present when the environment poses (or is perceived to be) a threat to the individual, either in the form of excessive demands or in the form of insufficient resources to meet the individual's needs.**
>
> **(Auerbach and Dolan, 1997)**

In the context of MBV, it is particularly important to understand which specific values are uniquely activated when an individual is reacting to stress in an 'optimal manner.' As shown in Figure 2.4, there are values associated with high performance that tend to be inhibited when the individual is either

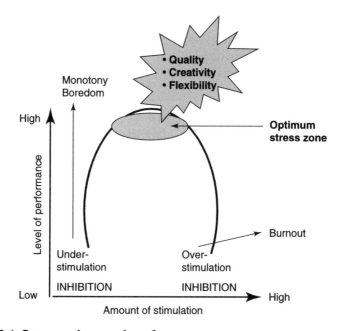

Figure 2.4 **Stress, values and performance**

under-stimulated or over-stimulated. Values associated with high perform-ance may include friendliness, creativity, achievement, or commitment to the company. The results of under-stimulation are usually boredom and a sense of monotony, while over-stimulation may lead to hyperactivity and result in exhaustion and what is commonly referred to as 'burnout'.

The increasing need to develop work environments where stress is reduced to a level that does not negatively impact or impair the individual means that leaders themselves need to understand the serious toll stress can have on their own lives. Further, they need to know how negative lev-els of stress impact their workforce and ultimately business outcomes. In essence, leaders need to learn how to lead less stressed lives. One challenge in this respect is the difficulty of measuring the level of stress or stimuli. However, some diagnostic tools have been published and validated in the course of the past several years (Dolan, 2006).

In more developed countries an interesting phenomenon has occurred over the past several years. In a culture where performance is highly valued and financially rewarded, people shift their behavior in order to become a 'super-achiever.' Although they may have other values such as family hap-piness or harmony, for example, they begin to place an emphasis on the dominant cultural values. This 'super-achiever' behavior has led to what is widely known as Type A Behavior; it is characterized by the following, and typifies many North American managers:

1. A constant feeling of time urgency, and an obsession with time limitations.
2. This sense of pressure is handled by high levels of activity and high levels of competitiveness to the point of being hostile to people who challenge their ideas.
3. Workaholic tendencies; i.e., the person may work endlessly, leading to the exclusion of relationships and leisure activities.
4. Impatience with anyone or anything that interferes with goal attainment.

This cluster of behaviors has given rise to a large body of research attempting to understand the determinants and consequences of Type A behavior. For instance, it has been found that people with these personality traits tend to create stress for themselves or make stressful situations worse than they otherwise might be. Furthermore, particular aspects of the Type A personality (specifically anger, hostility and aggression) are not only associated with increased stress, they may also lead to heart attacks. It should be noted that values in and of themselves are neither good nor bad. It is the extent to which an individual expresses the value via behavior that creates negative or positive affect. For example, an individual who values power may demonstrate this value by dominating or controlling others, or through the relentless pursuit of financial acquisition; while someone else may value power but use it judiciously to achieve shared organizational goals or to promote a fair and just workplace. Figure 2.5 provides some examples of how typical beliefs and values can lead to harmful behaviors and outcomes (column A), or how we can alter our beliefs and values to produce positive behaviors and outcomes (column B).

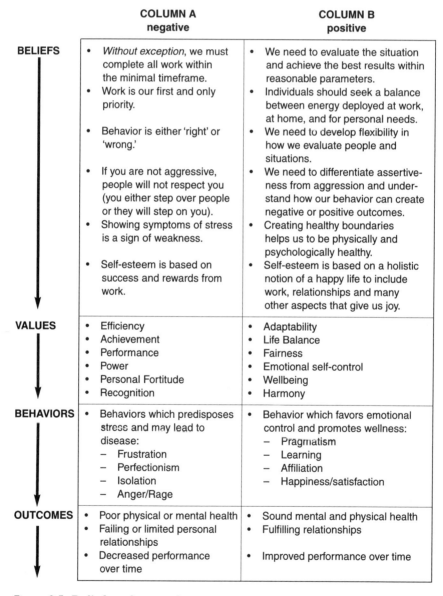

	COLUMN A negative	COLUMN B positive
BELIEFS	• *Without exception*, we must complete all work within the minimal timeframe. • Work is our first and only priority. • Behavior is either 'right' or 'wrong.' • If you are not aggressive, people will not respect you (you either step over people or they will step on you). • Showing symptoms of stress is a sign of weakness. • Self-esteem is based on success and rewards from work.	• We need to evaluate the situation and achieve the best results within reasonable parameters. • Individuals should seek a balance between energy deployed at work, at home, and for personal needs. • We need to develop flexibility in how we evaluate people and situations. • We need to differentiate assertiveness from aggression and understand how our behavior can create negative or positive outcomes. • Creating healthy boundaries helps us to be physically and psychologically healthy. • Self-esteem is based on a holistic notion of a happy life to include work, relationships and many other aspects that give us joy.
VALUES	• Efficiency • Achievement • Performance • Power • Personal Fortitude • Recognition	• Adaptability • Life Balance • Fairness • Emotional self-control • Wellbeing • Harmony

BEHAVIORS	• Behaviors which predisposes stress and may lead to disease:
	  – Frustration
	  – Perfectionism
	  – Isolation
	  – Anger/Rage
		• Behavior which favors emotional control and promotes wellness:
		  – Pragmatism
		  – Learning
		  – Affiliation
		  – Happiness/satisfaction

OUTCOMES	• Poor physical or mental health • Failing or limited personal relationships • Decreased performance over time	• Sound mental and physical health • Fulfilling relationships • Improved performance over time

Figure 2.5 **Beliefs, values and stress**

ACTION/REFLECTION

Based on the information provided in Figure 2.5 on beliefs, values and behaviors in relation to stress, consider the following questions with regard to your own life:

1. To what extent do your beliefs and values resemble more of column A or B?
2. To what degree can you identify yourself with some of the specific points mentioned in either column A or B?
3. To what extent do you think that your beliefs and values affect your current level of stress?
4. Based on the profile detected in response to the above questions, do you think that you are predisposed or vulnerable to developing some stress related illness?

Value formation in an organization

While it is known that individual values are formed from basic learning in infancy, childhood and adolescence based on our models of parents, teachers and friends and other influential people, determining how values are formed in an organization is a complex phenomenon that depends on many variables:

*   **The beliefs and values of the founder.** Every company starts its life as an impulse from an idea and some principles of action that are more or less implicit. Assembling the required financial, human and material resources to implement the idea is a subsequent step. Summarizing the arguments of Schein (1988); firms are created by business (people) having the intuition that the combined efforts of a selected group of people can create a new product or service in a market. These founders, in general, determine how the company is defined, how it resolves its problems, and how it adapts externally and integrates internally. The founder not only possesses a high degree of determination and self-confidence but also usually has very firm ideas on how the world works, the role that different people can play, how to arrive at 'the truth,' and methods of control over time and space. Logically, the ideas and principles of the founding group tend to be dissipated over time as the company grows, unless special efforts are made to encourage their continuation. The reality is that many of the companies showing an especially strong cultural identity maintain a coherence and strength of principle inherited from their founder.

- **The beliefs and values of the current management**. At any given time the management of the company can decide to perpetuate, revitalize, or even radically modify the beliefs and values of the founder. One of their tasks is to manage the perennial conflict between the traditional and the modern in all aspects of its operations. This is one of the basic problems underlying generational succession in companies.
- **The beliefs and values of the employees**. One of the strongest formative influences on beliefs and values in employees is constituted by the existing mechanisms of compensation. For example, it is pointless for management to make speeches about the importance of innovation if they do not stimulate and compensate creative effort.
- **Training and the influence of consultants**. An essential mechanism for modifying beliefs and values is training. In fact, true learning consists of 'unlearning' irrelevant beliefs and replacing them with new ones. Such training may take the form of attendance on courses, reading suitable publications (such as this book) or interaction with consultants. It is equally important to focus on senior managers with professional development designed to activate or legitimize the implementation of values that have previously been learned and partially forgotten. This type of development ensures continuity throughout the lifespan of an organization. Clearly it would be unrealistic to think of promoting values like honesty and initiative through attendance at seminars.
- **The existing legislation**. Legislation covering employment, the environment, taxation, etc. in each country will also significantly influence the process of establishing beliefs and values in companies.
- **The rules of the game in particular markets**. The degree of free competition in any market, as well as accepted conventions or customs, will impose certain 'rules of the game' that condition the beliefs and values of companies. Among the beliefs most influenced by competitive pressure is the importance of beating your rivals and of gaining short-term advantage or benefit, whatever the means used to achieve this, regardless of the long-term effect on the viability of the business or even society.
- **The prevailing social values of the period**. At the beginning of the 20th century, the predominant social values in the developed countries were different from those now, which in turn will be different in the future. For example, transparency is a relatively emergent value whereby confidentiality was previously of the utmost importance. Employees are now referred to as 'organizational members' where in earlier times people were merely 'cogs' in the metaphorical organizational machine.
- **The cultural tradition of each society**. In every society, the social values and business values influence each other mutually. For example, a large part of the economic success of Japan is due to its urge to 'show' the

Western world its collective strength. This is achieved through the incorporation of its traditional social values, such as the drive for continuous improvement, harmony, loyalty and pride in belonging to a family or group, into its industrial society.

- **The history of success and failure of the company**. Lastly, it must be stated that the systems of beliefs and values of the company are self-sustaining if its results are considered good. If a company does well profit-wise and explicitly includes values such as dealing honestly with its customers in its systems, then it will tend to perpetuate that value as essential for its business. This is the 'winning formula' factor. In contrast, however, if this company obtains losses, it is likely or at least possible that it will reconsider its system of values.

VALUES AND POSITION IN THE SYSTEM

In every company, three possible positions playing different roles with respect to its principles or essential values can be differentiated (Oshry, 1977):

1. *The level of the generators of values of the system*: The generators of values are the owners or representatives of the company, those who have overall responsibility for it and essentially determine the 'rules of the game.' In the case of the privately-owned company, the representatives of the ownership tend to follow much more faithfully the beliefs and values of the shareholders than in the case of the publicly-owned company, whose true 'owners' are obviously the citizens through the taxes they pay, but who are only very indirectly represented (and often effectively unrepresented) in its center of power.
2. *The level of the managers of values*: The roles of the managers of values or the managers of valuable resources correspond to the senior executives and intermediate professionals, situated between those who represent the owners and the members of the system. This position is also typically oriented to manage conflicts of values between those above and below them in the hierarchy.
3. *The level of the members of the system of values*: In this position are those who work in a company constituted according to the principles and structures that have been generated by others. The members of the system tend to defer to the set of principles and values generated by those above them only when a system of rewards and punishments is linked to compliance or non-compliance. But they may never come to feel the values to be really their own, like those who have directly generated them or those who are managing the values.

An innovative alternative within the framework of the organization oriented not towards the hierarchical control of people but rather to the development of their capabilities is possible. This would be an organization in which the members of the system feel themselves also to be managers and even generators of the set of principles and values that should govern the life of the company.

The power of values towards generation of knowledge and success in organizations

In essence, values are words and therefore relatively simple structures of thought which nevertheless encompass complex ideas about the reality desired by people. Values have the capacity to transcend the perception of what now exists around us, enabling us to conceptualize a vision of the future that is better, or even ideal. This conceptualization of what is desirable can manage to encapsulate in a few words more knowledge than an entire strategic plan, especially when one considers that usually there is no one in the organization capable of reading and assimilating the plan.

Peter Drucker, the father of modern management, discussed how knowledge, not capital, is the new basis of wealth in his classic book *The Post-Capitalist Society* (1993). In one of the passages in the text he asserts that the emerging society will have to integrate the power of capital with the power of humanist knowledge (not mere knowledge) if it wishes to survive:

> Post-capitalist society will be divided by a new dichotomy of values and aesthetic perceptions (… beyond the dichotomy between 'intellectuals' or thinkers, and 'managers' or do-ers), the first of these concerned with words and ideas, the second with people and work. The successful individual will need to be prepared to live and work simultaneously in these two cultures.

Logically, capital tends to be attracted to where there are ideas, values, knowledge and opportunities for business. Yet, organizations are now being challenged to see beyond the bottom line and to create more humane work environments that also contribute to social good. This ideal organizational type may seem beyond the reach of even the most optimistic business/social visionary. Yet an example of one corporation, Mondragon Corporacion Cooperativa (MCC), is flourishing precisely because it has adhered to its core values centered on the intersection of business and society and the balance of people and profit.

MONDRAGÓN CORPORACIÓN COOPERATIVA: A MODEL OF SHARED VALUES

Tucked away in the beautiful green hills of the Basque country, about one hour outside of Bilbao, Spain, resides Mondragon Corporacion Cooperativa (MCC) believed to be the largest and most successful cooperative in history. What began as a 'social experiment' with only a handful of people is today an international cooperative corporation with approximately 70,000 worker-owners. The corporation is comprised of 168 enterprises including MCC Worldwide (i.e., 7 corporate offices and 38 plants) and a yearly revenue of eight billion dollars. MCC is especially significant however not only because of its cooperative business structure, which may seem at odds with a world dominated by competition, but because of its success at enacting a shared mission focused on both people and profit.

Unlike most corporations, MCC does not subordinate people to capital gain. Instead MCC expresses their philosophy of balancing human, business and societal needs through its corporate values, specifically co-operation, participation, social commitment and innovation. The corporation's values are concretely expressed through its focus on developing people by providing work opportunities, career advancement through democratic processes and ongoing education.

One person at MCC's corporate headquarters succinctly defined the cooperative's concept of values. He stated, 'Values are things to put into practice, not to talk about. They should not be just a piece of paper you put on a wall.'

(*Source*: B. Richley, 2006. A study of Mondragon Corporacion Cooperativa and its influence as an exemplary business/social model: An inquiry into the diffusion of values-based innovation. Unpublished doctoral dissertation. Case Western Reserve University, Cleveland, OH.)

Values form part of the power of knowledge to the extent that they guide daily behavior, provide cohesion, and give meaning to the collective will; when they serve to resolve conflict and take decisions for change (Rockeach, 1976) when they stimulate development and when they enable complexity to be coped with creatively much better than manuals of procedures.

In short, it cannot be denied that an organization's vitality and success depend crucially on the existence of values such as creativity, initiative, vitality, confidence, courage, readiness to face risk, flexibility, and autonomy – both psychological and financial. Precisely for this reason, MBV proposes the need to manage values and to guard them as the critical resources they undoubtedly are. As we shall see in the next chapter, managing values means managing the culture of the company, strengthening it day by day and always revitalizing it to face an unpredictable future.

WHAT ABOUT YOU?

ACTION/REFLECTION

Take a few moments and engage in an analysis identifying the traditional values that are operating in your organization.

Which values continue to serve the company and its stakeholders?

_____
_____
_____
_____
_____
_____

Which values hinder the organization and its members?

_____
_____
_____
_____
_____
_____

Which values do you know need to change in order to create a thriving and vital organization?

_____
_____
_____
_____
_____
_____

What would the difference be if these values were changed? To the company? To the lives of people who work in the organization? To other stakeholders? To society?

_____
_____
_____
_____
_____

Summary

- Values are not only words; values guide and direct our behavior and affect our daily lived experiences
- Values, according to the MBV concept, can be categorized into three dimensions: **ethical-social** (one's beliefs about conduct), **economic-pragmatic** (orientation to efficiency, performance standards and discipline) and **emotional-developmental** (provide motivation for personal fulfillment).
- The relationship between beliefs and values is extremely close; within the practice of MBV, the 'unlearning' of some beliefs is essential in order to replace or renew values, change behavior and exert a positive influence for individuals and organizations.
- When people feel either under-stimulated or over-stimulated due to values incongruence, stress rises and impacts both individual performance and organizational performance.
- Values form part of the power of knowledge to the extent that they guide daily behavior, provide cohesion, and give meaning to the collective will; when they serve to resolve conflict and take decisions for change when they stimulate development, and when they enable complexity to be coped with creatively much better than manuals of procedures.

NOTES

1   All in all, it is difficult to see great differences between 'Value Analysis', 'Total Quality' and 'Process Re-engineering'. Even the ISO standards on quality are nothing more than a standardized procedure for re-thinking things in order to do them as well as possible or to generate the maximum value.
2   Source: D. Batstone, *Saving the Corporate Soul & (Who Knows?) Maybe Your Own*. Jossey-Bass, 2003.
3   *Ibid.*
4   *Ibid.*
5   In practice, most authors use the terms 'ethical' and 'moral' indistinctly (Freeman, 1990).

3 Renew or Die: The Importance of Culture Change

'It is not necessary to change. Survival is not mandatory.'

(W. Edwards Denning)

'The organizations most capable of confronting the future do not believe in themselves for what they are but for their capacity to stop being what they are.'

(E. Gore)

Understanding organizational culture and why it matters

Organizational culture develops over a period of time and is largely entrenched in the values embraced by the organization. Ed Schein, a noted scholar on organizational culture from MIT, defines organizational culture as:

> A pattern of basic assumptions, invented, discovered or developed by a given group as it learns to cope with its problems of external adaptation and internal integration that has worked well enough to be considered valid and therefore is to be taught to new members as the correct way to perceive, think, and feel in relation to those problems. (1985, p. 9)

But what does this really mean and does it matter? While many may consider discussions of organizational culture merely to be the amorphous fodder that sustains academic journals and consulting practices, its presence and impact cannot be denied. For example, think of a large traditional law firm or financial institution. Now think of a successful software company during the nineties IT boon or the dynamism exhibited on the trading floor at the New York Stock Exchange. How does the 'feel' of the environment differ from one image to the next? Imagine yourself in the midst of each place and think about what you might observe. What stories do you overhear? How are people dressed? How do they communicate? Your responses to these questions reflect aspects of the culture known as artifacts. Artifacts are visible organizational structures and processes (Schein, 1999), or the things most apparent that allow you to begin to 'read' an environment (Siegel, 2001).

If you were to stay in any of these environments for a period of time you would then begin to move toward a deeper understanding of the culture. You would learn about the organization's values through its norms, ideologies, strategies, goals and philosophies that are expressed either implicitly or explicitly. Eventually you would uncover what are perhaps paradoxically the most elusive yet definite aspects of any organization, namely, the unconscious and taken for granted beliefs, the habits of perception, the thoughts and the feelings of its members. These collectively held assumptions represent the bedrock of organizational life.

For decades the nebulous nature of organizational culture has been considered through multiple points of view as a way to both concretize its abstract nature and to convey its seemingly Svengali-like influence on people and situations. Culture has been likened to a heritage that is passed down from older generations to younger ones, 'a large complex computer that programs the responses and actions of people', or as 'a collective programming of the minds of one group that differentiates them from other groups derived from one's social culture', and perhaps most succinctly and fittingly as the 'personality' of the organization (Dolan and Garcia, 2002).

The concept of organizational change involves modifying an organization's culture – a difficult task involving not only superficial aspects but entrenched components as well. In order to appreciate the significance of a culture change, ponder for a moment how easy it would be to change some part of your own personality. When was the last time you succeeded in changing a trait or habit of yours for the better? Was it easy, or difficult to alter a part of your identity? What we generally know about human behavior is that people change when they are motivated to do so either by some extrinsic or intrinsic force that creates an alignment among one's value system, bringing them closer to their image of their true or authentic self. If we think of an organization's culture as its personality then might the same be true for bringing about change in a company?

Why should an organization change?

MBV is a management philosophy that suggests organizations are dynamic entities that should engage in continuous renewal. But the

> **MBV provides a way to engage in cultural change involving incremental and drastic change processes.**

renewal process is not about change simply for the sake of change, or keeping up with the latest management fad. From a 'values perspective,' true change is about effectively managing and maintaining the organizational culture in order to bring it in alignment with its core values and the demands of its environment. MBV provides a way to engage in cultural transformation involving both incremental and drastic change processes sometimes referred to as first and second order change.

As stated earlier, initiating a culture change is tough. It requires many factors to successfully implement MBV but as a starting point one should begin by giving thoughtful consideration to the following:

Before initiating MBV answer these three questions:

- Why should we engage in organizational change? Specifically, what are the benefits to the organization and its stakeholders?
- What should the change involve and how far should we go?
- And lastly, when is the right time to change?

In the 21st century businesses around the world are struggling to coexist amidst a complex and volatile system. Organizations, and hence its members are under a two-fold and unrelenting pressure: the need to adapt in order to survive in an increasingly competitive market and to simultaneously innovate if they want to differentiate and to succeed. The bottom line: if an organization wants to thrive, and not merely stay alive, it must engage in an ongoing process of renewal.

It is well-known that classical Greek philosophy proposed that 'change is the only constant.' The beliefs and values that support the structures and processes of an organization must also be continuously transformed

> **The stress from such an unstable environment can cripple organizations who believe they do not need to change based on their success in the past.**

if they are intended to be the guiding force that will allow it to adapt to an unstable business climate. The stress from such an unstable environment can cripple organizations who believe they do not need to change based on their success in the past. To state that everything alive is in perpetual change and interchange with its surroundings is the same as stating that the only thing that does not change is what is dead. Death is the only invariable.

STRATEGIC OPTIMIZATION AND ETHICAL REASONS FOR CHANGE

The top executives of today's most competitive companies, not only the large ones but the medium-sized and small too, are very conscious that change must be understood as an opportunity to be able to continue to develop. However, until well into the second half of the 20th century, a business organization was understood as an autonomous body shielded from its environment. And even today there are companies that remain impervious to changes happening around them and even inside them, continuing with ways of thinking and doing things essentially identical to those of the bureaucratic and formalized organizations of the beginning of the century.

At the risk of over-simplifying, there are basically two types of organizations today that have resisted large-scale change in response to the environment:

(a)   Public institutions and companies that are cut off from the real dynamics of free markets, not subjected to competitive and customer pressures, and protected politically even though they contain large areas of economic inefficiency and demonstrate notorious indicators of dissatisfaction, both by their customers and their own employees. This can be especially true for many sectors of public administration such as energy, education, and justice. In the case of public companies quoted on the stock market, this resistance to change is especially evident when the shareholders of these companies are satisfied with its profitability, and thus short term satisfaction can lead to inaction and risk of not surviving for the long term. One of the celebrated examples is the case of IBM. The later quasi dominated the market of large frame computers and was ultimately blindsided by the growing and shortly thereafter personal computer explosion. However, because IBM was willing and able to change it took drastic measures to climb out of a situation that nearly caused its extinction.

(b)   Privately-owned companies, particularly family ones, governed in an autocratic and marginally professional way, but which continue to achieve acceptable economic results due to a niche market usually maintained since its founding.

However difficult change may be it is not impossible to imagine even for an industry as established as healthcare. Much of the medical profession has implemented a culture shift in order to remain competitive and to respond to stakeholder demands. Consider some of the changes that many healthcare providers have implemented while still remaining true to its core purpose (see Table 3.1).

To navigate successfully through the demands of the 21st century, and to continue growing successfully thereafter, means knowing how to

Table 3.1 **An example of a culture change in one public sector: Healthcare**

From only	To also
• Considering patients and immediate system users	• Considering patients and multiple stakeholders internal and external to the organization
• Treating disease	
• Bio-clinical approach	• Promoting healthy behavior
• Managers' control	• Bio-psychosocial approach
• No confidence between administration, healthcare workers and other stakeholders	• Managers lead
	• Efforts to build collaboration and trust between administration, healthcare workers and other stakeholders
• Bureaucratic philosophy	
• View change as threat	• Entrepreneurial philosophy
• Hierarchical structure	• View change as an opportunity and challenge
• Management by instruction and/or management by objectives	
	• Networked structure
	• Management by values

WHAT ABOUT YOU?

ACTION/REFLECTION

Which of the following motives serve as a potential catalyst for initiating MBV in your organization?

1. **Strategic survival motives**
   - Increasing profits
   - Adapting to changes in the environment
   - Change in leadership
   - Preparing for the future
   - Manage gap between future vision and present reality
   - Exploiting business opportunities
   - Protection from environmental threats
   - Avoiding authoritarian changes

2. **Optimal motives**
   - Taking full advantage of new technology
   - Diminishing cost of production
   - Taking full advantage of employee creativity
   - Instilling a culture of continuous improvement
   - Implementing a program of total quality management
   - Give meaning to work (job enrichment)

3. **Legal-normative motives**
   - Legislation concerning the ecology/environment
   - International norms of quality
   - National legislation per occupational health and safety
   - International norms for preventing occupational health or safety problems
   - Legislation about equal opportunities and equal rights

4. **Ethical motives**
   - Being effective in using public funds
   - Protecting the environment
   - Respecting principles of equality
   - Respecting clients/customers rights
   - Being consistent in what the firms says and what it does
   - Improving quality of life via work
   - Respecting the democratic principles/values of society
   - Respecting professional code of ethics

5. **Other motives**
   - Increasing personal commitment
   - Changing because everyone else in the industry thinks it is important
   - Following advise of experts/consultants
   - Other

monitor changes in the environment, to move forward into the future and to renovate the company. Renovation or corporate renewal ensures that an organization will be viable, profitable and competitive. It is well known that those who fall behind cannot survive in a market of free competition. Those companies that do not learn how to 'unlearn' and to continuously readapt to the new demands of their environments tend to lose vitality and die. As a director of a very large company once said, *Either we change of our own accord now or we will be forced by outside events to change, and the shock will be much worse.*

However, in addition to the strictly strategic reasons of survival, other motives for change can be considered. Which of these do you think most executives identify as the principal motives for changing the way of thinking and doing things in their company: strategic, optimizing, regulatory-legal, ethical or other? The box on page 55 contains reflections for action, in which we present some of these motives collected from the views of numerous participants in seminars on strategic management and management of change.

As might be guessed, few people believe that the need for change is attributed to ethical motives. The main motives to change are typically considered to be strategic, such as for protection against market threats or to take advantage of opportunities in the environment. Nevertheless, changes induced by ethical motives (e.g., efficiency in the use of public money, protection of the natural environment) may also be considered to be strategic changes as would those intended to comply with new regulations and standards particularly those related to quality and safety even though they may primarily be regarded as a way to avoid sanctions and litigation.

INDICATORS EMPHASIZING THE NEED TO CHANGE IN RESPONSE TO THE BUSINESS ENVIRONMENT

If the environment neither posed threats nor offered opportunities, then the life of companies would be purely vegetative. There may be some who would welcome such placid calm but if they were honest, most executives/professional managers would be bored to death. There are innumerable factors and circumstances that are changing at an accelerating speed in today's business environment. It is virtually impossible for companies or managers to insulate themselves from this upheaval. The following can be listed among the more significant. Take time to determine which of the elements listed are increasing the need to drive change in your environment?

ACTION/REFLECTION

Which of the following do you consider as influencing your organization? Check all that apply.

❏ An increasing demand for quality guarantees and reduced production costs to be able to enter and compete in new markets, or even just to stay in existing markets.

❏ An increasing awareness that all workers at all levels need to be stimulated, that the organization must make better use of their creativity.

❏ Excess production capacity and saturated markets in many sectors.

❏ Pressure from consumers and taxpayers for efficiency in the management of public resources and services, etc.

❏ The problem of maintaining benefit levels under the welfare state.

❏ The tendency for passive users to become active customers with criteria for choice and criticism.

❏ Diminishing job security, increasing self-employment, more temporary and seasonal jobs.

❏ Accelerating technological development, especially new information systems, industrial 'robotization', telecommunications, etc. All contributing to more atomization of processes.

❏ Faster introduction of innovative products in all sectors.

❏ Faster pace of competition.

❏ New regulations regarding ecological impact of business activities affecting all developed countries.

❏ Shorter product life-cycles.

❏ Increased levels of education among the working population, leading to ever-higher expectations of job-satisfaction, job-interest, career paths, income growth, etc.

❏ Privatization of virtually all areas of public administration.

❏ Globalization of markets.

❏ Emergence of countries and regions with lower production costs in all continents.

❏ Extension of economic power from around the globe.

❏ Appearance of 'post-materialist values' in the richer, more developed countries, with people attaching more importance to free time, health care, respect for nature and the environment, aesthetic considerations, participation and direct democracy, individual freedoms, etc.

❏ Faster turnover of companies in all sectors, through start-ups, mergers and acquisitions, brand failures and management failures.

❏ Growth of tele-working from home via computer networks.

□ New strategic alliances between looser networks of companies, even between apparent 'competitors.'

□ Closer integration between suppliers and customer companies in many different areas of activity, from design to production, from logistics to distribution and after-sales services.

□ Greater awareness of risk management, leading to risk sharing and offsetting

□ And many more trends specific to particular markets and sectors.

Total number of responses: _____

CAN YOU AFFORD NOT TO CHANGE?

INDICATORS EMPHASIZING THE NEED FOR CULTURAL CHANGE

The policies and plans disseminated by the management of the company are, in effect, messages to their employees carrying a 'sell-by' date; their relevance and validity are strictly limited in time. But even the brightest of ideas are often abandoned or their utility short lived. In essence, they reach the expiration date. Thereafter disillusion sets in, skepticism about change increases and the next set of directives, even those with good intentions, must overcome increasing obstacles of internal resistance.

> **What people need are ideas, projects and values to inspire and to motivate them to want to get up and go to work every morning.**

What people need are ideas, projects and values to inspire and to motivate them to want to get up and go to work every morning, especially Monday mornings! But it is often difficult to find any significant meaning to work in a company that has lost its vitality.

How many of the following indicators of 'lack of cultural vitality' are evident now in your company? Complete the following two **ACTION/ REFLECTION** assessments.

Even more specifically there are certain kinds of behaviors to look out for in your company. If they are present on an ongoing basis they signal a warning that the cultural vitality is in jeopardy. Further, these behaviors may be blocking cultural development and creating the tending to repeat dysfunctional patterns. If these behaviors are not changed the company will very likely stagnate and be unable to develop the creativity and innovation necessary for its future.

ACTION/REFLECTION

I   Assessing your organization's vitality culture and environment

❑ Employees talk about customers as if they were an obligation (or worse), rather than an opportunity for work and service yielding mutual benefit.

❑ Honesty and trust seem to be absent from the culture; instead there exists a tendency towards superficiality and excessive 'political' precautions.

❑ Bosses who only want to supervise outnumber managers and leaders trying to develop people and ideas.

❑ Daily pressures are accepted as excuses for foregoing important team-building practices like periodical sessions for longer-term thinking, gatherings to mark departures and retirements, educational forums, staff meetings, etc.

❑ The vision of where the organization hopes to go in the future is expressed in financial bottom-line figures (e.g., next year we will achieve an ROI of 13.5%, etc.). It is directed only according to technical or rational rules, rather than developing human capital, or social and environmental good.

❑ The leaders see structures and technologies as answers, rather than trusting in people as individuals.

❑ Economic returns and goals are seen as the same thing.

❑ There is an unspoken tension between the key personalities of the organization, often even obvious animosity.

Total number of responses: _____

ACTION/REFLECTION

II   Assessing your organization's vitality culture and relationality

To what extent do you believe that the following behaviors are present in your organization and that they need to be changed because they are negatively impacting your organization? Use the following scale to rate your responses:

[1 – Never   2 – Sometimes   3 – Always]

1. People generally do not trust one another   _____
2. People are outwardly and consistently cynical   _____

3. Aggressive behavior is present on a regular basis   _____
4. People conform to norms rather than trying something new   _____
5. People remain silent than risk telling the truth   _____
6. Apathy and/or the absence of initiatives are typical   _____
7. People at all levels say one thing but do another   _____
8. An inability to delegate is typical   _____
9. People are constantly postponing important meetings   _____
10. Poor planning frequently leads to poor work outcomes   _____
11. Feedback is only provided during performance reviews   _____
12. Feedback is just another way of saying, 'You've messed up!'   _____
13. People hide their mistakes for fear of reprimand   _____

Total number of responses: _____

What should the change involve and how far should we go?

In thinking of the need for change there are two main questions to consider: (1) What should be changed? Specifically, what levels of change are needed: strategic, operational (structures/processes) or individual? (2) What depth of change is needed: adaptive or transformational?

WHAT IS IT THAT SHOULD BE CHANGED?

In a company oriented towards continuous improvement, innovation is needed in practically every aspect of organizational life, or at least a certain degree of renewal. However, in order to illustrate the possible levels of change clearly, three distinct levels may be considered (Table 3.2 and Figure 3.1).

Table 3.2 **Levels of change in a company**

Level of change	What to change
Change of strategy	In effect, a reformulation of 'Where are we going, and why?'
Operational change	Change of organization structures and of internal systems and processes.
Individual change	Change of leadership style, of the way of thinking, and of the values shared by all the members of the company as a group.

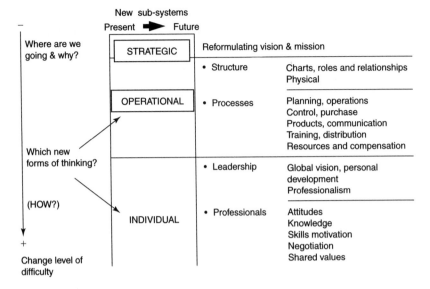

Figure 3.1 **Levels and difficulties of change in a company**

Figure 3.1 is intended to make an important point: the lower you descend in the scheme, towards the base (i.e., the dimension of the individual employee), the more difficult it is to effect real change. Obviously, changing values shared among individuals is far more difficult and transcendental than just modifying an organization chart or changing technology in a company.

> Changing values shared among individuals is far more difficult and transcendental than just modifying an organization chart or changing technology in a company.

The need for 'gearing' between strategy, structure, processes and people: the role of values

Every business organization is an 'open system' which is in constant adaptive interchange with its environment. It receives inputs of 'energy' and processes outputs or productive responses that add value to the 'energy' received. The energy inputs are constituted by the capital, ideas, prior history of the firm, its personnel, technologies, and whatever else goes into making it function. The productive outputs are not just the products and services but they also include the personal development of people.

The process of adding value depends on the correct 'gearing or linkage' of four mutually dependent 'drivers' of the organization: the strategy, the structure, the internal processes and people. If one of these fails, remains static or is not integrated, it is practically impossible for the others to work well. The notion of interdependent organizational factors resonates with the idea put forth by Nadler and Tushman (1980) who postulate the need for a 'fit' or 'correct shaping' between all the subsystems of a business organization. MBV adds to this notion of 'fit' by suggesting that the essential beliefs and values of the operative culture act like a lubricant facilitating the enmeshing of these gears. A values fit will enable the constant transformation of positive energy as the critical elements of an organization interact in harmony with its environment.

For example, a bureaucratic type of organizational structure cannot easily fit values system oriented towards development of human potential; a strategic vision of sector leadership is not compatible with the existence of redundant processes that add no value. The existence of an operating culture that clearly legitimizes shared values such as agility, quality internal communication, or the stimulation of creativity of people is needed in order to ensure the positive transformation of shared energy.

Perhaps another comparison will help to explicate how energy is transformed in an organization. Human biology allows us to establish some analogies to illustrate the interdependence of all the critical sub-systems:

- The strategy is the vision of the future, located in the brain.
- The culture, as already mentioned, is equivalent to the personality or form of behavior. This is based on the set of beliefs and values learned through interaction with the environment and from the integration of internal tensions. Like strategy, this is also located in the brain.

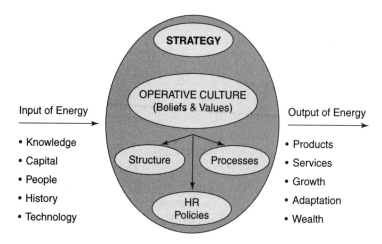

Figure 3.2 **The business organization as an energy transformation system**

- The structure is the skeleton and arteries that sustain and channel the processes of movement and internal communication between functional areas (muscles and nervous system).
- The productive processes are the observable behavior, which executes intentions harmoniously.
- The people in an organization are like the heart pumping blood needed to fuel the system and to maintain the whole body in operation.

Comparing a company to a human system allows us to reconsider and perhaps identify with organizations in new ways. Rather than thinking of businesses as stagnant and lifeless entities we can see them for what they really are, or have the potential to be; dynamic and vital environments permeated with the energetic processes of mutually supporting purposes. Imagine your organization as a human system. What is its personality? Where is it in its lifespan? How does it interact with the environment? How does it manifest its values? What do you hope it will become? What can you do to help it to flourish?

NEED TO ADAPT OR TO TRANSFORM?

The depth of change in a company can reach two levels: the company can adapt (i.e., a gradual form of change), or transform (a major or rapid form of change) (see Table 3.3). However, in practice it is often difficult to distinguish where the one ends and the other starts. In broad terms, we can talk about changes as adaptation or transformation depending on the difference or 'gap' to be bridged between the strategic vision of where the company wants to go and its situation or condition at the present time. *How close, or far apart, are the present state and the desired future state?*

For example, a company that is obtaining acceptable results, that enjoys a stable and competitive position in its segment of the market, and that

Table 3.3 **Different levels of change in the organization**

Adaptive change	Transformational change
Small gap (small difference between future vision and present situation)	Large gap (big difference between future vision and present situation)
Type 1 – Incremental or first-order change (more of the same)	Type 2 – Drastic or second-order change (a change in the way of changing)
Reducing gap or optimizing	Re-inventing
Change of image or procedure (e.g., new Coca Cola and Coca Cola classic)	Change of culture (e.g., new Chrysler corporation – the Lee Iacoca style)
Micro changes	Macro changes

operates well internally, is not likely to generate a future vision very different or distant from its present situation. Therefore, the degree of change needed in response to its strategy is a more adaptive change that will enable it to consolidate and respond better to the needs of its markets. This type of adaptive change may involve, for example, the redesign of some of its products, certain cost reductions in certain departments, or modifications to its information systems. In contrast, a company that formulates a particularly ambitious vision with respect to its present situation, such as a small family company setting out to become a small multinational with professional management, will without a doubt have to undertake a major transformation. This will imply profound changes in its structures, internal processes and personnel policy. In short, this company will need a complete culture change.

More of the same or 'a change in the way of changing'?

The reflection put forward by Watzlawick (1989) is not only interesting, but useful when thinking about organizational change. Drawing from psychotherapy and mathematics he differentiates between 'Type-1' and 'Type-2' changes: the first being 'more of the same' while the second is a 'change of change.' Let us look at what these concepts mean.

Which represents a deeper change: when a car accelerates from 0 km/h to 5 km/h or when it accelerates from 5 km/h to 500 km/h? According to the approach of 'the solution of Type-1 change' and 'the solution of Type-2 change' formulated by Watzlawick, the second change, from 5 to 500 km/h is a change within the same frame of reference. The increase in the speed of the car, despite its spectacular scale, is more of the same since the car is already in motion. However, the change from being stationary to being in motion despite the slow speed, is more profound and is designated 'meta-change' or 'change of change.'

Cases of Type-1 change often arise when an attempt to solve a problem is made from within the situation originating the problem. In the business arena, searching for a stricter and more authoritarian Human Resource Manager to deal with problems of apathy and absenteeism would be a Type-1 change. By contrast, to create an environment that supports more autonomy and responsibility throughout the organization would be a Type-2 change. Another example of a Type-2 change would be the meta-negotiation or re-negotiation of the rules of the game for solving a problem or making a deal. Instead of being trapped in an endless tactical game of 'I win and you lose', two negotiators might sit down to agree to a collaborative style of negotiating, 'I win and you win', rather than the initial competitive style.

An important and peculiar characteristic of 'changes of change' is that they cannot be instigated from within a specific system. They need to be driven by someone from outside the organization who is not a member of the group

> **'Changes of change' cannot be instigated from within a specific system. They need to be driven by someone outside, who is not a member of the group needing to change, someone with an external perspective.**

needing to change, someone with an external perspective, and with no 'axe to grind.' This is a necessary condition for a change embracing all the members of a system.

The policy of reducing the size and costs of an organization is given a variety of names in management jargon: you have probably come across the concepts called re-structuring, rationalizing, re-adjustment, re-floating, right-sizing, and even re-dimensioning. Most typically, such policies are reactive responses in the context of a sudden crisis. The survival of the organization is claimed to depend on reducing the fixed costs of personnel, and is implemented by dismissals (if possible), retirements (often 'early') and recruitment bans that effectively force organizations to shrink through 'natural wastage.' Some headline-hitting examples of this kind of change were the spectacular reductions in global staff levels by IBM (63,000 workers in 1993), Sears Roebuck (50,000 workers in the same year) and AT&T (40,000 workers in 1996). When these cases are inevitably seen as a 'change for the worse' by employees, the discussion of beliefs and

ACTION/REFLECTION

What changes of the type 'more of the same' have occurred in your organization in the past several years (i.e., Type 1)?

_____

_____

_____

Can any of the changes in your organization in the past several years be characterized as Type 2 – drastic or second-order change?

_____

_____

_____

values becomes especially salient. Such decisions often imply a change in the culture of the company, where there had previously existed the belief that 'no one ever gets sacked in this company' the reality causes a 'values check' among stakeholders.

THE IMPORTANCE OF PRESERVING KEY TRADITIONAL VALUES

It would be frivolous to think that a company should embark on culture change simply because it wants to 'shake things up.' When thinking of the introduction of new values, perhaps for increasing company efficiency, such as flexibility, creativity, autonomy or speed of response, it must not be ignored that the company will have reached its present situation because of the existence of a certain way of thinking and doing things that have embraced certain worthwhile values. These probably are worth retaining, or certainly should not be thrown overboard precipitously, since they are a part of the company's identity and undoubtedly regarded with pride by its stakeholders, internal and external to the organization.

Not infrequently, the resistance to change when new styles or procedures are hurriedly introduced stems from a common feeling in the organization that people want to preserve some of the values that make up the cultural identity of the company. The loss of these key values may have much more negative results than many managers imagine or understand.

> By definition individual values serve as a guide to a person's intentions and actions. Similarly organizational value systems provide guides for organizational goals, policies and strategies. Thus the nature of the values is a crucial factor in the impact that culture will have on organizational effectiveness. If the prevailing values support appropriate goals and strategies the culture is an important asset. Conversely the *wrong* values can make the culture a *major liability*.

All too often change is viewed as a destructive force placing additional demands on already overworked individuals, teams and departments. This perspective of change is not what is meant by a culture change. All change can be a powerful source of learning. Learning means first unlearning old ideas, and putting new ideas into practice. If we ask ourselves when we should learn, rather than when we should change, it will be much clearer that the probable answer is 'always.' In fact, talking of undergoing change can sound quite stressful, but to talk of continuous learning is more likely to relieve stress. But remember we are also talking of permanent 'unlearning' often of ingrained habits. This type of change reflects a change in culture. Continuous learning is about being open to questioning our beliefs and assumptions about the way we have become accustomed to functioning and our interactions with the world around us.

When is the right time to change?

Deciding when to change is a crucial question for the strategic development of a company. Change can be reactive and by nature defensive or it can be proactive and anticipatory. While reactive change is usually the consequence of an unfolding chain of events, such as a crisis, threatening legislation, or loss of market share, proactive change is that which is generated by true leadership and is the response to informed consideration of trends, forecasts and expectations. Anticipatory change pre-empts both favorable and adverse phenomena in the future internal and external situation of the company.

The projects for change you initiate in response to observed trends add a special competitive advantage, since not all your competitors will have sufficient capacity for the same sort of change. In contrast, those companies that focus only on survival will have no alternative but to accept reactive change in situations of crisis. It is clear that when a company that is obtaining good results initiates a process of significant change, it is because it has high quality leadership that is moving ahead into the future, and thus trying to gain competitive advantage and significant differentiation.

Another time dimension with regard to cultural change is that of the rate or speed of change attempted. Many executives assume that once a decision has been made to change it is better to implement it as fast as possible under conditions perceived as urgent. One reason for this approach is that they believe the change will be perceived as negative by employees but if the initiative bears management's 'stamp of approval' it will more

- **Anyone working to bring about lasting culture change will attest to the enormity of the task. Without a framework, culture change appears hopelessly complex. MBV, thus may provide such a framework.**
- **Changing culture in many ways parallels farming. The first phase, Analysis and Objective Setting, is dedicated to analysing and preparing the soil. Phase II, Systems Introduction, plants the seed of change. The third phase, Systems Integration, is the cultural equivalent of adding fertilizer and water so that the plant takes root and flourishes. And the fourth phase, Evaluation, Renewal and Extension, is similar to harvesting the crop and gathering new seed for the next planting.**

Source: Judd Allen, *Culture Change Planner*, http://healthyculture.com/Articles/CCplanner.html

likely ensure a timely and well executed plan. A change of culture cannot be achieved in weeks or even in months. If one compares it with the development of personality on the individual level, it is more a question of progressive episodes of combined experience and learning.

Summary

- Organizational change in the context of MBV involves modifying an organization's culture.
- From a 'values perspective,' true change is about effectively managing and maintaining the organizational culture in order to bring it in alignment with its core values and the demands of its environment.
- MBV provides a way to engage in cultural transformation involving both incremental and drastic change processes sometimes referred to as first and second order change.
- To navigate successfully through the demands of the 21st century, corporate leaders need to know how to monitor changes in the environment, to move forward into the future and to renovate the company; failure to so can result in corporate premature death.
- In thinking of the need for change there are two main questions to consider: (1) What should be changed? and (2) What should be the scope (depth) of the needed change (adaptive or transformational)?
- An organizational change requires you to make a decision about the scope and the level of change.
- Deciding when to change is a crucial question for the strategic development of a company.

4 The Logic of Two Different Cultures: Control versus Development

'The coordinating authority must act from the apex and must continue being distributed more widely the lower one descends down the pyramid. For this reason, each role must be clearly defined.'

(Fayol, French manager, 1945)

'The fuel that is needed for the journey into the future is not money: it is the emotional and intellectual energy of each and every one of the employees.'

(Hamel and Prahalad, *The New Logic Half a Century after Fayol*, 1995)

'Before we said: trust is good but control is better; today we say: control is good but trust is better.'

(Diener, German Industrialist)

To what extent are the beliefs and values inspiring the organizations of the beginning of the 20th century the same as those persisting today in most companies? What are the new beliefs and values that will inspire the necessary changes in structures, processes and personnel policies so that companies can hold on to their markets and develop new ones in the 21st century? Do we cling to a culture of control, or do we cultivate an environment that fosters development throughout the organization? Ask yourself what is needed, control or development, in order not only to survive, but to thrive.

So far we have proposed a model for MBV including the importance of values and organizational culture along with why a company should be open to changes in its ways of thinking and operating. In this chapter we will more closely explain two dominant types of culture, namely control versus development and why a shift in management orientation is necessary for MBV to be successful.

Basically, we can describe two broad general orientations that reflect the different currents of thought on the ideal way of thinking and doing things

69

in the management of business organizations since the middle of the 19th century:

- Those that aim to rationalize the company by traditional values of hierarchical control (i.e., order, obedience, loyalty, security, etc.); and
- Those that aim to drive the company forward by new values of personal development and continuous learning (i.e., creativity, autonomy, variety, risk-taking, etc.).

A great majority of companies today are strategically designed based on traditional organization models with an orientation towards hierarchical control. An over reliance on control and rational processes, while relatively comfortable and predictable, contributes to an environment where employees are indifferent, uninspired and excessively dependent on leadership. While we do not suggest that control is bad, we do argue that a more integrated (i.e., relevant aspects of control and development woven throughout the organization), flexible and learning-oriented design will contribute to a robust culture and therefore a successful business.

A new cultural logic oriented towards development and continuous learning is not just one more organizational 'designer label' fashion. MBV proposes that this strategic evolution 'away from oppressive control and towards development' should not be regarded as another management fad, but rather as a dynamic continuum along which each company has to find its own position and style and at its own pace. It is our intention in the following sections to facilitate this process.

> MBV proposes that this strategic evolution 'away from oppressive control and towards development' should not be regarded as a fad, but rather as a dynamic continuum along which each company has to find its own position and style, and at its own pace.

The necessity to alternate and integrate control-oriented management with development-oriented management

The resolution of the dilemma between security and risk (between control and development) is essential for the survival and growth of a company. Both options imply certain distinctive but related systems of values. MBV posits the need to not abandon one value set in favor of the other, but to know how to integrate them according to specific conditions within your company's unique profile.

It may seem obvious but the integrated framework of MBV is somewhat novel in the world of management theory. Until now theory has tended to

Table 4.1 **Control orientation versus development orientation**

Control orientation	Development orientation
Survival	Self-actualization
Focusing/concentrating	Expanding/diversifying
Company first	People first

recommend frameworks either oriented toward the bureaucratic-formal organization or toward humanist, socio-technical models – but rarely are the two incorporated into a singular and perhaps more importantly, practical model. MBV aligns itself with what the renowned scholar Kurt Lewin wisely proposed: 'There is nothing so practical as a good theory' (1951).

As shown in Table 4.1, we can identify various sets of apparently opposite values distinguishing control orientation versus development orientation. In essence, the control orientation focuses on the company whereas the development orientation is centered on the individual within the organization. We now provide some detail to explain each of these points demonstrating two ends of a continuum.

SURVIVAL AND SELF-ACTUALIZATION

As we know, Maslow's motivation theory (1943) suggests we have different needs. Through the lens of MBV these needs could be considered as two overarching groups of values: survival (lower-order values) and self-actualization (upper-order values) (Figure 4.1).

Under Maslow's theory of motivation it is only when the lower-order values are fulfilled that most people are able to think about upper-order values. An interesting point regarding how Maslow's theory comes to life in today's organizations is highlighted through a research finding: when a person perceives one's self to be denied upper-order values, they focus even more energy on obtaining and ensuring the presence of lower-order values (e.g., security, safety, etc.). An example of this 'theory in action' might be an individual who places a high value on autonomy but works for a company that places inordinate amounts of control over their job (i.e., policies, procedures, running all decisions 'by the boss'). In this case, denying such a person a fair amount of autonomy and responsibility might make them overly concerned about following the rules in order to avoid sanctions that could jeopardize their value for job security. Over time, this adherence to 'the rules' could reduce

> When a person perceives one's self to be denied upper order values, they focus even more energy on obtaining and ensuring the presence of lower order values (e.g., security. safety, etc.).

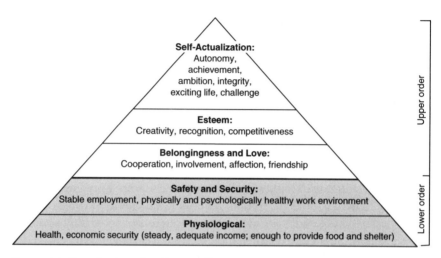

Figure 4.1 **Survival and self-actualization values**
Source: Adapted from E. Nevis (1983).

the person's self-confidence, risk-taking and even negatively impact their performance. If a person is bound by control, how likely will they be to bring problems to the attention of management, or to suggest improvements that would reduce bureaucracy in place of efficiency? Not likely when they revert to ensuring the presence of lower-order values.

The psychological concept of 'self-actualization' or fulfilling one's ambitions is especially relevant in MBV. MBV seeks to enjoin the development of both lower and upper-order values as a way to realize the 'potential' of individuals throughout the organization. While initially this may seem to be an unrealistically lofty goal, a closer look will reveal that it is indeed achievable. At the macro level this integration is made manifest through the intentional design of the organization's culture that supports these objectives through articulation of its core values. These core values may take many forms to include statements and actions around organizational learning, participatory processes or a belief in education. At the micro, or individual level, this integration is achieved more concretely. For example, through job design enhancements, training and development initiatives, or even 360° feedback assessments to build competencies that are important to one's personal and professional growth.

As with so many other aspects of values, certain similarities can be observed between what happens on the individual level and on the organization level. While some companies may be immersed in a system of values oriented toward maintenance and survival through control, others may focus on values that attempt to realize the company's potential through the development of employee capabilities. Rather than putting forward the logic of an 'either, or' choice between management control or management development, MBV advocates a dialectic from which emerges a philosophy and practice of the integration of these two.

WHAT ABOUT YOU?

ACTION/REFLECTION

Take a few moments and review Figure 4.1. Check all the values that apply to you within the context of your organization.

Lower to upper-level categories	Specific values
❏ **SELF-ACTUALIZATION:**	❏ Autonomy ❏ Achievement ❏ Ambition ❏ Integrity ❏ Exciting life ❏ Challenge ❏ Other:_____
❏ **ESTEEM:**	❏ Creativity ❏ Recognition ❏ Competitiveness ❏ Other:_____
❏ **BELONGINGNESS:**	❏ Cooperation ❏ Involvement ❏ Affection ❏ Friendship ❏ Other:_____
❏ **SAFETY/SECURITY:**	❏ Stable employment ❏ Physically and psychologically healthy work environment ❏ Other:_____
❏ **PHYSIOLOGICAL:**	❏ Health ❏ Economic security (steady, adequate income; enough to provide food and shelter) ❏ Other:_____

To what extent does your organization integrate lower-order values and upper-order values? Do you think that an act of balancing values from one end of the continuum to the other is needed? Try to give specific examples of how these two aspects are integrated in your organization at the following levels:

You as an individual

_____

_____

_____

Your team (*if applicable*)

_____

_____

_____

Your department (*if applicable*)

_____

_____

_____

Throughout the organization

_____

_____

_____

TO CONCENTRATE (CONTRACT) OR EXPAND (DIVERSIFY)?

> The proof of having superior intelligence is the capacity to keep two opposing ideas in one's head and still continue functioning.
>
> (F. Scott Fitzgerald)

Although the analogy may appear incongruous, the development of the universe and of an organization has at least one dynamic aspect in common: the fluctuation between contraction and expansion. What the universe repeatedly and consistently demonstrates is the co-existence of both dynamics (e.g., expansion from the Big Bang and contraction through gravity). For companies, this same sort of balancing act can be seen in those organizations that correctly manage the creative tension generated by the variability between adopting values of expansion and of concentration (Table 4.2).

The choice between concentration and expansion is influenced by which stage of the economic cycle the company is currently experiencing. In times of depressed demand or profits most companies are likely to adopt values of concentration, tending to maintain their presence in markets or

Table 4.2 **Integrating values related to expansion with values related to concentration**

Expansion	⇔	Concentration
1. Open territories (many opportunities)	+5 +4 +3 +2 +1 0 −1 −2 −3 −4 −5	1. Close territories (limited opportunities)
2. Fluid structures	+5 +4 +3 +2 +1 0 −1 −2 −3 −4 −5	2. Rigid structures
3. Merging/buying	+5 +4 +3 +2 +1 0 −1 −2 −3 −4 −5	3. Keeping/Staying put
4. Differentiation	+5 +4 +3 +2 +1 0 −1 −2 −3 −4 −5	4. Integration
5. Diversity	+5 +4 +3 +2 +1 0 −1 −2 −3 −4 −5	5. Homogeneity
6. Multitasking	+5 +4 +3 +2 +1 0 −1 −2 −3 −4 −5	6. Specialized tasking
7. Innovation	+5 +4 +3 +2 +1 0 −1 −2 −3 −4 −5	7. Maintenance
8. Risk	+5 +4 +3 +2 +1 0 −1 −2 −3 −4 −5	8. Safety, security
9. Global vision	+5 +4 +3 +2 +1 0 −1 −2 −3 −4 −5	9. Focused vision
10. Process oriented	+5 +4 +3 +2 +1 0 −1 −2 −3 −4 −5	10. Results oriented
11. Participation	+5 +4 +3 +2 +1 0 −1 −2 −3 −4 −5	11. Acceptation/ Conformity
12. 'Unlearn' climate	+5 +4 +3 +2 +1 0 −1 −2 −3 −4 −5	12. Retention
13. Broadminded	+5 +4 +3 +2 +1 0 −1 −2 −3 −4 −5	13. Inward-looking
14. Exploring	+5 +4 +3 +2 +1 0 −1 −2 −3 −4 −5	14. Dominating
15. Opting for change	+5 +4 +3 +2 +1 0 −1 −2 −3 −4 −5	15. Opting for permanency
Total (max 80 points) – CHAOS	⇔	**Total (max −80 points) – ORDER**

capacity, or reducing overheads by rationalizing, or restructuring. But it is often the case that companies who go against the current, or buck conventional wisdom, are the ones that later benefit from differentiation or are seen as bolder and more self-confident than their rivals.

A company that clings to values of concentration, preferring rigid departmental boundaries and a parochial view rather than an open-minded or forward-thinking vision is very likely to stagnate because it will not be receptive to changes in the environment (i.e., market demands, new technologies, resources, etc.). Excessive order and control

> **Companies have even been known to die of boredom, not just figuratively, but literally in the sense that their best people get bored and quit.**

causes loss of vitality and drive. Companies have even been known to die of boredom, not just figuratively but literally, in the sense that their best people get fed up and quit. Try the exercise in Table 4.2. The closer your total score is to the negative maximum of −80, the greater the probability that your company is devitalized by an excess of values of concentration. It is also likely that you may be bored and at times wonder, 'What am I doing in this company?'

On the other hand, a company may also be at risk by being excessively oriented toward values of expansion and change. For examples, too much diversification, versus specialization, too many risks taken versus security, too many acquisitions versus investment, too much exploration of new fields, at the expense of mastering core competencies. The chaos likely to result from this orientation could also lead to loss of vitality, to loss of identity, to effort and resources dispersed too widely and thinly, to over-stimulus and chaos. If your score in the exercise in Table 4.2 tends towards the positive maximum of $+80$, your company may be heading for a fall through an excess of values of expansion.

As in so many other things, equilibrium does not consist of staying static at some supposed mid-point between two extremes, but rather in knowing how to alternate sensibly between one and another kind of value as indicated by specific contexts or situations (this is the essence of the concept of dynamic equilibrium or homeostasis). But neither does this mean rapid oscillation between contradictory values. For example, on point 14 of Table 4.2, a company that tends to conduct ongoing market research and attaches high importance to being alert to changes in its environment may be scored as $+2$; however, this does not imply that it does not also build its core competencies on continuing to dominate its 'old' markets.

DETERMINING PRIORITIES: STAKEHOLDERS AND THE ORGANIZATION

Another dilemma within companies is the tension between views that support the primacy of the system or those that promote the primacy of

Table 4.3 Examples of primacy of the company and of the individual

Values indicating the primacy of the company	Values indicating the primacy of the individual/stakeholders
Priority focused on identification with the company (normally associated with collective expressions such as 'we' or 'in our place we…')	Priority on self interests (i.e., profession or other personal characteristics)
Maintaining present structure and systems	Flexibility and adaptability based on individual or stakeholder demands
Strict obedience to company policies and rules	Breaking the rules for personal advantage or appeals to stakeholder needs
Maintenance of norms	Stakeholder-driven actions leading to inconsistent or unclear procedures

individuals. If the interests of the organization's survival and growth are given exclusive or long-term priority over the interests of stakeholders (e.g., employees, customers, suppliers, the communities in which it operates, etc.), or the other way around, this imbalance will ultimately lead to inefficiency or instability for both (see Table 4.3 for examples of each). Clearly, the system and its stakeholders are inextricably linked and the neglect of one, over time, leads to the demise of the other. Finding the way to balance what is good for the organization and its stakeholders are the very essence of the art and skill of management. The successful manager of the 21st century knows that their primary function is to continuously create convergence between organizational goals and objectives and those of its stakeholders through the articulation of shared values.

The meaning of values in control-oriented and learning and development-oriented organizations

We have mentioned before that values are words that may be used in very different ways according to the context in which they are formulated and the meaning that is attributed to them. For some being good means being resigned and patient, whereas others will consider a good person to be one who is enterprising and original, one who is not afraid to say what they think or believe (Savater, 1991). Therefore values such as support, respect, integrity and efficiency can take on a variety of meanings depending on whether they are formulated in an organizational culture oriented towards control or in a culture focused on learning and development. A culture of learning and development is rooted in values that support and encourage both organizational and human potential. Often these distinctions are thought of as 20th century versus 21st century organizational cultures or simply, old versus new, or traditional versus innovative cultures. Table 4.4 compares how these values take on entirely different meanings under both cultural types.

> A culture of learning and development is rooted in values that support and encourage both organizational and human potential.

An example of an organizational culture centered on learning and development is Cisco Systems. Cisco is a world leader in supplying networking equipment and network management for the internet. Their philosophy has translated into a culture of success balancing the goals and objectives of the organization and their stakeholders.

CISCO: A CULTURE THAT MAKES IT ONE OF THE 'BEST PLACES TO WORK'

Once again, Cisco Systems has landed high on Fortune magazine's annual 'best places to work' list. This time the company is ranked #4 among large companies – those with more than 10,000 employees. Fortune applauded Cisco's efforts to make the workplace fun, mentioning the nearly famous 'nerd lunches' (technology-talk lunches) and the movie-themed food available in some cafeterias on Oscar day. Cisco, #27 on the overall Fortune list, has now made the elite ranking eight straight years. That's no accident. Company officials say that enriching the work – and non-work – experience of employees is a core commitment.

Cisco is proud to be recognized by Fortune Magazine for the eighth consecutive year as one of the 100 Best Companies to Work For, says Kate DCamp, senior vice president, human resources. We strive to create a culture of open communication with employees so that we can create programs and services that will meet the needs of our diverse work force and increase employees' commitment to Cisco.

The much sought-after Fortune list is based on an evaluation of the policies and culture of each company and the opinions of the company's employees. Two-thirds of the score comes from employee responses to a 57-question survey going to a minimum of 350 randomly selected employees from each company. The survey asks about things such as attitudes towards management, job satisfaction and camaraderie. The remaining score is based on an evaluation of each company's demographic makeup, pay and benefits programs and culture. Companies are scored for credibility (communication to employees); respect (opportunities and benefits); fairness (compensation, diversity); and pride/camaraderie (philanthropy, celebrations).

Source: G. Patrick Pawling, 'Company Makes List for Eighth Straight Year,' 14 January 2005, News@Cisco; http://newsroom.cisco.com/dlls/2005/ts_011405.html

**CISCO
BALANCING ORGANIZATIONAL AND STAKEHOLDER NEEDS**

REALITY CHECK

CISCO SYSTEMS – FOSTERING A CULTURE OF DEVELOPMENT

Cisco Systems' culture is an amalgam of management directives and the individuals who make up Cisco.

Cisco purpose: To shape the future of global networking by creating unprecedented opportunities and value for our customers, employees, investors, and partners.

Cisco mission: To be the supplier of choice by leading all competitors in customer satisfaction, product leadership, market share, and profitability.

Communications:

- Cisco encourages communication through all levels of the organization.
- Cisco regularly communicates its vision, mission, strategies, and goals to ensure a common direction and empower employees with information to make decisions.
- All employees are given the necessary decision-making responsibility to achieve results.
- Teamwork is supported and rewarded at Cisco.
- Communications meetings (company-wide, department-wide) are held quarterly.
- Regular newsletters and e-mail communications are distributed.

Flexibility: Cisco supports flextime, flexwork (telecommuting), and part-time work schedules, depending on the particular work requirements in the department and the manager's discretion.

Diversity: We encourage a work environment characterized by respect for each individual, where people from diverse cultures and ethnic groups work together in harmonious and heterogeneous teams. Diversity supports and represents the values of cultures worldwide and creates an open environment for all employees.

Work environment: Cisco strives to provide a stimulating environment for all employees by providing high levels of motivation, empowerment, and recognition and removing obstacles that hinder creativity. The Cisco environment is highly energized with employees who share successes while striving for excellence.

Source: http://www.cisco.com/jobs/culture.html

Table 4.4 **Meaning of certain value terms, under the old culture of control and the new culture of development**

Values	20th century: culture of control	21st century: culture of learning and development
Control	Supervision focused on control geared toward correcting deviations from anticipated results. Results are determined by top management. Hierarchical structure.	Managers encourage autonomy and employee responsibility. Control is interwoven in policies and procedures to ensure quality assurance, safety, etc. Results are derived through participatory processes that are inclusive and aimed at getting appropriate and accurate information. Flatter organizational structure.
Support	Saying what you believe others want to hear; approving and praising; helping to hide errors.	Helping others to check the effectiveness of their work and learning from their errors.
Integrity	Staying put in one's own principles, values and beliefs; not giving in.	Open disposition toward situations and others with different belief systems.
Respect	Not questioning the rationale of other people and more specifically those in positions of authority.	Show consideration for others regardless of organizational 'rank' and being open to their opinion, ideas, perspective, etc.
Self-confidence	Demonstrating self-confidence through persuasion and 'winning.' Admission of errors is akin to 'losing face' and status. Posturing is a way of life.	Demonstrating self-confidence as well as accepting other opinions. Capacity to admit mistakes, learn from others regardless of position.

The rational-economic culture and why it fails

The logic of 'rational-economic' thought predominant in management from the beginning of the Industrial Revolution until the end of the 20th century tended to be based on controlling the performance of people more than on strengthening it, on reducing costs more than on creating new ideas, and even on producing more than on selling.

The cartoon below is affectionately dedicated to the fair number of bosses who are driven to control every detail of the working lives of employees. This might be termed 'the Zeus complex'. Usually – but not invariably – such bosses are unaware that their management style is inhibiting, if not damaging. However, one should not jump to conclusions. Firstly, the logic of the beliefs and values of the traditional company should be properly understood. Many of the values apparent in the traditional models of

Mythological fantasies of the 'Zeus Boss'

organizations are worthy of merit and thus retaining. Others may benefit from being changed or revised.

As we have proposed before, these traditional organizations were designed in accordance with a set of beliefs about human nature in relation to work that was the legacy of the early theoreticians of the market economy, starting very early on with Adam Smith who proposed that societal conditions would be improved if everyone pursued their own self interests. These are the beliefs we term *rational-economic* and support the doctrine that human nature is rational with respect to economic decisions. (Research into the workings of the human mind – particularly from recent mind/brain studies – has discovered that the assumption of rationalism as the basis for human thought and action is significantly less valid than previously thought.)

Frederick Taylor's term 'the Scientific Management of Work' (1911), was derived from the rational-economic model of organizing that developed a system of incentives limited to economic stimuli, by which the link between the person and the organization was reduced to a purely contractual relationship. In this model the employee was a passive entity dependent on and controlled by the organization or, more accurately authority figures.

Taylor was convinced that the laziness of workers, or their natural instinct of 'couldn't care less,' was an inherent part of human nature and should be controlled by the company through a strict system of definition of tasks and incentives. Before the First World War he put forward a model for the organization of work that is still widely in force today particularly in large industrial manufacturing companies or in industries in developing countries. One of the concepts he introduced was the idea of the individual 'task' which he proposed as the one most characteristic element of the then modern 'scientific management.' According to Taylor, the task of each worker should be completely planned. Each person should be provided written instructions describing precisely all the details of the work they must do, together with the means to be used to do the work.

ACTION/REFLECTION

Which of the following beliefs/assumptions about the model of 'economic man' do you agree with? (*Place an* x *in either 'yes' or 'no' column.*)

WHAT ABOUT YOU?

		YES	NO
1.	Man always pursues his own benefit at the expense of others.	___	___
2.	Employees are motivated basically by economic incentives and will always act in the way that brings them the maximum economic benefit.	___	___
3.	Given that the economic incentives are under the control of the company (although heavily influenced by market mechanisms), the employee is essentially a passive agent to be manipulated, motivated and controlled by the company.	___	___
4.	Feelings/sentiments are by definition irrational and unpredictable; therefore, they should be prevented at all costs from interfering in the rational manner of doing business by the company.	___	___
5.	The 'natural' objectives of employees are the opposite of those of the company; Therefore, they must be suppressed to ensure that employees work toward the organization's objectives.	___	___
6.	Owing to their irrational feelings, employees are basically incapable of self-discipline and self-control.	___	___
7.	Nevertheless, employees can be divided into two general groups: one, the larger, in which all the above assumptions apply, and another small group of self-motivated, self-disciplined, less dominated by sentiments, responsible, reliable employees who constitute a 'moral elite'; these latter should naturally assume the management of the rest of the employees.	___	___

The introduction of the idea of task is essential for the consolidation of the management of organizations since its effect is to transfer ownership and control of the process of work to the company and removing it from the worker who had hitherto 'owned' his craft (Weisbord, 1989). The idea of the task is very powerful because it accepted and systematized what was often assumed or implicitly known by the individual. The concept of 'the task' helped to legitimatize the 'work' that was to be accomplished and thus accounted for in a formal practice. According to Taylor, productivity would be generated through the idea of the precisely-defined task, because it collects, systematizes and transmits knowledge and skills in an orderly fashion throughout the organization. The organization then becomes the owner of the knowledge.

But, rather than passing on the old craftsmanship, scientific management was 'de-skilling' work. Tasks as actually defined represented a fragmentation of functions; jobs were diminished in terms of the scope and skills that workers could develop; the consequence of this, which was only initially favorable to management, was that workers could be treated and remunerated as increasingly less qualified and less 'professional' operatives.

The Taylorist focus has contributed to the degradation of work and to the loss of the employee's sense of psychological ownership over their work process and work result which characterized the industrial production methods. In fact, today when we speak of *empowerment* or the liberation of the creative potential of employees, this is nothing more than an attempt to correct this historical damage.

The true 'enchainment' of the industrial worker/ex-craftsman arises from the loss of this sense of psychological ownership and control over his/her work. Moreover, the vast majority of employees lost the ability to bargain for their financial reward based on the strength of their individual skills and the quality of their craftsmanship.

> The true 'enchainment' of the industrial worker/ex-craftsman arises from the loss of this sense of psychological ownership and control over his/her work.

However, it would be unjust to dismiss Taylor as a stereotype exploiter of the working man or a mechanistic inhuman theorizer. His principles are basically humanist on paper, but in contrast his biography reveals him to be described as a rigid and contradictory person, although pre-occupied about social justice in a paternalist way. In fact, there existed two different Taylors, and they exemplify perfectly the internal dialogue each one of us conducts, between social and technological impulses, between external control and self-control, between authority and independence (Weisbord, 1989). Some observers suggest that 'opposition to Taylor was a major cause of the rapid growth of unionism' in North America (Auerbach and Dolan, 1997, p. 10).

McGregor (1957) took these traditional rational economic beliefs and synthesized them in his Theory X (see below). Many organizations today, even industrial manufacturing or 'smokestack' companies, differ in many respects from those of the early 20th century characterized by the beliefs represented by Theory X. However, it must be recognized that these suppositions still deeply permeate the basic mental maps of many senior managers at the end of this century.

ESSENTIALS OF THEORY X: THE 'PERMANENT' BELIEFS ABOUT MANAGEMENT AND CONTROL IN THE COMPANY

[THEORY X]

- Ordinary people are basically lazy in work situations and will attempt to avoid working whenever possible.
- Most people work for necessity and thus they need to be closely supervised, and disciplined when their performance deviates from organisational goals and objectives.
- Most people are not very ambitious, they prefer to be assigned work but the responsibility will be left to managers.

The formal and bureaucratic structure: can it work forever?

Whereas Taylor was basically concerned with industrial organizations, Fayol in France, Urwick in England and Mooney in the USA were systematizing their own experiences as managers, formulating principles that would serve as good management practice in any type of organization. Their conclusions on the need for very formalized organization structures, with very clearly defined areas of responsibility lead to their designation as 'theories of the formal organization.'

In general terms, one can regard the ideas of Taylor at the level of manual jobs, and the formal theories at the level of administrative work, as having formed the ideological foundations of corporate management until the end of the 20th century. The photo of office workers is from the era when the theories of the 'formal organization' were put into practice as hierarchical control systems.

It must be emphasized that the companies studied by the proponents of these theories were operating in extremely stable, often static, commercial and technological environments. This was the case with General Motors

Images of the formal and bureaucratic organization

in its early years, studied by Mooney, and with an important French mining and metallurgical firm called Commentry-Fourchambault studied by Fayol (1949). In the UK, Urwick derived the basis for his ideas from military organization in time of war, when discipline and planning played a fundamental role.

The management principles according to these theories of the formal organization generally accepted around the middle of the 20th century can be synthesized under four headings (Dolan *et al.*, 1996):

- **Unity of command**: To avoid conflicts, it is essential that the worker, whatever his level, should receive orders from only one superior, not from various, at any one time. Another implication of the descending 'line of command' concept is that some senior employees outside the structure were designated 'staff', meaning they advised rather than managed others.
- **Pyramid model**: Management authority is exercised from the apex, descending down through the hierarchical levels of the pyramid structure. Each level consists of more employees but with less authority than the level above. It is thus important to define clearly on which level any particular job or employee is situated.
- **Principle of exception**: The more important a decision is for the well-being of the business of the organization, the higher up the hierarchical scale it should be taken. Conversely, only routine decisions may be taken at lower levels.
- **Sphere of control**: Within the pyramidal structure, where there is only one person, usually the Chief Executive, at the top exercising control over the entire organization, neither he/she nor any other manager should directly control the work of more than 10 other employees.

Max Weber, a theoretician of the relationships of power and authority in bureaucracies, understood power as the means of obliging individuals to obey even though it was against their will, whereas authority was seen in getting individuals voluntarily to comply with the instructions they received. Weber differentiates 4 kinds of authority (1946):

1. **Charismatic authority**: based on exceptional personal qualities such as demonstrating extraordinary insight or accomplishments that inspire loyalty and obedience from others. This is the essential authority of every true leader.
2. **Traditional authority**: based on precedent and custom. For example, this type of authority can be associated with the family owner of a business, a military officer or a monarch.
3. **Rational-legal authority**: based on a position legally empowered to issue rules and procedures. This is the authority of directors holding official positions in the public administration or formally assigned executive positions in companies.

4.   **Rational-expert authority**: based on the capacity to influence deci-
     sions, derived from knowledge and technical competence. This is the
     authority of professionals and consultants who act as advisers without
     necessarily having executive capacity.

According to his initial ideas, bureaucratic management arises as an attempt
to make the company more rational and professional, avoiding arbitrary and
'unprofessional' decision-making and behavior. *Bureaucratic management
basically means the exercise of control based on knowledge (technical competence) and it is this characteristic that makes it specifically rational.*

   The following are some of the main beliefs on which the bureaucratic
organization is founded:

1.   Employment is a 'career' which should be developed according to a
     pre-planned system of moves and promotions, normally based on
     length of service and age, or on the experience and technical knowl-
     edge gained over time, not on 'favoritism' (nor necessarily on the
     specific needs of the company in any given situation).
2.   A hierarchy of authority should exist to satisfy the needs for coordina-
     tion of work and compliance with procedures, policies and standards.
3.   Relationships between members of the organization should be
     'impersonal' and determined by formal criteria, not based on friend-
     ship, family relationships or membership of any social group, club,
     religion, political party, etc.
4.   All decisions must be recorded in writing.
5.   Each job or position should be described in detail, to facilitate super-
     vision, compensation or penalties according to the results obtained
     by the individual employee.
6.   A clear separation should exist between the ownership of the organ-
     ization and those who work in it, in order to facilitate the adoption
     of rational decisions in the interests of the organization as a whole,
     and avoiding the adoption of decisions seen to be mediated by par-
     ticular interest groups.

   One of the principal negative consequences of the bureaucratic organization is that the employee, whether senior or junior, is subjected
to powerful pressure to conform to the rules. This overdependence on rules,
policies and procedures tends to confuse the nature and purpose of the organization's rules as they come to be considered as ends in themselves. In this
way, the formal and instrumental aspects of the bureaucratic tasks – the
paperwork, the system – assume greater importance than the substantive
aspects related to the true purpose and objectives of the organization.

   Another basic criticism of bureaucracies is that they tend to fragment
into self-contained sub-units each with its own interests to defend, relegating

ACTION/REFLECTION

- **Based on the 6 points of bureaucracy on page 87, to what extent do you believe your organization is bureaucratic?**

_____

_____

_____

_____

- **List the corresponding values for the points above. Consider how these values help and/or hinder your organisation in the 21st century.**

_____

_____

_____

_____

the organization's objectives to second place after their own objectives. In other words, bureaucracies are especially prone to 'empire-building' and creating 'silos' that foster a vicious circle of inefficiencies and bad management from which it becomes increasingly difficult to undo. Once territories are formed the overriding objective is to keep people out and information in; guarding the 'castle gates' becomes the daily mission.

> Once territories are formed the overriding objective is to keep people out and information in; guarding the 'castle gates' becomes the daily mission.

Bureaucracy and formal rigidity of organizational structure is one thing, but another consideration is the need for some kind of control or supervisory system. An interesting study of British companies considered to be 'excellent,' concludes that they all accept the need for control according to various dimensions (Goldsmith and Clutterbuck, 1985):

- Control of all the financial aspects, to make sure money is directed to where it is most productive and creates most wealth, and that assets earn a suitable return.
- Simplified controls using a small number of key ratios, so that managers can react immediately and directly to anomalies and deviations.
- Demanding high levels of performance and contribution from all managers.

- Continuous feedback on the results of specific policies, activities and decisions.

Revisiting the Hawthorne studies

At the same time when Taylor was exemplified as the 'consultant engineer', the Harvard University psychologist, Elton Mayo, and his colleagues (Roethlisberger and Dickson, 1930) were conducting a historic research study in the Western Electric Company of Hawthorne, in the outskirts of Chicago (Mayo, 1933). This experiment represents the beginning of the management model oriented towards the development of employees and may be extrapolated to many current situations.

The objective of the experiment was to study the effects of different working conditions on a group of women working on a telephone instrument assembly line. As the experimenters introduced basic improvements such as better illumination, more frequent rest breaks, more opportunities for the women to organize their own methods of working, etc., they began to measure increases in productivity identifiable with each factor. However, at the end of these experiments, when the group of workers was returned to the original working conditions, the researchers were astonished to find productivity increasing again, to even better levels than under the improved conditions of the experiment.

What had happened? To explain this observation, they had to consider other factors underlying those conditions that had been deliberately manipulated. It was evident that the workers had been motivated to produce more and better results. And the reasons for their high morale could only be the following:

1. These women felt 'special' because they had been selected for this study. They interpreted this as meaning that they were important to the management and that they were being treated as people, not as numbers.
2. During the experiment the women had built good relationships among themselves and with their supervisor, since they had been given considerable freedom to control their own pace of work and to distribute their work among themselves in the most comfortable way. They had been given a degree of 'ownership' of their work.
3. The easier social contact among the women made the work more pleasant. Working relationships had become friendships.

The 'Hawthorne effect' has come to propose an essential truth: most people tend to work more and better, at least for a limited period, when they perceive that they are being treated in a personal way and that they are participating in something new and special. Virtually any change in the working situation can be considered as 'something new and special' provided that it is also perceived as well-intentioned (i.e., non-exploiting). In fact, every well-designed new project or objective stands to benefit from the Hawthorne effect.

WHAT ABOUT YOU?

ACTION/REFLECTION

Did you ever personally experience a 'Hawthorne Effect'? When? How did you and the work at hand benefit? Take time to elaborate. What about this experience made you feel special? What conditions supported the improvement?

_____

_____

_____

_____

_____

_____

Did you ever, even unintentionally, observe the 'Hawthorne Effect' in your workplace? What happened? How did people react? Did the effect last? If not, what could you have done to sustain the effect?

_____

_____

_____

_____

_____

_____

Revisiting the humanist beliefs

In corporate management the term 'humanist' should not be taken to mean that managers have to be 'soft' or simply 'do-gooder' types. Current management thinking described as 'humanist' (Mayo, 1933) aims to overcome the limitations of the formal bureaucratic approaches of the early and middle years of the 20th century. The humanist management philosophy focuses on the possibilities of personal and social development for the individual employee under a new organizational model.

The following paragraph by one of the pioneers of changing organizations, Warren Bennis (1970) had this to say as an example of the new way of thinking:

In contrast to the centralized solution of problems by the hierarchy in the bureaucratic organizations, there will arise in the future a new type of leadership, more complex and not concentrated in the person of one man, but distributed according to competencies and the specialization of various members of the organization. (pp. 269–82)

Furthermore, as exemplified by the following statement by Likert (1967), the humanist model takes into account the social and group attributes of human nature in relation to work:

The management of the company will only be making full use of the potential capacity of their human resources when each and every one of the employees are members of one or more work teams that are well-established and function efficiently; such teams should be capable of close interaction and should have high performance goals.

In his now classic work, *The Human Side of Enterprise*, McGregor proposed that many of the Taylorist beliefs that had up until then represented the most efficient possible method of directing people (what he termed Theory X as previously discussed) were erroneous. And following the concepts developed by the psychologist Abraham Maslow (1943) concluded that:

External management and control methods are of no use in motivating people whose physiological and security needs are fairly well satisfied, and whose needs for personal fulfillment are now predominant.

For Taylor, 'scientific management' of work meant the application of physical-quantitative methods for the rationalization of industrial productive effort, whereas for McGregor, the 'humanist or professional' manager adopted the scientific findings of psychology and other behavioral sciences, with the aim of serving the economic interests of the company.

In his 'Theory X', as described earlier, McGregor explains the consequences of management theories based on rational-economic and formal-bureaucratic beliefs. By contrast, the other assumptions represented by McGregor's 'Theory Y' propose that people can fully realize their potential when their work is meaningful and when their individual values and needs can be integrated with the objectives of the company.

> People can fully realize their potential when their work is meaningful and when their individual values and needs can be integrated with the objectives of the company.

The 'socio-technical' approach to management

The 'socio-technical' perspective puts forward something so self-evident that it is often ignored. The organization of the most efficient way of

---

ESSENTIALS OF THEORY Y

- **Employing physical and mental effort at work is as natural as playing or relaxing.**
- **External control and threats are not the only means to motivate people at work. Most individuals are capable of being self motivated towards the accomplishments of organisational goals.**
- **People will accomplish organisational objectives when it provides them with psychological compensation.**
- **After doing a job for a while people will begin to look for new opportunities and responsibilities.**
- **The capacity to learn, be creative and innovate does not characterize a small minority of people in organisations but rather a large majority of them.**
- **At present the standard conditions at work do not allow for maximizing the intellectual potential of human beings.**

---

working has two dimensions that are differentiated, yet mutually dependent: the technological-economic and the psychological-social dimensions.

Initiated in the middle of the 20th century by a group of writers with backgrounds in psychoanalysis from the Tavistock Institute of London, the socio-technical theory has provided conceptual support to the 'Quality of Working Life' interventions initiated in countries such as Scandinavia, Germany and Canada (Dolan and Schuler, 1994). These interventions aimed at optimizing conditions in a synergistic way, combining the appropriate organization and physical work installations (e.g., office or factory layouts) with the appropriate psychological and social conditions (e.g., shared eating areas, company sporting events, volunteer or charity events). At the end of the 1970s, Emry Trist (1978) of the Tavistock Institute published a comparative chart illustrating the socio-technical paradigm he envisaged for the end of the century, set against the classic paradigm of the beginning of the century.

The social system, according to Trist, includes people and their habitual attitudes, values, behavioral styles and relationships. It includes the reward system; and it is the formal power structure as depicted on organization charts and the informal power structure deriving from knowledge and personal influence.

The technical system includes machinery, processes, procedures and a physical arrangement. We usually think of a factory in terms of its technical system. To be effective, the social and technical systems must integrate and assist one another. A manufacturing workcell that requires high teamwork will not produce in an environment of suspicion, individual rewards and command-control. Businesses where people have isolated workstations, large inventory buffers and few sequential processes have difficulty with teamwork.

The engine component manufacturer did good things with the social system. However, the firm neglected the tools, metrics and processes required to improve quality. People wanted to improve, they simply did not know how. Nor could they recognize improvement, since meaningful metrics were not in place.

The truck manufacturer has the opposite imbalance. This firm's extensive analysis tools and knowledge are widely distributed. But the people lack interpersonal skills, common goals and trust. Nor could they hope to attain these qualities under their particular power structure and reward system.

Table 4.5 displays a summary of the principles of socio-technical system design distilled from the work of Eric Trist and many others.

Are organizations evolving?

It is apparent that, within a century, organizations will have become central to our lives. As researchers study these organizational systems, the knowledge

Table 4.5 **Socio-technical principles**

Social system	Technical system
● There is no optimum organization. ● As the environment, culture, people and technology change, so should the organization. ● When selecting people for a workgroup, strive for homogeneity in their backgrounds and work attitudes. ● Reduce wide variations in knowledge levels and variety through cross-training. ● Achieve high performance through commitment rather than minimal problem compliance. Use more carrot than stick. ● Build commitment by involving people in the shaping of their future. ● Provide opportunities to satisfy unfulfilled higher order needs. Use the intrinsic motivators. ● Adult learning occurs primarily through experience. Integrate learning on the job through advisors, facilitators, and guided application.	● Control variances at their source. ● Ensure that the detection of a variance and the source of that variance occur in the same work group. ● Maintain quality by detecting variances in the process rather than in the final product. ● Monitor inputs as carefully as outputs. ● Size work buffers large enough to allow problem solving but small enough to prevent problem avoidance. ● Match technological flexibility with the product mix. ● Match technology scale with production volume of the work groups.

(continued)

Table 4.5 (continued)

Integration	Managing the system
• Design the socio and technical systems simultaneously and jointly. • Give workers larger and more varied tasks and increase cycle time. • Integrate support functions within work groups to the largest possible extent. • Optimize the system rather than the system's components. • Begin and end a work group's technical boundary at a discontinuity in the material transformation process.	• Allow teams to manage the daily work. • Coach and facilitate rather than supervise. Coaches should manage the team boundaries. • Upper management should set goals, supply resources and manage the culture.

we obtain from how they evolve and function feeds into behavior of managers. Further, as managerial theories evolve so does the practice of management. Ultimately, we are beginning to see companies change from being extremely controlling and bureaucratic toward new models focused on individual and organizational development. However, organizations are not one extreme or another: most exist within these two ends of the continuum. The challenge to those wanting to implement MBV is to gain an adequate understanding of personal and professional experiences to make sense of how these related theories are actualized in today's workplace. Rather than rejecting previous theories and practices, MBV requires us to integrate knowledge available from the past and the knowledge available to us at present to move us to the future. Using MBV as the framework to evolve, organizations will engage in organizational development and change as part of its culture – a focus for the next chapter.

Summary

- Organizations are constantly struggling to strike a balance between their control orientated culture and the development oriented culture.
- An over reliance on control and rational processes in the 21st century organizations contribute to an environment where employees are indifferent, uninspired and excessively dependent on leadership.
- The classical paradigms of management developed over the course of the 20th century are no longer effective; the bureaucratic model works only in limited environments and the socio-technical systems needs more elements in order for it to work well.

Part II
Practices Associated with Management by Values (MBV)

5 The Relationships Between Organization Development (OD) and MBV

'What would life be like if you had not courage to attempt anything?'
(Vincent van Gogh)

'If you don't change, reality in the end forces that change upon you.'
(Stuart Wilde)

What is organization development?

Organization development (OD) can be defined as the application of knowledge adapted from the behavioral sciences that inspired the humanist and socio-technical movements. OD interventions are aimed at simultaneously increasing both short and long-term organizational effectiveness by means of improving processes and structures that support individual, group and system advancement. At the heart of OD is a focus on creating a learning environment designed to sustain improvements throughout the organization. As such, OD constitutes the conceptual basis of MBV.

Even in the 21st century, OD has not yet been generally understood nor applied in many countries. Some of the reasons for this are:

1. An excessive focus on economic objectives that emphasize short-term profitability at the expense of learning, creativity and innovation for long-term gain.
2. A desire for quick-fix or band-aid approaches to change management. In part this is exacerbated by a lack of education, training and practical OD content in MBA courses and similar programs.
3. Non-participatory or bureaucratic organizational cultures (e.g., dominated by hierarchy, control, power and authority). In essence, a

misfit between an organization's values and those promoted by the field of OD.

4. Managers and organizational leaders are confused about how to differentiate between: (1) OD practitioners that perform either 'hit and run' or 'one-hit wonder' interventions (i.e., selling the latest management fad); (2) OD practices aimed at creating a dependence between the organization and the consulting firm; and (3) OD professionals committed to co-creating an environment in participation with their clients to create short and long-term learning that serves the organization and its members (i.e., both internal or external stakeholders).

In the last couple of years, OD consultants around the world are making an attempt to render the intervention more systematic and professional. The OD network has thus developed a credo and a set of ethical standards as illustrated below.

ORGANIZATION AND HUMAN SYSTEMS DEVELOPMENT CREDO (JULY 1996)*

Our purpose as professionals is to facilitate processes by which human beings and human systems live and work together for their mutual benefit and mutual well-being. Our practice is based on a widely shared learning and discovery process dedicated to a vision of people living meaningful, productive, good lives in ways that simultaneously serve them, their organizations, their communities, their societies, and the world.

We are an interdependent community of professionals whose practice is based on the applied behavioral sciences and other related sciences, a human systems perspective, and both human and organizational values. We serve people at all system levels, ranging from individuals and groups to organizations, communities, and ultimately the global community.**

We believe that human beings and human systems are interdependent economically, politically, socially, culturally and spiritually, and that their mutual effectiveness is grounded in fundamental principles which are reflected in the primary values that guide our practice. Among those values are: respect for human dignity, integrity and worth; freedom, choice and responsibility; justice and fundamental human rights; compassion; authenticity, openness and honesty; learning, growth and empowerment; understanding and respecting differences; cooperation, collaboration, trust, diversity and community; excellence, alignment, effectiveness and efficiency; democracy, meaningful participation and appropriate decision-making; and synergy, harmony and peace.

> * The moral-ethical position on which the OD-HSD profession is based, along with the beliefs and values underlying that position, are more fully described in 'An Annotated Statement of Values and Ethics By Professionals in Organization and Human Systems Development.' This CREDO is based on that Annotated Statement.
>
> ** The global perspective does not mean changing the focus of our practice, but only the context within which we view our collective practice. And by shifting our paradigm of who 'we' are, we can become a global professional community whose collective action will have global significance based on both our practice and ways in which we 'walk our talk.'
>
> *Source*: http://www.odnet.org/credo.html

The philosophy behind OD is to motivate organizational stakeholders toward greater clarity, cohesion, creativity, flexibility, autonomy and well-being toward shared goals and objectives. The more committed the organization is to creating a culture centered on learning and development, the greater the likelihood that it will generate sustainable improvements.

To achieve the goal of increasing the effectiveness of the company, OD represents a powerful set of beliefs, values and techniques of intervention to stimulate changes in the way people inter-relate within the organization; changes that will favor the development and strengthening of individuals' creative capacities; changes that will favor the maximum contri-

> OD represents a powerful set of beliefs, values and methodologies centered on learning that are intended to stimulate changes in the way people interact with one another in order to improve the overall quality of life for its members and the work of the organization.

bution of people to the success of their organization. The beliefs and values that OD can bring to a company will constitute in themselves the kind of cultural changes that many companies need. Therefore there is every reason why OD should not only be accepted but positively legitimized and driven by the company's top management. In the following sections, we will take a look at some of these core values. In summary they are:

- *Core value I*   Courtesy and respect
- *Core value II*   Trust, communication, mutual support and legitimization of learning through the analysis of errors
- *Core value III* Team work
- *Core value IV*   Flattening the hierarchy and increasing autonomy
- *Core value V*   Participation for change
- *Core value VI*   Genuine interest in the quality of life

CORE VALUE I: COURTESY AND RESPECT

Respect for people is not the same as formal courtesy and good manners, although these can be signs of respect. One of the main causes of lack of cultural vitality and lack of personal commitment in many companies is the poor example from leaders and managers toward the opinions and feelings of employees throughout the organization.

> One of the main causes of lack of cultural vitality and lack of personal commitment in many companies is the poor example from leaders and managers toward the opinions and feelings of employees throughout the organization.

This disrespect shows itself in many dimensions of behavior, from the simple failure to greet people with a friendly 'good morning' to gross failures of communication during times of critical importance such as the need for re-structuring or layoffs. If a good example is set from leadership then there is a good chance that this behavior will spread throughout the organization, being reciprocated from the bottom up and extended outside as well, to customers, suppliers, the local community, and a behavior that is desirable to all those with whom the company has dealings. Good manners and respect at all levels is a golden rule for the good social functioning of any purposeful organization.

The intelligent design of an organization – its shape, the way it functions, the recognition of important inter-relationships between functions, etc., can facilitate this valuable form of behavior between individuals and can help each to acquire respect for their colleagues, not just for their expertise but also for their distinctive personal qualities. Cross functional designs are one OD example that can build mutual awareness, appreciation and respect.

CORE VALUE II: TRUST, COMMUNICATION, MUTUAL SUPPORT AND LEGITIMIZATION OF LEARNING THROUGH THE ANALYSIS OF ERRORS

Efficient and culturally vital organizations are characterized by living and working in a climate of trust, sincerity and mutual support between stakeholders. This type of environment enables individuals to take justifiable risks, inevitably to make some mistakes, and to learn from the outcomes of their decisions and actions, good or bad. Problems, failures, even disasters (e.g., 'I've just lost our

> Efficient and culturally vital organizations are characterized by living and working in a climate of trust, sincerity and mutual support between stakeholders.

best customer!') should be analysed, discussed and rectified as much as possible.

As we shall see later when we discuss 'the learning company', the detection of an error or problem, at whatever level, should not provoke the hunting-down and punishment of the guilty party, nor the search for scapegoats. Such behavior is ineffective at best and humiliating at worst. Errors and problems should be approached as, firstly, opportunities to learn, then as opportunities to extract something positive from a negative situation (i.e., future success from past failure). It is always worth remembering that only people who don't make decisions don't make mistakes.

Unfortunately, most companies still have a long way to go before there is open and honest communication, especially upwards, from subordinate to boss. We all know there is always a great deal of criticism of bosses' behavior, policies and decisions, but usually this is made in the corridors or over lunch. Bosses must be realistic enough to accept this because their success and that of the organization depends on knowing what the people throughout the system are thinking and feeling; they need accurate feedback. People throughout the organization need to learn how to encourage honest but constructive communication and feedback, including knowing what they have done, or are doing exceptionally well.

OD addresses the need for establishing and creating various communication channels, processes and systems, establishes forums for relaxed exchanges of views, and procedures for learning from feedback. OD also helps us to accept human nature for what it is: there will always be individuals who do not get along or who choose other ways of interaction. This is why it is equally important to create alternative channels and systems in the event of inevitable blockages, misunderstandings and disruptions to open communication.

CORE VALUE III: TEAM WORK

Perhaps more than any other time in history, organizations are depending more on teams to accomplish their work. The popularity of teams has resulted in numerous configurations to include work teams, parallel teams, project teams, management teams, *ad hoc* teams, virtual teams, hot groups, leadership teams, executive teams, *Kaizen* teams (i.e., Quality Control Circles), and many others types. (On management teams see Cohen and Bailey (1997), 'What makes teams work: Group effectiveness research from the shop floor to the executive suite', *Journal of Management*, vol. 23(3), pp. 239–90.) At the heart of the team movement is the philosophy that more minds are better than one. In today's work world of increased competition, ongoing change and the need for innovation, teams are proving to be more effective. Teams allow for the synthesis of diversity, learning, mindsets and expertise. If they span several hierarchical levels, teams can be effective in breaking down rigidities and artificial divisions between functions and levels within the organization. There is also a growing trend to include supplier and/or customer personnel in project teams.

The building and consolidation of groups of people into a cohesive team requires considerable investment in time, training and resources; real teams are not created overnight. Teamwork, however, is not a panacea to resolve all organizational problems, in fact, teams can be problematic. Consequently managers need to have a solid understanding of group dynamics, team learning, critical factors that contribute to developing healthy teams, and creating the context for teams to succeed (see for example, Balkin, *et al.*, 1997; Hackman, 1990; Lingham, 2004). Nonetheless, most companies consider such investment very profitable, and individual employees have been shown to prefer this method of working (Katzenbach and Smith, 1993; Mohrman *et al.*, 1995).

CORE VALUE IV: FLATTENING THE HIERARCHY AND INCREASING AUTONOMY

Efficient and healthy organizations actively work to reduce bureaucracy and hierarchical authority levels. Many OD projects have the specific aim of eliminating unnecessary layers in an organization, often referred to as 'flattening.' The idea behind flattening an organization is to create more effective processes such as communication, sharing of resources, faster response time, and autonomy for individuals, teams and departments while simultaneously increasing interaction between all levels of stakeholders. The ultimate goal of flattening is to create a more efficient, informed and flexible organization.

This does not mean that there should not be a basic structuring of levels of responsibility; rather that these levels should not become barriers to effective working and communication. The structure should reflect the needs of the organization by helping it to react quickly to events, to be as close as possible to customers, to counter the competition, to be up-to-date in technological matters, to ensure quality standards are maintained along the production chain and whatever else is needed to allow it to survive and to thrive.

Flattening also promotes the belief that the best work arises from conditions of self-supervision rather than external control. Organizations should be structured to allow for feedback, individual input about how their work should be achieved, and idea and information sharing. Central to

Core Value IV is the conviction that all people are responsible professionals, capable of independent and creative work.

The change toward treating all employees as adult individuals, each with their own criteria for success and needs for a sense of achievement, can be one of the most spectacular innovations to implement in any organization, producing surprising increases in the mental and emotional resources committed to corporate goals and overall wellbeing.

> The change toward treating all employees as adult individuals, each with their own criteria for success and needs for a sense of achievement, can be one of the most spectacular innovations to implement in any organization, producing surprising increases in the mental and emotional resources committed to corporate goals and overall wellbeing.

CORE VALUE V: PARTICIPATION FOR CHANGE

Commitment to real and effective change depends on the active participation of the people affected by the proposed change, well before reaching the stage of actually implementing the changes. Participation involves critical factors such as open communication (i.e., asking for opinions and then sharing the information), treating people with respect, and encouraging involvement in the design of change, eliciting information and listening to others. Without this approach, it is very easy for change to be seen as a threat or a possible deterioration of working conditions. This negativity spreads very fast throughout an organization, often condemning valuable ideas to total failure and leaving the organization weaker than before.

Lack of participation explains the high failure rate of many 'process re-engineering' projects and similar approaches to change management. These initiatives are often mere productivity-related 'neo-Taylorism' efforts. They are usually missing any authentic dimension of substantive improvement including the psychological relationship between the professional and the organization for which and within which he or she works.

CORE VALUE VI: GENUINE INTEREST IN THE QUALITY OF LIFE

High-quality performance at work requires attributes such as creativity, commitment and friendly relationships with customers, communication skills, continuous learning and self-improvement, plus a host of others specific to particular areas of work and business. They represent a better quality of life for employees and an important competitive advantage for the company.

The environment that simultaneously focuses on a high quality of performance and a high quality of life realizes that these conditions arise from a good psychological relationship between the individual and the organization as a whole. A healthy dynamic relationship is difficult to achieve in situations of stress. Stress occurs at the individual level when his or her workload or responsibilities are perceived to be too great or heavy for the available mental and emotional resources. One of the main sources of 'strength' for the individual in managing stress is the equilibrium of time dedicated to work, family and to oneself. Concern for working conditions, not only physical but even more importantly psychological, of all employees is an ethical and economic imperative for the true business leader.

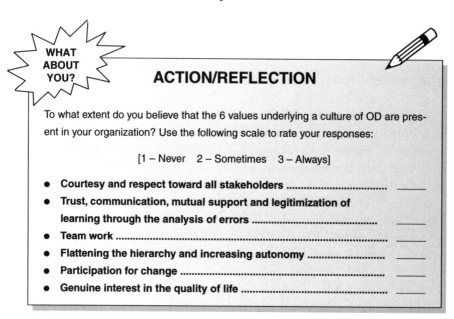

WHAT ABOUT YOU?

ACTION/REFLECTION

To what extent do you believe that the 6 values underlying a culture of OD are present in your organization? Use the following scale to rate your responses:

[1 – Never   2 – Sometimes   3 – Always]

- **Courtesy and respect toward all stakeholders** .... _____
- **Trust, communication, mutual support and legitimization of learning through the analysis of errors** .... _____
- **Team work** .... _____
- **Flattening the hierarchy and increasing autonomy** .... _____
- **Participation for change** .... _____
- **Genuine interest in the quality of life** .... _____

Managing by values is an investment in the present and future of your organization but one that requires time and resources. Fortunately a vast body of knowledge exists within the scholarship of OD interventions that are directly applicable to MBV. Figure 5.1 provides an illustration of the different targets and methods common to OD interventions that can be used in relationship with MBV.

Cummings and Huse (1989) grouped these interventions into four main categories:

1. *Interventions at the level of interpersonal processes.* These are the most typical of OD applications, and concern one of the most general and

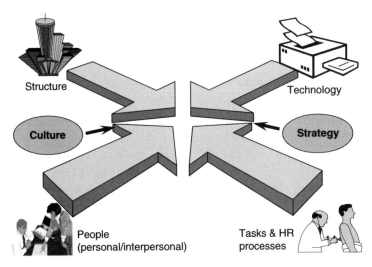

Figure 5.1 **Targets and methods for OD interventions**

basic aspects of an organization, interpersonal relations and communication. For this reason they appear at the base of the schematic. Among these interventions are an emphasis on communication processes by internal or external experts and trainers (more of this later when we discuss the role of facilitators in the process of change); coaching; team-building sessions; the analysis and management of inter-group conflicts; staff opinion surveys; data analysis and feedback of findings; and training programs on interpersonal communication (techniques, channels, problems such as distortion, dissonance, interference, etc.)

2. *Interventions in the management of human resources.* These are innovations or improvements in the techniques of HR management, dissemination of values into the culture, as well as skills and experience into selection methods; HR involvement in participative MBO schemes; redesign of tasks and incentive systems; career planning; training programs on dealing with job-stress; performance evaluation methods and programs.

3. *Technical-structural interventions.* These are more fundamental interventions to help restructure and re-shape an organization. The results may take many forms, such as work or project teams, matrix management schemes, networks, the re-design of work processes to increase motivation, quality, speed of reaction, and even highly technical programs of ergonomic and psychosocial study and improvement of the quality of working life.

4. *Strategy-level interventions.* These correspond to more recent developments in OD, closely integrated with changes or reviews of strategy by top management. They cover comprehensive change management

programs, organizational learning programs, development of networks and functional alliances between organizations and most of all
instilling new values for the entire organization.

The following are some of the main benefits from applying OD interventions:

1. Successful corporate change of all kinds is facilitated by means of sys-
    tematic, methodical management.
2. Genuine commitment of employees to the goals of the organization
    is revitalized; motivation to work to the best of one's capabilities is
    strengthened.
3. Interpersonal communication and the capacity for effective team-
    work are improved.
4. Creativity in the solution of complex problems is stimulated.

OD has a fundamental impact in enabling the company to orient its
beliefs and values towards a more psychologically healthy working environment for all employees. People are encouraged and helped to express
their ideas and feelings more openly, and to consolidate their commitment to the company's goals.

The innovative company: the learning organization

'A learning organization "is an organization which facilitates the
learning of all its members and continuously transforms itself." '

(Pedler, Boydell, and Burgoyne, 1988)

'A learning organization "builds and continually renews its competitiveness in all functions." '

(Penn, 1990)

The focus of OD, which we consider the supporting concept behind MBV,
can be set out generically under two forms of understanding a company:
the innovative company and the company capable of learning. Both ideas
are very closely related and are essential aspects of the truly dynamic company. An in-depth understanding of them will help you manage the evolution of your company from a culture of control oriented management
towards a culture of development-oriented management.

The main differences between static and dynamic organizations can be
summarized into eight dimensions or areas where innovation can be either
ignored and suppressed or stimulated and implemented (Table 5.1).

Table 5.1 **Static and dynamic organizations**

Dimensions	Static vs Dynamic aspects
1. Formal structure, as depicted in the company's organization chart	Rigid vs Flexible
2. Atmosphere at work; the general climate of ideas and relationships	Task centered vs People centered
3. The functions of roles (e.g., directors, managers, supervisors, etc.)	Command and control vs Facilitating and stimulating development
4. The style of decision-making	Centralized vs Decentralized
5. Internal flows of communication	Restricted flow vs Unrestricted flow
6. Economic-financial philosophy (e.g., accountability, measurement, etc.)	Cost focus vs Investment focus
7. Predominant values	Maintenance vs Change and risk
8. Tolerance of ambiguity	Low vs High

Another useful way of presenting the concept of a dynamic company orientated towards development under the OD approach is that of the company that is continuously learning new skills, new competencies, new behaviors – **the learning organization** (Argyris and Schon, 1978). A true learning organization is focused on legitimizing open and effective interpersonal dialogue in all directions, not just up and down. It also means the organization is continuously transforming itself so as to adapt to the demands of changes in the environment and of new internal tensions that must be integrated. Another important definition of a company that learns is one that is capable of 'unlearning' out-dated values, assumptions and forms of behavior, in order to adopt other new ones more relevant to achieving future goals.

The following description of the main characteristics of the learning company will give an idea of the enormous potential benefits, but also of the difficulties to be overcome in implementing this approach:

1. At any of the (preferably few) hierarchical levels, the organization is capable of periodically 'unlearning' beliefs, values and behaviors that previously had been regarded as permanent. For example, a company long steeped in the extreme forms of the 'hard work ethic' whose philosophy might be caricatured as 'we come here to work, not to enjoy ourselves' would need to abandon this in favor of a more relaxed belief that recognizes people's needs to derive satisfaction and pleasure from learning to work better, or from changing old unproductive habits.

2. The organization encourages open and effective inter-personal dialogue. This is based on the exchange of personal criteria for objectives,

quality of work, priorities, success and all the important 'process' factors that accompany the 'product' factors of work or task content. Equally important is continuous feedback on what has been achieved and how it was achieved. In fact, the style and content of daily communication between colleagues, irrespective of hierarchy, is one valuable context which produces effective learning and real change in a company.

Such communication for learning and change must be based on significant data, verifiable information, honestly held opinions – in effect, the content of dialogue must be meaningful, founded in reality – and the participants must be open to having their statements checked and perhaps contradicted by others. All views or assertions are based on assumptions and interpretations, which may be right or wrong. And even the language and words used in work dialogues can condition the quality of the communication and learning processes that follow (e.g., a comment that starts: 'Correct me if I'm wrong but ...' has a different quality from, 'You can't seriously expect me to believe that!'

3.   All its members have a global view of the company as a whole. There are no narrow isolated tasks or jobs. Everyone receives complete information on the strategic plans of the company and everyone participates according to their experience and knowledge in the analysis of problems and opportunities, and in the design of the strategy itself.

Using an architectural simile, we can visualize the stained glass window of a gothic cathedral. Imagine that the individual components were alive. Any one of the colored glass panes comprising the window has a monochrome vision of reality: it can only see itself as having one particular color and one simple shape. However in combination the glass panes together constitute a magnificent multicolored work of art.

4.   There are no closed territories, neither physically or conceptually. There are few partitions and lots of 'cross-fertilization' of ideas. In effect, there is good horizontal communication between divisions, departments, units and groups. 'Silos' are viewed as an unacceptable part of organizational life.

5.   Individual autonomy is legitimized. True learning takes place in the 'give and take' among mutually-respecting, mutually-trusting professional members of a busy team or department.

6.   One essential function of leaders and senior managers is to offer reassurance and emotional support. Anxiety derived from ambiguity or excessive insecurity blocks learning. In many companies, one of the main complaints of employees is the 'lack of support' from their bosses, who themselves probably feel they have enough to do to contain their own anxieties.

7.   People are permitted to learn from mistakes, from taking justifiable risks which sometimes work out and sometimes don't. Without this

legitimizing of mistakes, it is practically impossible for a company to encourage learning and innovation among employees. It is very typical of bureaucratic and non-dynamic organizations that the occurrence of mistakes is inevitably followed by the hunting down and punishment or humiliation of those seen as guilty. In such situations, people react naturally by avoiding risks, not taking decisions, hiding mistakes and blaming others.

REALITY CHECK

BILL GATES ON LEARNING

'Microsoft puts into practice a very simple and yet revolutionary principle: You can learn significantly more from your errors rather than your success stories.'

Source: Translated from the Spanish as appeared in *El Pais*, 2 May 1995

The structures and processes to be re-designed for cultural evolution from control towards development

In this section we shall discuss in more detail two areas of OD action for moving an organization's culture away from hierarchical control and towards the development of employees. These two areas for implementing constructive change are: Loosening and flattening the structure of an organization and, conversely, strengthening team-building, and re-designing work processes and communication processes to improve motivation.

GIVING THE ORGANIZATION LESS STRUCTURE AND MORE TEAMS

According to the old logic, control required formal and rigid hierarchical structures, so that everyone 'knew their place.' However, in order to realize the potential of all employees, the pyramidal structure needs to be reconsidered. The 'new' logic of OD requires less hierarchy, fewer compartments, more freedom of action and communication. This generally translates into a 'flattening' of the pyramid, the underlying aim being to make the structure fit the needs of efficient working, rapid reaction to events, continuous learning, and enabling fluid communication rather than letting the structure hinder these desirable attributes. Under the new flexible structure, roles will be defined with reference to the development of small groups or mini-businesses, instead of the traditional professional categories and individual functions. It is not sufficient just to create teams to solve particular problems, along the style of total quality programs for example, nor is it sufficient just to reorganize people around processes, as recommended under the interesting approach of re-engineering the company.

The reduction and loosening of hierarchical levels must aim to give people at all levels more autonomy and responsibility for faster thinking and decision-making, not just on their immediate work processes but on wider issues of importance to the whole company. This is what is implied by the classic precepts of OD on job enrichment and job enlargement, which are the conceptual bases of empowerment initiatives and process re-engineering.

Such structural change involving alterations in roles and relationships is of course accompanied by physical changes; for example, new distributions of working space, ergonomic redesign of plant layouts, open planning of offices, sometimes the disappearance of 'one person – one desk' assumptions, or sometimes the creation of team meeting spaces, and 'virtual offices.'

REDESIGN OF WORK PROCESSES AND COMMUNICATION METHODS TO INCREASE MOTIVATION

The organizational process is understood to mean the sequence of functions or interdependent variables which have to be organized and coordinated in order to give meaning and the capability of adding value over the course of the productive transformations carried out by the company in response to customer needs. Changes in such internal processes are technical changes, for example, automating data transmission around the organization, creating new channels of communication, delegation of functions, new production systems, decentralization of decision-making, simplification of administrative channels, new systems of compensation, etc.

The 're-engineering of processes' now being considered and implemented in many organizations is an excellent opportunity for gearing up the productive processes in such a way that they increasingly add more value to the final product or service that the customer buys (Hammer and Champy, 1993). However, process re-engineering does not always explicitly integrate the human dimension into such changes: the opportunity also exists to add more motivation, more job satisfaction, more commitment, more consistency between corporate and individual goals and values, when productive processes are re-engineered. In short, MBV can go hand in hand with these changes.

There are two specific internal processes whose optimum functioning is essential for achieving high levels of professional performance:

1. Those associated with the psychological characteristics of the job or position.
2. Internal communication processes.

Process improvements integrated with psychological motivation

The motivating features of the jobs of directors and senior professionals, which are so often considered critical for the success of a company, do not consist only of their higher salaries and the satisfaction from the intrinsic content of their work, but also include a wide range of psychological working conditions and 'rewards.' And very often it is assumed that these kinds of conditions and rewards are unsuitable for or cannot be offered to the rest of the employees. Some of the more important of these motivating psychological characteristics of jobs include:

- Autonomy – auto organization of work processes, breaks, work habits, etc.
- Variety – possibility to have variety in performing work.
- Identity – perception of owning of work processes and outcomes.
- Importance – belief that work outcomes are useful for self and for the lives of others.
- Equity – perception of justice, fair play.

WHAT ABOUT YOU?

ACTION/REFLECTION

Answer the following questions using the scales below:

Motivating psychological job characteristics	Which of the following psychological characteristics of work apply to your current situation?					Which of the following psychological characteristics are presently absent for the vast majority of employees in your firm?				
	Very absent				**Very present**	**Very absent**				**Very present**
Autonomy	1	2	3	4	5	1	2	3	4	5
Variety	1	2	3	4	5	1	2	3	4	5
Identity	1	2	3	4	5	1	2	3	4	5
Importance	1	2	3	4	5	1	2	3	4	5
Equity	1	2	3	4	5	1	2	3	4	5
Feedback	1	2	3	4	5	1	2	3	4	5
Social support	1	2	3	4	5	1	2	3	4	5

- Feedback – symmetry (both positive and negative) and coherence in getting feedback.
- Social support – belief that support will be given by colleagues, superiors and others when things get rough.

Improvement of internal communication processes

Most companies that carry out any kind of internal survey (sometimes called 'climate studies', 'communication audits', or 'organizational diagnoses') find that the complaint most often voiced by employees is the 'lack of communication.' This does not necessarily mean a lack of information but rather not being able to interpret it clearly (perhaps there is too much, perhaps it is contradictory, perhaps it is only partial). In any event, as Lee Iacocca (former Chief Executive Officer of the Chrysler Corporation) has stated, 'The only way to motivate people is to communicate with them.' And communication is not as simple a process as most managers assume; for a start, it is a two-way process; secondly, all communication has to pass through a series of filters; and thirdly, receiving messages is not the same as understanding them.

Internal communication within organizations essentially flows in three directions:

1. **Descending communication**: This is fundamentally used to pass down information from upper levels of the organization to lower levels. Its effect is moderately motivating and orientating for the work of employees. It is based on bureaucratic-formal theories of management and is most typical of large organizations. It takes the form of internal magazines, electronic mail, corporate videos, conventions and similar 'retreats' away from the work site.

2. **Ascending communication**: However, even with sophisticated systems of descending information why do employees still feel that they are not receiving important information necessary to understand the company or to perform their jobs adequately? These types of complaints or feedback usually reflect the absence of an established channel for upward sharing of information, comments or feedback, or because employees cannot easily exchange views and opinions throughout the system other than between those who work closely together.

   One of the most significant actions to promote an innovative company culture is creating a system that legitimizes the right of all stakeholders to express themselves and that those opinions/ideas/feedback, etc. will be considered as critical data for consideration in managing the organization. This one single action (which is not easy to put into practice) can produce a dramatic cultural shift throughout an organization, even if the company is still oriented toward hierarchical control.

3. **Horizontal communication**: This includes not only communication between individuals at similar levels in different parts of the organization, but also between teams and groups. One of the most serious disadvantages of the compartmentalized company is that there are barriers to this valuable and essential cross communication. One useful practice in this area is the holding of regular meetings between those responsible for the different operating or functional units in a company to exchange ideas, provide mutual support, and keep up-to-date on progress towards organizational goals.

WHAT ABOUT YOU?

ACTION/REFLECTION

Which of the following processes of communication are present in your organization? Does one process dominate the others? Which additional processes would benefit your company and why?

		Low.....to....High
(1)	Descending communication	1 2 3 4 5
(2)	Ascending communication	1 2 3 4 5
(3)	Horizontal communication	1 2 3 4 5

What process(es) can you implement within your own sphere of influence in your organization that will positively enhance your communication channels? Be specific, list the benefits:

_____

_____

_____

_____

Surviving and thriving in the 21st century

Changing means unlearning and getting rid of old beliefs that were probably very valid in the past, when the company had other customers, other employees, other technologies and, above all, other environments. We have looked at how the humanist approaches to management proposed since the middle of the 20th century have tended to counteract some of the limitations of the rational-economic and bureaucratic-formal approaches predominant in business and administrative organizations since the beginning of the century. However, even now, this humanist view of work and way of working has still not been fully understood or accepted by most companies or administrations.

Today it is universally acknowledged that all competitive and public service organizations must be oriented towards the customer, and many put this into practice. However, what is not commonly accepted is that employees are also important as individuals and that the organization benefits from orientation towards their needs, and by regarding them as

WHAT ABOUT YOU?

ACTION/REFLECTION

Place a checkmark by the following beliefs that embody your current organizational culture? Next place a checkmark by those beliefs that are not currently a part of your current culture but should be developed in order for your organization to succeed in the 21st century?

Beliefs	Present today	To be developed
Improving the quality of life of employees is a critical objective.		
Change is viewed as an opportunity not a threat.		
Excess of order kills creativity.		
More and more we are operating in a world without frontiers.		
A good leader inspires and trusts the employees in his/her surroundings.		
Employees' decisions are based on decisions that are free from pressures; they are considered to be internal clients.		
Training and development throughout the organization is imperative for success today.		
If given the appropriate conditions, employees will seek to demonstrate their creativity.		
An imaginative and adaptable workforce is critical to our company's success.		
Autonomy and less restricted tasks increases motivation and improves our outcomes.		

'internal clients', if not as equal partners with the owners and managers of the enterprise. In essence this is the coming revolution in competitiveness and effectiveness. This is the creation of the dynamic organization by harnessing the dynamic capabilities of all the people in it.

Despite organizations wanting to move forward and incorporate organizational change as part of its culture, many organizations experience ambivalence to change. While OD provides a roadmap, various methodologies and tools for the implementation of MBV, it is equally important to be able to identify clear roles to lead and to manage the process and to deal with resistance to organizational change. The next chapter deals with laying the groundwork for a culture change and dealing with possible barriers.

Summary

- Organization development (OD) is defined as the application of knowledge adapted from the behavioral sciences that inspired the humanist and socio-technical movements; OD interventions are aimed at simultaneously increasing both short and long-term organizational effectiveness by means of improving processes and structures that support individual, group and system advancement.
- Six families of values are proposed as a core for an organization and development culture: (1) courtesy and respect; (2) trust, communication, mutual support and legitimization of learning through the analysis of errors; (3) team work; (4) flattening the hierarchy and increasing autonomy; (5) participation in change; and (6) genuine interest in the quality of life.
- OD interventions can be grouped into four main categories: (1) interpersonal processes; (2) management of human resources; (3) technical-structural; and (4) strategic.
- OD has a fundamental impact in enabling the company to orient its beliefs and values towards a more psychologically healthy working environment for all employees.
- Organizations which will survive in the 21st century will have their employees capable of constantly 'de-learning' and 're-learning'; MBV provides a culture for reinforcing these capabilities.

6 Creating a Culture Shift: Roles and Managing Resistance to Change in Your Company

'Willingness to change is a strength, even if it means plunging part of the company into total confusion for a while.'

(Jack Welch – Former CEO, General Electric)

'Sometimes the situation is only a problem because it is looked at in a certain way. Looked at in another way, the right course of action may be so obvious that the problem no longer exists.'

(Edward de Bono)

The implementation of MBV involves changing the culture of the company. As we recall in Chapter 1, the Triaxial Model of MBV involves economic-pragmatic values (related to the organizational performance, effectiveness and strategic planning), ethical-social values (related to transparency, respect and honesty) and emotional-developmental values (related to learning and learning flexibility, trust, generating emotions and realizing and releasing potential of organizational members). Creating a culture shift in an organization using MBV is a process embracing these three value sets across levels of an organization, and as with any organizational change process, there are roles and responsibilities critical to the success of implementing cultural change.

Roles and responsibilities in implementing culture change

A process of culture change involves people capable of managing this complexity in specific ways that may be related to their roles. There are five basic roles that are involved in the change process. As the customers (clients) are the individuals (or organizations) that are directly affected by the change process, they are placed in the position that is affected by the other four roles as shown in Figure 6.1.

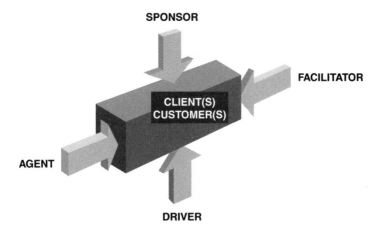

Figure 6.1 **Roles in the process of culture change**

1. **The driver**. The driver may be an individual or team that detects the need for change from within the organization based on their position or expertise. The driver argues for change, advocates change, mobilizes emotions and reasons for change and is usually also the sponsor so as to have weight and power to actually legitimize the change. Examples of those who often fulfill this role are the human resources professionals who argues for a fundamentally different, better way of treating employees; and the marketing professional whose driving philosophy is that all employees play an active part in satisfying customers, not just those specifically responsible for marketing and selling the company's products or services (Dolan and Schuler, 1994). Unless you have performed this role yourself, it will be hard to appreciate the range of negotiation and political skills and the strength of personality required to argue for a fundamental change in the face of reluctant, resistant or hostile 'colleagues' of higher up in the corporate ladder. And if the driver is unsuccessful in obtaining sufficient sponsors for 'his/her' change, his/her own position in the organization becomes untenable and he/she has to leave. The driver's role is often converted into that of a facilitator or agent once the process of change has been planned and begins to be implemented.
2. **The sponsor**. The sponsor also usually carries the final responsibility for the success or failure of the change. The sponsor applies his or her legitimate power and authority to endow the change with political legitimacy to allocate the resources necessary (in terms of people, time and money).
3. **The agent(s)**. These people (as it usually takes several individuals) execute, implement, troubleshoot, and generally put into practice the many technical aspects of the change (new technologies and systems, training, performance evaluation, communications, process reengineering, etc.).

These are the people with the executive and technical authority to help initiate the culture change. These agents of change may work from their individual positions of responsibility or as members of project teams. They put into practice the systems and infrastructure that push the change process forward such as technology, training, focus groups and other projects that align with the strategic vision of the organization as a result of this change.

ACTION/REFLECTION

- Which of the following roles in the change management process have you assumed in your organization?

    _____ **A driver**   _____ **A sponsor**   _____ **An agent**

    _____ **A facilitator**   _____ **A customer**

Which of the above roles do you think that you should assume in order to implement change in your organization? Be as descriptive as you can.

_____

_____

_____

_____

Which of the above roles contribute most to the bottom line of the organization? Why?

_____

_____

_____

_____

Which of the above roles require most effort? Explain.

_____

_____

_____

_____

4. **The facilitator** (or consultant). This person is more of a thinker than the agent. The facilitator provides advice, methodical and methodological reflection, and intervenes in the communications process in effecting the change. This person's role is to make the mechanisms of the change work more fluidly and the transitions more smooth. An experienced internal or external consultant can fulfill this role. The facilitator helps the top management to reflect and define the change needed; takes part in the design (through the provision of tools or

methodologies and experience in other contexts), implementation, and monitoring of the change (as part of the feedback loop to inform the process); and facilitating communications during the process. To perform this role effectively, the facilitator has to concentrate people's attention specifically on the human processes involved – interpersonal communication, relationships, stress management, reconciliation of individual and organization interests, etc.

5. **The customer**. This person(s) are on the receiving end of the change. Hence, everyone in the organization plays this role to a greater or lesser extent and is affected by the change implemented and therefore should be part of the process in recognizing the need for change, the design, implantation and the monitoring of the change process.

Roles to be assumed by the change leader(s)

The results of too many change projects are mere adjustments of image or tinkering with technological processes because there is no leader 'in the front line' to govern and legitimize authentic (and often much-desired) changes of beliefs and values in organizations. The members of the organization are left feeling that they have only got 'more of the same' and expect situations to revert to the status quo when the 'dust' has settled after a flurry of cosmetic or technical changes.

> The results of too many change projects are mere adjustments of image or tinkering with technological processes because there is no leader 'in the front line' to govern and legitimize authentic (and often much-desired) changes of beliefs and values in organizations

There are many senior managers or 'bosses', particularly in medium-sized or small companies where they may be proprietors or owners of a family business, who are uncomfortable with the idea of leadership let alone being equipped with the skills to initiate and facilitate change. However, they do not recognize that it is precisely for leading and inspiring people, for governing the dynamics of their organization, and for mediating the tension between stability and change, that they earn their professional remuneration.

Behind every successful company – of whatever size or sector – there is a truly transforming leader, and a story of effective leadership to be told. Well known examples include Bill Gates in Microsoft, Percy

> Behind every successful company – of whatever size or sector – there is a truly transforming leader

Table 6.1 **Main differences between the complementary roles of managers and leaders in MBV**

Role of a manager in managing MBV	Role of leader in legitimizing MBV
• Ensures that things are done correctly	• Explains why things need to be done
• Implements strategy	• Develops vision and mission
• Introduces operational plans	• Instills values
• Manages available resources	• Develops new resources
• Controls costs	• Creates values
• Maintains status quo	• Innovates, develops vision for change
• Systems/structures/control	• Process/people/confidence
• Short-term thinking	• Long-term thinking
• Gets people to conform with the prevailing values	• Gets people to internalize the vision and new values
• Controls dysfunctional behaviors	• Harnesses peoples energy
• Organizes	• Reorganizes
• Believes in the system	• Questions the system
• Task-oriented, commands	• Mobilizes people with ideas
• Avoids chaos at all costs	• Champions creative chaos

Barnewick in ABB, Richard Branson in Virgin. All these transformational leaders are considered visionary entrepreneurs in their respective business areas, and some are now globally recognized as leaders of change.

Leadership can be defined as the capacity to influence others' behaviors so as to channel their efforts toward the achievement of new goals. And as proposed by MBV, values are an essential element for channeling such efforts. Change leaders incorporate all three value sets of the Triaxial model of MBV using Economic Values at the organizational level, and Ethical and Emotional-Developmental Values throughout the organization (at the organizational, department (team or group), and individual levels).

In Table 6.1 we contrast the different functions of the director-manager and the director-leader, incorporating the ideas of various other authors on this subject (Bennis, 1989; Burns and Stalker, 1961; House 1971). Obviously, both roles are necessary and complementary for putting MBV into practice.

The responsibilities of the leader of culture change can be summed up as helping and enabling people to bring about change in the way of thinking and doing things at work. This kind of leadership role cannot be adopted or assumed overnight; it is not a question of 'nominating' or 'appointing' a person to this role. Such leaders tend to emerge and are gradually recognized and acknowledged as the best person to lead the organization. It is a long-term development process. Very few have what it takes to fulfill this role with any degree of success. The qualities required in a leader that embraces and legitimizes MBV in the process of culture change (to bring

WHAT ABOUT YOU?

ACTION/REFLECTION

Which of the above mentioned characteristics best describes your style: More of a manager or more of a leader? Which of the three sets of Values in the MBV model do you tend to focus on? How does this help you understand yourself better?

_____

_____

_____

_____

_____

_____

_____

_____

_____

_____

_____

_____

_____

_____

about the new ways of thinking and doing things under MBV) cannot be improvised: they must be developed. We identify three fundamental areas for such development, and list some of the qualities and responsibilities in each area:

PERSONAL DEVELOPMENT

1. **Affirming values honestly, coherently and consistently**. A leader has to adopt and defend the values that employees believe to be the life giving force of the organization. He/She must maintain honesty and transparency in his/her role (doing what he or she preachers) thereby achieving a high level of integrity and credibility. The credibility of a leader who embraces MBV begins with the clarification of his/her own values and those of the organization.

2. **Maturity and tolerance of ambiguity**. A leader has to get used to acting without the support of rules and regulations, without systems of instruction and control. He/She must live with a considerable degree

of uncertainty and risk. A leader must know how to assess and strengthen their own maturity and that of their colleagues and collaborators. (By maturity, we mean the extent to which a person is willing and able to assume responsibility for their own behavior and decisions). The mature leader/manager has to know how to help others live with complexity, uncertainty and ambiguity and has to start with himself or herself (Leigh, 1988).

3. **Knowledge of oneself**. Leaders must know their own strengths and weaknesses, assessing them realistically, and engage in self-renewal and self-improvement. They have to know where and when to get help or assistance and interact efficiently with others in situations of conflict. They have to recognize and control personal tendencies that may not be in line with professional interests. Honesty with oneself, however painful, is essential.

4. **Adaptability**. The capacity to adapt to new situations can be improved by training and practice, not just in sports but in professional activities as well. This ability is closely linked to one's self-confidence, self-esteem and learning flexibility.

5. **Intuition**. Often there is no time or no need for prolonged rationalizing before making a decision. A key characteristic of true leaders is that they know when to trust in their own intuition which usually is informed by personal relevant experience.

6. **Energy**. Exercising transformational leadership is hard work, calling for much physical and emotional energy – usually in intensive bursts, at critical stages – but also stamina and determination. The leader sets the standard for their colleagues to follow, and if any colleague weakens under the pressure, the leader must be prepared to take over some of the load or function as a coach in such situations to develop their employees.

7. **Communication skills**. Leaders also have highly developed interpersonal and public communication skills.

> A leader paralyzed by an excess of stress may block the entire change process in an organization.

8. **Resistance to pressure**. The application of all the above qualities will consume a great deal of a leader's personal resources, so he must be exceptionally resistant to stress. A leader paralyzed by an excess of stress may block the entire change process in an organization. Such 'hardy leaders' have the capacity to get excited by new stimuli, to regard new situations and problems as learning experiences and opportunities, and the belief in one's own capacity to modify adverse circumstances and change tactics or directions that aligns with his or her strengths (Kobasa *et al.*, 1982)

GLOBAL VISION

1. **Exploring**. A manager wishing to go beyond the role of administering or maintaining the company's system must venture beyond the boundaries of their own work. A leader needs to take a genuine interest in everything that goes on throughout the organization. Such behaviors extend beyond the office and requiring leaders to be present in all areas of the organization, talking and listening to everyone. It means finding out what is going on with customers, suppliers and competitor companies, in other industries, and even in other countries.

2. **Keeping informed, keeping in touch**. The leader must be able to set up and operate good channels of communication and systems of information, both formal and informal. They need to monitor events in the immediate organizational situation, as well as in the business, political, economic and social environments. This requires the development of political skills, and the creation of professional and social networks.

3. **Keeping on top of things**. It is essential for an effective leader to have an overview of the diverse activities at all levels in the organization, to ensure that the employee and organizational values are aligned.

4. **Visualizing**. A transforming leader must be skilled at visualizing scenarios of possible results from alternative policies and practices.

5. **Innovating**. This is not exclusive to R&D and marketing departments. A dynamic leader is constantly looking for and assessing new ideas for doing things, considering problems from unlikely angles, and must allow for time to just sit and think creatively.

STRENGTHENING AND DEVELOPING COLLABORATORS

1. **Create and sustain enthusiasm**. To do this, leaders have to connect emotionally with their colleagues, generating in them the expectations that will excite and encourage them to work toward the change. This calls for empathy or the ability to understand things from their colleagues' diverse points of view while at the same time projecting inspiring images of the future. The use of metaphors and symbols is useful in arousing enthusiasm.

2. **Developing maturity**. A leader must know how to evaluate and strengthen the level of maturity, the capacity for autonomous action and independent judgment of his or her collaborators. Being an example is probably the best way to influence the maturity of those who work most closely with the leader.

3. **Listening**. Sufficient time must be allowed for the leader to listen individually and collectively to the views of their collaborators, who are

most likely to include the other key role-players in the culture change – the drivers, agents and facilitators/consultants. Listening is essential to true team-work; and it permits the leader to test out ideas before making decisions and to check constantly that the actions proposed are really feasible and desirable. Knowing how to listen is essential to be able to formulate the values that are truly meaningful to people.

4. **Mobilizing creativity**. A leader of change who wants to enable others to achieve results and success, must create a climate of innovative thinking, creativity and experimentation within their top team and legitimize the process of learning from mistakes.

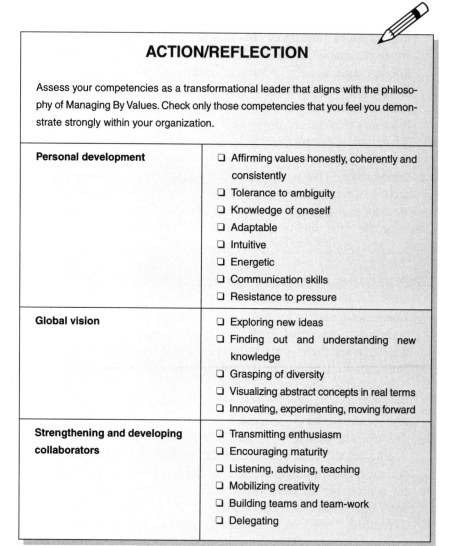

ACTION/REFLECTION

Assess your competencies as a transformational leader that aligns with the philosophy of Managing By Values. Check only those competencies that you feel you demonstrate strongly within your organization.

Personal development	❑ Affirming values honestly, coherently and consistently ❑ Tolerance to ambiguity ❑ Knowledge of oneself ❑ Adaptable ❑ Intuitive ❑ Energetic ❑ Communication skills ❑ Resistance to pressure
Global vision	❑ Exploring new ideas ❑ Finding out and understanding new knowledge ❑ Grasping of diversity ❑ Visualizing abstract concepts in real terms ❑ Innovating, experimenting, moving forward
Strengthening and developing collaborators	❑ Transmitting enthusiasm ❑ Encouraging maturity ❑ Listening, advising, teaching ❑ Mobilizing creativity ❑ Building teams and team-work ❑ Delegating

5.   **Delegating**. Strengthening effective delegation means that leaders must constantly be asking themselves: 'Why do I have to do this?' and 'Who else could do it?' This requires the leader to suppress tendencies to expect perfect performance (and high standards that only they may be capable of) and to want to be the protagonist of every important task.

REALITY CHECK

Jack Welch, former General Electric's legendary CEO, accidentally blew up a factory early in his years as an engineer. He was experimenting with a new product when suddenly the roof went. In most organizations, that would have ended his career. Jack's boss was surprisingly calm, walking him through the issues involved: Was it a reasonable risk he had taken? Was the project consistent with the values and goals of the company? The corporate culture supported what Jack had been doing, and both he and the product line went on to thrive.

Culture is often described as 'the way we do things around here.' In fact it is more complex. It is also feelings, underlying beliefs, values, history, and assumptions about an organization. Those are rooted in experiences, stories, and behavior patterns sometimes decades or centuries old. The culture tells people what is and is not okay. Culture is enduring, difficult to develop or reshape. Thus changing a culture or reengineering it, involves delicate and complex competencies, planning and procedures.

An organizational leader must know what are the collective values truly felt by the members of the company. The leader must be able to formulate them clearly, enthusiastically and honestly. Given today's social context of business organizations and the general levels of education and social-political awareness, it is practically impossible for a leader to 'manipulate' basic values, or to propound negative or dubious values.

REALITY CHECK

BERNARD BASS ON THE ROLE OF TRANSFORMATIONAL LEADERSHIP

Bernard Bass is a distinguished Professor Emeritus of Management and Director of the Center for Leadership Studies at the State University of New York (Binghamton). He has published over 400 articles and technical reports, and has written 18 books, concentrating on leadership, organizational behavior and human resources. For the past 20 years he has focused on research and applications of transformational leadership (see for example, Bass 1990a and 1990b).

Leadership is recognized as of prime importance to all forms of endeavour from ancient Egypt to modern times. It is universal in appearing in every culture and society. Until recently it was studied as an exchange between the leader and the follower. The leader clarified what needed to be done, or in discussion with the follower reached agreement about what needed to be done. If the follower carried out what needed to be done, he or she was rewarded or avoided punishment. But this transactional leadership failed to explain why followers were willing to sacrifice themselves for the benefit of the greater good or to commit themselves to goals beyond their own self-interests. Such required *transformational leadership*. The transformational leader 'asks not what your country can do for you, but what you can do for your country'. The transformational leader raises the consciousness of followers about what is right, what is good and what is important, moves followers toward achievement and self-actualization, raises followers sense of self-worth, and motivates the followers to go beyond their self-interests for the good of their group, organization or society.

Four components are seen in the behavior of the transformational leader. Different leaders may never display these components, display them sometimes or display them very frequently:

- A first component is charismatic behavior. Followers want to identify with the leader. The charismatic leader displays competence, confidence and determination. They are role models for their followers.
- Inspirational behavior is a second component usually found among charismatic leaders. They articulate an attainable vision with optimism. They use emotional appeals and metaphorical imagery. They provide meaning and challenge with simple messages.
- Intellectual stimulation is the third component which moves followers to become more innovative and creative. They question assumptions, reframe issues and suggest new solutions to old problems.
- Individualized consideration is the fourth component. They focus on their followers as individuals with individual needs for growth and opportunity.

Source: Dolan *et al.* (1996), pp. 256–7. Excerpt used with authors' permission.

The 3 phases of change

Kurt Lewin, experimental social psychologist, is one of the fathers of the ideas of democratic leadership, participative management, group decision-making, and the theory of social change. One of the main contributions of Lewin is his analysis of the three phases of change, which have been

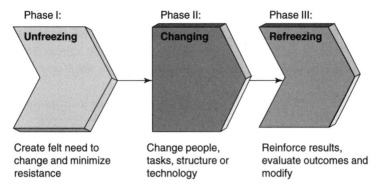

Figure 6.2 **Lewin's three phases of managing planned change**

converted into one of the classic theories of change and subsequently taken up by Schein (1987) and others (Burke, 1994) who labeled the intervention as 'process consultation'. A process of planned change consists of three basic phases: 'unfreezing', change itself, and then stabilization as depicted in simple terms in Figure 6.2.

PHASE I: UNFREEZING OF ATTITUDES OF PEOPLE CONTENT WITH THE CURRENT STATUS QUO

This is the initial phase during which the drivers of change must generate a need to change established and accepted ways of working to 'unfreeze' the status quo. In effect, the leaders must generate dissatisfaction in the specific areas of thought and behavior they wish to change. There are three consecutive mechanisms involved:

1. *Disconfirmation.* Securing recognition (or at least countering denial) that the status quo will fail to result in the future successes expected by individuals and the organization.
2. *Dissatisfaction.* Inducing a feeling of guilt at not maintaining desirable values and a sense of anxiety that objectives will not be met. No change can ever be based on a condition of satisfaction with the status quo.
3. *Reassurance.* Transmitting some emotional security and acceptance of the failure to meet certain expectations, with the aim of helping people to tolerate the negative aspects of the situation and the message. The purpose of this intervention is to maintain the self-esteem of the people who are being asked to change.

> One of the marks of an effective leader is that they can present 'bad news' in such a way that people interpret it as 'possibilities for change.'

If we want to reduce people's resistance to change, we cannot tell them that they are doing everything wrong. Everyone is driven to preserve their own ego, and this impulse would lead them to reject equally comprehensively the rational messages that the leaders are trying to communicate regarding the behavior that needs to be changed. If change is to be accepted and positively implemented, it is always necessary to balance the negative evaluations of certain kinds of behavior with positive evaluations of others that are valuable, worth preserving and worth developing. In fact, one of the marks of an effective leader is that they can present 'bad news' in such a way that people interpret it as 'possibilities for change', and it is always possible to be constructive and forward-looking, however negative a situation may appear. In this phase of the change process, it is very typical to feel uncertainty and distancing from established ways of working.

PHASE II: CHANGING BEHAVIOR BY MEANS OF 'COGNITIVE RESTRUCTURING'

Cognitive restructuring is change at the mental level of individuals involved in the change. To achieve cognitive restructuring two activities must be stimulated:

1. The person must explore their surroundings to obtain new, relevant information. Questions such as 'how do our competitors do this?' or 'how does it work in other countries?' are good start questions.
2. The person then identifies possible new ways of acting. This has been used as part of the technique of *benchmarking* (Karlof and Ostblom, 1993).

As indicated in Figure 6.2, it is in this intermediate phase of cognitive restructuring that the forces of technical, psychological and social resistance are most influential.

PHASE III: STABILIZATION (OR RE-FREEZING)

Once the change project has been put into practice/implemented, it has to be stabilized or 're-frozen'. This involves substituting the temporary policies and actions by more definitive ones. This phase may be considered as the formalization or institutionalization of the change. Now efforts must be directed to promotion of the change and to removing or reducing the obstacles. For example, interventions such as establishing a permanent profit-sharing scheme or the removal of the requirement for employees to 'clock-in and out' could help to reinforce a new climate of commitment and trust between the management and the rest of the employees.

When the organization and its systems have settled down again, its members have to be able to integrate the new ways of thinking and behaving into their personal self-image and their significant relationships with other people and groups. Organizational changes must be presented to employees as discrete processes, limited in time and extent. In any event, the management practicalities of implementing changes in complex organizations almost always demand that they be treated as projects with a clear definition, a beginning and an end.

A LEADER'S KEY FUNCTIONS IN THE CHANGE PROCESS

Bennis (1989), one of the early writers and advocates of Organization Development, differentiates four key functions of the management job of a leader:

1. Management of attention. Before we can start to communicate or lead, we first have to get people's attention. All the members of the organization must be shown a vision of the future that is inspiring and that embodies values that people will believe are worth working for – and changing for.
2. Management of meaning. The leader of a change process must know how to de-codify signals and data, in order to give real, almost tangible meaning to the important internal and external variables that are the underlying justification and reason for the organization change. This ability is inextricably bound up with the talent for communication, and mastery of communications techniques we see in successful leaders.
3. Management of trust. If we understand changing as having the courage to confront the uncertainties and unknowns of the future, then the leader must be able to lead in the most literal sense of the word, and his followers must trust the leader first before they even think about following. Trust must be created if it is absent, and must be continually maintained and renewed. The leader needs an instinctive 'feel' for all the factors that affect his/her trustworthiness in his/her organization.

4.   Management of oneself. The processes of change are a source both of enthusiasm and of uncertainty and tensions, and consume large doses of personal energy. It is essential that the leader who has to legitimize the change should be capable of containing their own anxieties and of maintaining an emotional equilibrium, so that he/she can confront the situations of conflict and desperation that may arise.

Moving from 'doing things' and 'getting things done' to 'enabling things to happen'

Figure 6.3 shows three alternative ways of governing culture change. The first way, the approach or style of 'doing things', represents the tendency for the top managers of a company to do things themselves during the change process. A large portion of expressed work overload causing stress at upper management levels is the incapacity or the unwillingness of these 'leaders' to delegate or share the most novel or strategically significant functions.

The second possible way of governing change is the 'getting things done' approach, characterized by less concern for who does things or even with how things are done. The critical concern is 'to get things done.' In the context of culture change, leaders following this approach would be concerned to ensure that employees change in the required way. This entails giving instructions, applying 'carrots and sticks' methods and generally trying to motivate employees to comply with plans and objectives.

a) **Making things myself**
('Hacer las cosas uno mismo')
('Faire les choses moi meme')

b) **Making things happen**
('Hacer las cosas a otros')
('Faire faire les choses')

c) **Let things happen**
('Facilitar que las cosas lleguen a suceder')
('Laisser les choses arriver')

Figure 6.3 **Three alternative ways of governing culture change**

Table 6.2 **The change process and MBV**

Components of the change process	Alignment with MBV
Selecting people for jobs based on values and personal characteristics, rather than by paper qualifications and previous experience	Economic-pragmatic values (performance and effectiveness)
Experimenting and facilitating participation in the design and implementation of projects as part of the change process	Ethical values (respect and honesty) and emotional-developmental values (learning and realizing potential)
Effective delegating – through giving people real freedom of action and decision, accepting that mistakes will be made, clarifying the objectives and responsibilities 'handed down' and maintaining good communications	Ethical values (transparency, respect and honesty) and emotional-developmental values (learning)
Developing the skills of interpersonal communication among the entire management team. These skills are critical for all managers to be effective in business today, which is becoming ever more specialized and complex	Ethical values (transparency, respect and honesty) and emotional-developmental values (learning)
Developing work teams that really function as teams instead of a collection of individuals	Economic-pragmatic values (performance and effectiveness), ethical values (respect) and emotional-developmental values (learning)
Giving meaning to the work and responsibilities for every member of the organization. In other words, expressing goals and objectives in terms of values and beliefs, so that the organization's purpose and the individual's job are felt to be worthwhile	Economic-pragmatic values (performance and effectiveness), ethical values (transparency, respect and honesty) and emotional-developmental values (learning and realizing potential of organizational members)

Unfortunately, this approach to leadership is not compatible with participation and dialogue. As shown by the symbolic arrow, the ultimate direction of change under such a style will very likely be for the worse rather than for the better.

There is a third way, compatible with the principles of MBV, which is the 'enabling things to happen' approach. This approach involves helping all the members of the organization to be active participants of the change process – the leader being an orchestrator or facilitator. We list the components of the process and present their relation to MBV in Table 6.2.

ACTION/REFLECTION (SELF EVALUATION)

Competencies of a leader in a change process (check only if you have demonstrated the competency STRONGLY)	Examples from your experience
❏ Selecting people for jobs based on values and personal characteristics, rather than by paper qualifications and previous experience.	
❏ Experimenting and facilitating participation in the design and implementation of projects as part of the change process.	
❏ Effective delegating – through giving people real freedom of action and decision, accepting that mistakes will be made, clarifying the objectives and responsibilities 'handed down' and maintaining good communications.	
❏ Developing the skills of interpersonal communication among the entire management team. These skills are critical for all managers to be effective in business today, which is becoming ever more specialized and complex.	
❏ Developing work teams that really function as teams instead of a collection of individuals.	
❏ Giving meaning to the work and responsibilities for every member of the organization. In other words, expressing goals and objectives in terms of values and beliefs, so that the organization's purpose and the individual's job are felt to be worthwhile.	

Resistance to change

Managing or governing an organizational change involves dealing with resistance to change. If there is no resistance, there is probably no need to manage the change process – no pain, no gain. However, rather than 'managing' the change in beliefs and values from the top down, what we are concerned with is dealing with the change process using the Triaxial MBV model.

However as much as the necessity for change may be evident, it is also normally evident that there is at least some resistance. Any kind of change is a stress or effort to adapt, and people tend to react with defensive behavior – from inhibition to hostility. When faced with situations of change perceived as threatening even if it may be accepted and recognized as 'for the better' resistance would surface as it usually detracts people from the familiar anchors that we have become comfortable with. Change is therefore usually associated with uprooting certainty and predictability especially during transition phases.

> **If there is no resistance, there is probably no real need to manage change.**

Clearly, resistance to changes can sabotage the implementation of strategic decisions through causing delays or failures to achieve objectives, waste of human and financial resources, and loss of confidence in the leadership of the company. Resistance to change does not always manifest itself explicitly and immediately, in forms such as loud complaints, threats of strikes or non-cooperation, etc. It may show itself implicitly, immediately or much later.

1. *Implicit resistance to change.* This often is manifested as a more subtle loss of motivation, increases in mistakes, more unjustified absenteeism and unproductive psychological behavior that the change was probably intended to correct.
2. *Deferred or postponed resistance.* Negative behavior in reaction against proposed or actual change can often appear 'unexpectedly' and in 'disproportionate' ways, weeks, months or even years afterwards. Resentment may simmer under the surface and only erupt into active resistance when some minor event triggers it.

It is therefore important to be aware that deferred resistance is more difficult to detect and deal with than more open and immediate kinds of resistance. However, it is also emphasized that resistance to change is not always dysfunctional or unjustified. Some positive results emerging from resistance include:

- As a forum for employees to express frustrations that have long needed attention, some of which may be extremely important;

- Highlighting practical problems that have been overlooked or not understood by management.
- As a reinforcing mechanism for the cultural stability of the organization: It may constitute a warning to top managers that the proposed change goes against common values that have worked well in the past and could be worth preserving.

What is certain is that resistance to change should be taken seriously. Managers should listen to counter-arguments, should analyze people's reactions, and should accept constructive criticism. They should never assume automatically that resistance is necessarily irrational or malintentioned.

The role of communication in managing resistance to change

> Communication is the only tool we possess to achieve the 'miracle' of authentic change.

In any company, good communications are essential not only for processes of change but for efficiency in general. People can change in two ways: by compulsion or voluntarism. However, forced change is most unlikely to improve dimensions of behavior such as creativity and friendliness towards customers that all businesses need to obtain results. Communication is the only tool we possess to achieve the 'miracle' of authentic change.

Logically, the more a company disregards the role of the individual as the fundamental factor in the organization, the less it is likely to recognize the need for a change of culture towards the personal development of employees, and the less effective will be its internal communications.

It is also necessary to take the size of the organization into account when considering how to communicate well internally. A larger organization will have a greater need to dedicate resources to communications in the management of any type of change process. One of the most noticeable features of successful young organizations that have grown very fast to their current large size such as Microsoft, is the careful attention paid to maintaining open channels of communication between the leaders and all the members of the organization.

'COMMUNICATION FOR CULTURAL CHANGE': WHAT DOES IT MEAN IN THE COMPANY?

First, good communication is two-way, in contrast to the mere issuing of instructions, however well-explained and justified these instructions.

Disseminating information in itself is not a process of communication, although adequate information is a vital ingredient of communication. It should be recognized that much of the information that circulates within an organization is counter-productive and can be damaging.

The concept of communication for cultural change in a company may be understood on three different levels (D'Aprix, 1996; Ford and Ford, 1995):

1. *Communication as a tool for 'levering' change.* Communication plays a critical instrumental role for organizational change. The more persuasive the communication, both rationally and emotionally, the more effective it is in the achievement of change. However, persuasion should not be confused with manipulation. Persuasion in this sense has more to do with clarity and logic, with sincerity and the proper expression of values, goals and individual's roles related to their capabilities. The line between 'honest' communication and mere internal 'advertising' is often a very fine one.

> The more persuasive the communication, both rationally and emotionally, the more effective it is in the achievement of change

2. *Communication as the 'medium' in which the change phenomenon takes place.* Cultural change is co-created, produced and sustained interpersonal communication inside the organization.
3. *Communication as the objective of change.* Cultural change essentially involves interactions between people within and between groups, departments and divisions of an organization. In fact, communication has been treated as conversations that are central to the organizing process.

Managing the political dynamics of cultural change

All processes of change in the way of thinking and doing things in a company have two critical dimensions that must be properly addressed: the political dimension and the emotional dimension. To speak of the management of the political dimension of change is essentially to speak of the management of power; whereas, the emotional dimension concerns the management of dissatisfaction, of fear and of optimism. But communication is the basic tool for dealing effectively with both these dimensions.

In a process of strategic cultural change, management power should be utilized for three separate ends or purposes:

1. *To focus the direction of the change effort.* This is done by constructing a collective mental 'map' or statement of the strategic direction of the company. Essentially, it means preparing, in the most participative way possible, a consensual definition of 'where we are going' (the corporate vision) and 'why we are going there' (the corporate mission).
2. *To align the change process with shared values and principles.* This means the construction of a limited set of shared values and principles that will make it possible for all the members to devote their professional and personal energies to achieving the strategic goals.
3. *Maintaining the new system.* This involves dealing with resistance to change, countering the possible efforts of others to 'sabotage' the process or to hijack the process for other sectional or personal interests.

Any significant change in the company always represents the possibility of modifying the 'balance of power' between the 'collaborating yet competing' interest-groups or stakeholders. Change increases the ambiguity and disturbs established relationships, thus generating political activity. Communication is essentially necessary to resolve potential conflict and to realign this ambiguity in accordance with the best strategic interests of the whole organization.

The political dimension of communication for change can be considered to have various areas of application:

1. *Communications from the drivers of the proposed change and those who legitimize the change.* Those individuals driving the change, arguing for it from the perspective of their professional capacities, and justifying it for specific reasons (competition, market change, legislation, etc.) need to be supported by those who can legitimize the change (usually top management and those in authority). Hence the communications strategy must be based on helping these leaders (drivers) to be more effective in their various roles.
2. *Communications to define, in a participative way, the collective mental image of the desired future.* The proper management of participation is one of the key challenges of strategic management. Some of the more important activities to be organized are sessions for situational analysis by representative members of the organization and forward-focused seminars to map out possible futures (Weisbord, 1992) in which various different levels of people among the stakeholders of the company participate.

3. *Communications to generate a 'critical mass'.* Analysing the willingness and capacity for change of individuals and groups who are critical to the success of the change and deciding on specific communications actions to influence them so as to achieve the 'critical mass' required for the change to become reality. An organizational change comes about when there exists a 'critical mass' of sufficient people to 'radiate' the social persuasion that this change is necessary and desirable.

4. *Playing clean.* Although it may seem strange to some (or even to many managers), it is strongly advisable to maintain standards of honesty and integrity when it comes to mobilizing social networks and persuading others to join in a corporate change project. This means respecting legitimate interests in the status quo, and listening to the arguments of those resisting the changes proposed. The exercise of pressure, whether overt or subtle, is always counter-productive to changes based on values.

    Apart from being ethical, honest communication is valuable from a methodological perspective, since it contributes directly to increasing confidence of drivers and to reducing the fears of those affected by the change. The feedback from good communication is invaluable for the success of the change.

5. *Punitive action may sometimes be necessary and justified.* Leaders must, however, reserve the right and capacity to transfer, isolate and even to dismiss individuals who are completely dysfunctional with respect to the process of change.

6. *Developing the moral authority of those legitimizing the change, through actions aimed at strengthening two key variables: their training and their internal credibility.* The training and development of those legitimizing the change is essential for successful change, but is particularly difficult for two main reasons:

    - Those who have to legitimize change in an organization are usually people who consider that they have already achieved significant (or even sufficient) professional success. They often do not accept the need to 'expose themselves' to any sort of training experience related to the improvement of their leadership skills.
    - To devote an adequate amount of their precious time to training in as 'strategic management' or 'the management of change' is seen as a waste of time by many top executives with diaries fully booked with 'more important' day-to-day activity.

7. *Structuring the legitimization process as a 'cascade' descending down to the base of the organization.* It is very important that the commitment

Figure 6.4 **An example of a graphic representation of change**

to change and enthusiasm for change spread through all the levels and areas of an organization, like a waterfall. Blockages and weaknesses at certain levels can substantially reduce success. Dialogue must be encouraged, especially up and down, and changes to the proposed changes must always be open for discussion. There is no such thing as a perfect plan for change.

8. *Strengthening collective identification with the change.* All worthwhile change is an intangible concept, a collection of future possibilities. It is therefore important that people have some concrete and positive symbol of the change with which to identify. One way to do this is by assigning a meaningful name to the proposed change that can be readily adopted throughout the organization. This can be reinforced with a graphic image (e.g., a logo). An example is shown in Figure 6.4. This is the logo entitled 'Leadership and vision' devised by Boehringer Engelheim, intended to inspire ideas of team-spirit and the integration of diversity, with each of the elements having a different color in the original.

Managing the emotional dynamics of cultural change

The emotions aroused by change are usually both positive and negative, such as inspiration or disenchantment, ambition or fear, enthusiasm or irritation. But in the final analysis of functions and competence, the management of employees' emotions is the single most important task for many top managers. We shall now look at some key ways of using communication to handle three predominant emotions: dissatisfaction, fear and optimism.

COMMUNICATION FOR DEALING WITH DISSATISFACTION

No change has ever been generated on the basis of total satisfaction with the *status quo*. There are at least two effective ways communication can be used to 'unfreeze' rigid old beliefs and to promote constructive dissatisfaction:

1. Communicate convincingly the reality of the circumstances obliging the company to change.
2. Communicate convincingly the likely consequences of not changing. The more employees participate in forecasting this scenario, the greater will be the emotional 'unfreezing' of negative attitudes and the more disposed people will be towards change. Often only this dramatic presentation of the awful consequences of not changing can adequately explain and justify certain decisions (such as the re-structuring of the entire workforce of the company).

However, dissatisfaction is a necessary but insufficient condition for deciding to change. Somewhat anecdotal evidence of the weakness of this emotion as a motivator of action can be found in the results of a social psychology study undertaken on the mutual commitment of couples who have been together for several decades (Rusbult, 1988). It was observed that the commitment to the continuation of the relationship (usually matrimonial) tended to depend largely on the belief that there was no alternative and on the feeling that the investment (in the material and emotional senses) that had been made in the relationship could not be written off, rather than on the evaluation of intrinsic satisfaction of the relationship. It may well be that commitment felt by individuals to their employing organization is subject to similar factors. In addition to a sense of dissatisfaction with the status quo, the motivation to change also requires the belief that the individual is capable of changing and the belief that this particular proposed change will be effective in eliminating that dissatisfaction.

USING COMMUNICATION TO DEAL WITH FEAR

The success of a change depends on avoiding attitudes of excessive anxiety since these inevitably inhibit action in the change process.

Figure 6.5 is the Chinese word that represents 'crisis.' While the left character signifies danger or threat, the right character represents the concept of hidden opportunity or challenge. The combination of both symbols mean 'crisis'. When a company has to face up to a significant change it goes through a situation of transition and uncertainty that is often felt

> The psychological viability and success of a strategic cultural change in a company depends on the manner of which the majority of stakeholders view the change as a threat or as an opportunity.

危 險
THREAT-DANGER

機 會
OPPORTUNITY

危 機
CRISIS

> In Chinese, the word 'crisis' is composed of elements derived from the word '*threat-danger*' and also from the word '*opportunity*'.
>
> The very old Chinese wisdom symbolizes in this manner that every crisis entails elements of danger. Nonetheless, when the crisis is brought to the surface, a fountain of opportunities emerge.

Figure 6.5 **The word 'crisis' in Chinese script**

as a crisis, particularly when there is no clear and convincing strategic vision established in the organization. The US company ODR – Organizational Development Resources – which defines itself as expert in the implementation of change, and whose President, Daryl Cooner, is particularly imaginative and effective in devising tools for managing change, has these characters is its emblem and displays them on the covers of all its training and publicity material.

> The psychological viability of a strategic cultural change in a company depends on it being perceived more as an opportunity than a threat, by the greatest number of individuals at all levels of the hierarchy.

Obviously the psychological viability of a strategic cultural change in a company depends on this being perceived more as an opportunity than a threat, by the greatest number of individuals at all levels of the hierarchy. This matches one of the models of stress most widely accepted internationally: the cognitive-behavioral model (Dolan and Arsenault, 1980; Dolan *et al.*, 2005). When people perceive a variable in their environment as threatening, this tends to inhibit their action – as a defense mechanism.

A variety of different communication techniques can be used to reduce the fear associated with change:

- Try to balance the change with information about things that will not change.
- Communicate precisely what is expected of each person involved.

- Communicate any specific difficulties foreseen, so that nasty surprises are avoided.
- Try to eliminate or reduce irrational fears (correct any misinformation circulating within the organization).
- Generate confidence in the intentions of the leaders.
- Demonstrate that the first steps of the process, at least, are feasible.

1. *Try to communicate information about things that will not change.* This is easier said than done, taking into account the turbulent times in which we live and the lack of control we have over many changes in our technological and business environment. Nevertheless, the transmission of a sense of security that certain important values held in the company are not going to change would eliminate fear – a function of high quality leadership.

2. *Communicate what is expected of each individual.* It is necessary to communicate to each and every member of the organization (both individually and collectively) a clear description of the type of attitudes and behavior that they are expected to develop. They should have the opportunity to exchange opinions and to learn new skills.

3. *Communicate any specific difficulties foreseen.* If one can anticipate the difficulties expected to arise in the course of the change process, it is more likely that these can be minimized when they emerge. The anticipation and resolution of difficulties is critical for the success of the process. A realistic warning that the new situation cannot be expected to be 'a bed of roses' can even add to the credibility of the project and its promoters and help in dealing with the inevitable reactions of defeatism when problems have to be confronted during the intermediate stages of the implementation phase.

4. *Reduce irrational fears.* In every process of change, individuals can become very focused on what is going to happen to them during this process. Such worries, if kept unspoken, will fester into irrational fears. In the case where fears are justified and individuals will lose their jobs, the very minimum managers should do is to show courtesy and respect in the way they explain to these people, individually and honestly, the reasons why this is happening to them. Many companies employ purpose-designed programs and techniques, often run by outside agencies or consultants, to help ex-employees cope psychologically and to give practical help such as in finding new jobs, becoming self-employed, and early retirement. Regrettably, many senior managers are unable or unwilling to rise even to this minimum level of decency when 'getting rid' of surplus employees. In such cases, it is hardly surprising that the employees remaining react not with relief and gratitude that they have been spared, but with pessimism and de-motivation, with mistrust of the management, expecting that their turn might come next.

The findings from numerous training workshops on the management of change show that employees resist changes in their company for a variety of fears, some more irrational than others. These include:

- Fear that they will have to work harder or more hours, in the new situation.
- Fear of the unknown.
- Fear of losing the personal efforts or 'investments' made to reach or maintain their present status.
- Fear of losing status, income, friendships, and other personal benefits.
- Fear that rivals will be promoted or get more attention from superiors, leading to envy and resentment.
- Fear of being incapable of responding to the expected new skills, knowledge and behavior in the new situation.
- Fear that their existing deficiencies in job performance and competence will show up in the new situation.

5. *Generate confidence in the intentions of the leaders.* It is well-known that confidence is a powerful factor for assuaging fear. An essential element in the whole process of change is that people should have confidence in the intentions of the leaders of the process. Confidence is very easily destroyed (particularly by inconsistency) and therefore it is important that all communications made about the change should meticulously preserve consistency between what is said and what is done.

6. *Demonstrate that the first steps are feasible.* A valuable mechanism for reducing fear and generating confidence is the demonstration by the leaders that at least the first steps in the process can be taken without too much difficulty. And it helps if the first steps in the new direction, bring some early benefits or results.

COMMUNICATION FOR DEALING WITH OPTIMISM

Optimistic expectations are the fuel of change. Although the communication of these optimistic expectations will require use from variety of channels (from the publication of brochures and internal newsletters, to the production and showing of videos), it seems that no one ever emphasizes sufficiently the overwhelming importance of face-to-face communication. This calls for the expenditure of considerable amounts of personal energy by the leaders of the company, reaching into all the corners of the organization to promote and practice new behaviors aligned with the change.

The generation of an optimistic and positive feeling towards change depends in large measure on the creation and presentation of a clear and attractive vision of the future, one that satisfies the basic requirements of the individuals involved: pride of belonging to a successful company; social prestige; security of employment; personal development; economic well-being; and opportunity to prove one's worth. The strategic vision may be considered as nothing more complicated than the optimistic projection of a desirable future.

WHAT ABOUT YOU?

ACTION/REFLECTION

Aspects of managing change	Rate the communication practices in your organization (circle the most appropriate)	
Political	**Very frequent**	**Not frequent**
Communications from the drivers of the proposed change and those who legitimize the change	5 4 3 2 1 0 −1 −2 −3 −4 −5	
Communications to define, in a participative way, the collective mental image of the desired future	5 4 3 2 1 0 −1 −2 −3 −4 −5	
Communications to generate a 'critical mass'	5 4 3 2 1 0 −1 −2 −3 −4 −5	
Playing clean (transparency)	5 4 3 2 1 0 −1 −2 −3 −4 −5	
Punitive action may sometimes be necessary and justified	5 4 3 2 1 0 −1 −2 −3 −4 −5	
Developing the moral authority of those legitimizing the change, through actions aimed at strengthening two key variables: their training and their internal credibility	5 4 3 2 1 0 −1 −2 −3 −4 −5	
Structuring the legitimization process as a 'cascade' descending down to the base of the organization	5 4 3 2 1 0 −1 −2 −3 −4 −5	
Strengthening collective identification with the change	5 4 3 2 1 0 −1 −2 −3 −4 −5	

Emotional	
Communicate convincingly the reality of the circum- stances obliging the company to change	5 4 3 2 1 0 −1 −2 −3 −4 −5
Communicate convincingly the likely consequences of not changing	5 4 3 2 1 0 −1 −2 −3 −4 −5
Try to communicate information about things that will not change	5 4 3 2 1 0 −1 −2 −3 −4 −5
Communicate what is expected of each individual	5 4 3 2 1 0 −1 −2 −3 −4 −5
Communicate any specific difficulties foreseen	5 4 3 2 1 0 −1 −2 −3 −4 −5
Reduce irrational fears	5 4 3 2 1 0 −1 −2 −3 −4 −5
Generate confidence in the intentions of the leaders	5 4 3 2 1 0 −1 −2 −3 −4 −5
Demonstrate that the first steps are feasible	5 4 3 2 1 0 −1 −2 −3 −4 −5
Communicating optimistic expectations	5 4 3 2 1 0 −1 −2 −3 −4 −5
Communicating to generate optimistic and positive feelings by creating a positive image of the future	5 4 3 2 1 0 −1 −2 −3 −4 −5

REALITY CHECK

THE IMPORTANCE OF CONVERSATION IN ORGANIZATIONAL CHANGE

A department in a university was undergoing a complex organizational change initiative involving major structural alterations to a building (which included moving offices and people to different locations); an expansion of work for individual members beyond their established scope; downsizing and transferring of employees; informing stakeholders (including students) about the change; and creating new policies and procedures. During the change intervention, conversations and feedback from the organizational members expressed an important central need: the need for a space to have conversations across all levels where members could voice their experience during the process. This aligns with recent research on organizational change that highlighted the importance of conversations. As the Team Learning and Development Inventory (TLI) provides the possibility to both measure and map out conversational spaces, it was agreed that the three groups where conversations are central to this change initiative would fill out the TLI: the professional staff team, the renovations team, and the department itself (across all levels). The professional team met to plan, discuss, and work out the more intangible aspects of the change; the renovations team met with the architects, the top management team of the institution, and planned, discussed and work out the more tangible aspects of the change. The department head also had meetings with her entire staff (sometimes representatives of staff at all levels) to discuss and obtain feedback about the change process.

The TLI was administered to the three teams. When the department head saw the cross-organizational mapping, she was surprised as most of the aspects of the experienced conversational space were rated low (she had also filled out the TLI for this mapping) even for the Shared Leadership Space. She called for a meeting with the staff to discuss the findings and found out that most of them mentioned that during the meetings she had usually given them information about the change to keep them updated but did not ask if they could or would like to be involved in the process. Others pointed out that they did not feel safe to voice out their own opinions or experiences based on how the change initiative was handled while others mentioned that it was the first time that they had been asked about the change process and felt that the department head was genuinely interested in what they had to say. The department head informed me later on that she had not realized that she was merely disseminating information and that key skills for leaders and managers included the ability to promote collaboration and conversation during such a major change initiative. This insight offered the organization the opportunity to create adhoc teams that members volunteered for and many reported that there had been a good change in the organization with more lively and productive meetings that were safe and where members felt they were really listened to and could also help generate some action steps to help with the change process. In essence, they felt that they were part of the change.

Source: Lingham, T., & Richley, B.A, and Soler, C. (2005).
Used with authors' permission.

Culture shift and MBV

By way of a summary, there are three central variables that form a sequential chain:

- The appeal of the change
- The decision to change
- The chances of successful or real change

1. The appeal or desirability of the change is conditioned by the trade-off between its perceived costs and benefits. The greater the dissatisfaction with the present situation, and the clearer the perception of the negative consequences of not changing, the greater will be the perception of the benefits and values associated with the change. On the other hand, the greater the fears of the consequences of the change, together with the inertia and the attachment to present comforts, the greater will be the perceived cost of the change. This cost can be reduced in function of the calming effect induced by emphasis on those factors that will not change. Lack of participation and involvement in the design of the change also reduces its appeal.
2. Although the cost/benefit trade-off is positive, this does not mean that the appeal of the change automatically determines an individual's buy in and decision to go with the change. Deciding to change depends directly on the belief in one's own capacity to be involved and to carry out the change. The demonstrated feasibility of the first practical steps facilitates this belief that one is capable of deciding to change.
3. The chances of successful cultural shift in organizations as part of the change process depend on the effectiveness of the roles, phases, and communication of the change process. As discussed, when the cultural shift aligns with MBV, such change can be both successful and sustainable.

The next chapter deals specifically with how to implement MBV in an organization – putting it into practice. MBV does not happen overnight: the process involves distinct phases incorporating the distillation of values, establishing consistency through teamwork and creating polices and procedures to keep such a system in place.

Summary

- The implementation of MBV involves changing the culture of the company along three axes of values (the triaxial model): economic-pragmatic, ethical-social and emotional.

- Changing the culture of an organization requires competencies in managing changes and clear roles and responsibilities of the 'change agents'; without careful attention to the latter the success of implementing cultural change may be in danger.
- Amongst the various roles that are involved in the change process, the transformational leader role is critical; strong leadership, a vision, and a change team or guiding coalition charged with implementation is also needed.
- The change leader needs to understand the current culture, where the resistance will come from; and be prepared to persevere and to tackle resistance head-on.
- The three phases of managing planned change which also include a phase of managing the resistance to change can be labeled: unfreezing, change and refreezing.
- Additional factors that assist the process of successful change implementations include: managing communication intelligently, creating political alliances and mobilizing/reinforcing emotions.

7 A Step-by-Step Process for Putting MBV into Practice

'To change and to change for the better are two different things.'

(German proverb)

'Stand upright, speak thy thoughts, declare the truth thou hast, that all may share; be bold, proclaim it everywhere: they only live who dare.'

(Lewis Morris)

As proposed throughout this text, change for the sake of change has never been the philosophy of MBV. Nor does it make sense to consider a culture change just because you may not like the current state of affairs in your company. Every organization has an overriding mission, and MBV must serve that purpose. A company that decides to put MBV into practice, that is to make it a part of the culture, must do so as part of its strategic plan and process.

MBV is a process of deliberate culture change that represents a collective or organization-wide experience of creative and distinctive learning.

> Every process of strategic culture change represents a collective or organization-wide experience of creative and distinctive learning.

A key difference between MBV and other value-centered initiatives is that it is a dynamic and evolving process that must be developed and allowed to unfold over time. The nature of MBV and its relationship to organizational learning is made explicit. Each experience is unique, so there can be no prefabricated recipes for success. However, the essential architecture of a planned culture change rests on two pillars: one is the implementation of the change process (i.e., putting it into practice), and the other involves aspects of maintenance and sustainability through ongoing evaluation. For the purposes of this chapter we divide the work of erecting the first pillar into three separate phases, and the second pillar requires two more distinctive kinds of work, making five in all.

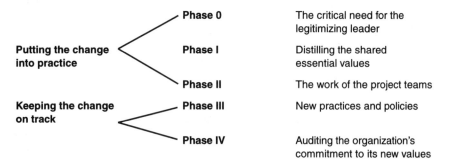

Figure 7.1 **The distinct phases in implementing MBV**

Phase 0: pre-change

We call this phase 0 because it really is an essential prerequisite, a *sine qua non* for the whole process. Many projects of strategic revitalization of the ways of thinking and doing things in an organization turn out to be mere intentions – sometimes even pseudo-intentions – not founded on solid arguments or rationale, nor funded with adequate resources. In other words, *good intentions are not enough for the management of change.*

The fate of the initial phase of implementing MBV resides with the answers to the following questions:

- Are we serious about a culture change?
- Are we in this for the long term? How do we define long-term?
- Do we have the right type of leadership to initiate and sustain the process?
- Do we have the necessary resources? What resources will we need?

A negative or even tentative response to the questions indicates that more thought, time and discussion should happen before attempting to implement MBV. The key to a successful change process is dependent on (more than any other factor) the presence of one or more true leaders who can legitimize MBV by demonstrating the will, commitment and capability to deploy all the necessary resources. Regrettably experience shows that this 'make-or-break' condition is not all that frequently met and is the reason for many failures related to cultural change. An effective leader, and a leadership team, must have the authority to allocate resources of three different types in order to mobilize the process:

1. The personal energies of the leader and her or his support team (i.e., long-term commitment, desire, shared beliefs, etc.).
2. Specific financial resources.
3. The most precious resource of all: time.

ACTION/REFLECTION

Question/reflection	Response (circle one answer for each question)	List specific indicators that demonstrate an affirmative response
Are we serious about a culture change?	Yes/Maybe/No	
Are we in this for the long term? How do we define 'long term?'	Yes/Maybe/No	
Do we have the right type of leadership to initiate and sustain the process?	Yes/Maybe/No	
Do we have the necessary resources? What resources will we need (i.e., tangible and intangible)?	Yes/Maybe/No	

ACTION/REFLECTION

- Which of the resources mentioned *would be the most costly* for the development and support of MBV?

_____

_____

_____

- How will you obtain and allocate these resources?

_____

_____

_____

- Which of the resources mentioned *would be the most unpredictable* for sustaining success in an MBV culture change?

  _____

  _____

  _____

- What are some ideas for how will you manage or stabilize these unpredictable factors?

  _____

  _____

  _____

THE FUNCTIONS OF THE CHANGE MANAGEMENT TEAM

A process of real change in any organization (i.e., especially a large company) where traditional ways of thinking and doing things are deeply engrained, calls for great professional capacity and the application of considerable physical and mental energy by the leader and the leadership team. Most management systems are designed to work under conditions of stability, so it is easy to overlook the special and different requirements needed in a change process. It can be particularly difficult for the same executives to manage the productive continuity of work processes and, simultaneously, concentrate intensively on changing those processes.

> It can be particularly difficult for the same executives to manage the productive continuity of work processes and, simultaneously, concentrate intensively on changing those processes.

In order to properly manage the dynamics of the transition between the present and the future of the company, specific structures and resources must be deployed. This means the setting-up of a 'task force or working party' – the name can be chosen to suit the way the change is being presented in the organization. But it should have the success of the change as its first and only priority, meaning belief in and support for MBV is critical. Such support will be not only technical and operational, but the team should also be equipped to give emotional and psychological support as well.

Should the leader be a member of this team? This depends on the personal style of the leader and the work load they are prepared and able to undertake. It is usually better for the leader to preserve some distance from the detailed work. The leader will need to balance the need (or even desire) to intervene and the need to be seen as a collaborator in the change process. At the same time, the leader and the leadership team will need to make decisions and to facilitate conflict resolution.

Logically, depending on the size of the organization, its resources of people and money and on the magnitude of the change, the size and responsibilities of this team will be more or less extensive, but its work will always be complex and intensive. Even in the largest of organizations, however, it is recommended that the team should have only a small number of permanent members, not more than five or six in any case. In larger or more diverse organizations, it will be helpful for the team to constitute one or more subordinate teams focused on specific task areas and reporting directly to the main team. This is always preferable to over-staffing the main team and perhaps hindering its ability to function smoothly, at a maximum level of interpersonal effectiveness.

The following considerations are important for the composition of the team:

- There should be two or three professionals, dedicated full-time to the project. They should preferably be managers who already have a good knowledge of the organization from their roles in the existing management structure. It will help if they have some prestige inside the organization, based on long service and recognized performance in their specialist areas. They should come from different functional areas but have shown a clear interest in all the other main areas of operational activity. And they need experience of working closely with others in a team.
- One of the professionals should act as team coordinator, taking responsibility for its efficient functioning (although in a small or medium-sized company, the Chief Executive may want to fulfill this role).
- One or two consultants, in the facilitator role, from either inside or outside the company. Their special responsibility would be the methodology for the process of change. Their involvement may well be part-time, for the duration of the project.
- The team should also have the power to co-opt additional temporary members, internally or externally, for specific purposes. Such needs are likely to arise for tasks of information collection and analysis, opinion surveys, communications and presentation, and training.

> **The generic purpose of a team or a task force is to give impetus to the change, to guide and monitor the whole process.**

Logically, the team will work very closely with the Board and the most senior operating executives: in fact, its work is an extension of the general management of the company. Its generic purpose is to give impetus to the change, to guide and monitor the whole process, and its activities can be detailed as follows:

1. Helping to control the specific budgetary allocation to the change plan.
2. Strengthening and coordinating the various different role-players in the process, and making sure that all members of the organization participate to the fullest extent possible.
3. Designing and supervising the implementation of a training plan for the change, on three main levels:

   (i) Development of the skills of transforming leadership, among the senior managers.
   (ii) Techniques and procedures for the internal facilitators.
   (iii) The specific and specialist techniques for reaching consensus and securing commitment to new beliefs and values throughout the organization.

4. Designing and supervising the implementation of the plan for communications. It is important that this plan is successful in keeping all the different interest groups, both inside and outside the organization, in permanent, reliable communication, both during the phase of adopting the new set of basic and operational values, and during the process of implementing the change.
5. Coordinating the project teams that will do the detailed work of incorporating the changes into the day-to-day operating processes in the different functional areas of the company (Phase II).
6. Designing and coordinating the work of Phases III and IV in the areas of Human Resource practices and internal values auditing.

ALLOCATING A REALISTIC BUDGET FOR THE COMPLETE CHANGE PROJECT

Curiously for the world of business, one of the elements less frequently found in actual culture change projects is a specific budget. The creation of a new culture, in fact the creation of anything, surely cannot be expected to emerge out of nothing. In business terms, anything not budgeted simply does not exist (or if it does, it is by definition marginal or peripheral). We have argued that culture change is of strategic importance for the survival of a company – and survival cannot be considered peripheral!

The following are the main components of a budget for a culture change project:

(a) *Direct items*
   • training in the new areas of knowledge, new values and new skills;

- internal and external communication related to the change (written material, videos, presentations, etc.);
- internal consultancy (time of staff involved that is not already allocated to their normal work);
- external consultancy (Some companies think they can get by without this but an objective professional viewpoint can be tremendously helpful and add credibility).

(b) *Indirect items*
- time dedicated to participative activities, such as meetings, in preparation for the change;
- time dedicated to training and receiving information on the change initiative for all employees in the company.

SETTING OUT THE NECESSARY TIME EXPECTATIONS – REALISTICALLY

A true leader of culture change is a strategic thinker, par excellence, and this kind of thinking is medium-to-long-term. A culture change is a profound change for any organization. Culture change is not a project to measure in weeks or months but in years; at least three years should be realistically envisaged.

Time is a scarce and more precious resource than money since it is non-recoverable. Therefore, no one wants to waste time, and we all know the pressures in business to achieve results as fast as possible. But if you have understood the discussion of values and their managed change we have presented so far, you will realize that the various stages in a project of this kind are too important to rush, nor can they easily be run simultaneously or overlapped. Each stage must be completed (completely!) before the next is attempted. Unexpected obstacles will be encountered, mistakes will surely be made and numerous factors will affect the momentum and pace at which the project can advance.

Phase I: distilling the essential values

Once the political will to change is confirmed as a serious intention, and resources are ready to allocate the resources required, the first phase of work on MBV consists of reformulating values, with the maximum participation at all levels.

As already stated in discussing what MBV actually is, most of the books and articles dealing with strategy, and in real-life cases of corporate strategic plans, are notoriously confusing in their use of terms like 'vision', 'mission statement', 'strategic purpose', 'objectives', 'ambition', 'progress reports', 'behavior guides', 'values', 'goals' and other related terms. MBV proposes a conceptual approach to facilitate strategic

> Corporate strategic plans are notoriously confusing in their use of terms like 'vision', 'mission statement', 'strategic purpose', 'objectives', 'behavior guides', 'values', 'goals' and other related terms.

action, by differentiating between vision and mission (both final values) and strategic operating values (operating culture). These three concepts (vision, mission and operating values) form the constitutional nucleus of the company. And like the contents of a constitution in the political or institutional sense, they should only be modified after legitimized processes of careful consideration, undertaken at infrequent intervals of time.

There are three basic sequential activities for this first phase of an MBV project:

1. Collective visualization of the kind of future desired, described and expressed as the final values to be incorporated in the organization's vision and mission.
2. Participation in the diagnosis of the strengths and weaknesses of the organization's current set of values, and how these measure up against the opportunities and threats of the organization's environment (this activity can be more vividly presented as a SWOT analysis conducted on the level of values instead of competencies).
3. Building a consensus on the lines to be followed in the path to change (new operating values to constitute the ruling culture of the organization).

This distillation of propositions, situational analyses and 'rules of the game' that command common and enthusiastic support, may be seen as the generation of a massive dialogue on the basis of the values and shared perspectives of as many as possible of the committed members of the organization, including the associated interest groups such as the main suppliers and customers, trades unions and professional associations. In essence, involve as many stakeholders as possible.

The classic approach to formulating strategy is to base decisions on a situational analysis. However, the MBV approach is in some ways the reverse: first the essential values of the organization's vision and mission are agreed (rather than decided), because these are needed to set the perspective from which the reality of the organization's situation and context is studied in order to reach decisions on strategy and tactics. The need for change has to be justified by the demonstrated existence of a gap between

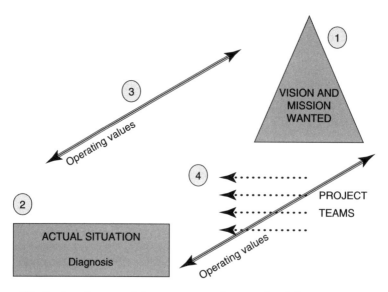

Figure 7.2 **Basic scheme of the sequence for putting MBV into practice**

the desired future reality and the reality as seen from the 'unsatisfactory' present. The culture change is the bridging mechanism.

If we begin the strategic reformulation by analyzing the present situation, we run the risk of being overwhelmed or getting stuck in 'problem-solving mode' to an excessive extent. What is required instead is the projection of a truly revitalizing business vision. The process, as we suggest in Figure 7.2, is more like a self-sustaining circuit: the people involved need to be able to relate the vision of the future they are projecting to a certain tangible reality, otherwise it can appear (or disappear) like a mere optical illusion.

Two essential challenges need to be dealt with in working through this phase:

1. A fair number of companies do not have any explicit formulation of their strategy, beyond the obligatory annual financial planning. Therefore, in most cases, we are in fact talking about a 'first time' strategic plan, rather than the revitalization of strategy. This represents an enormous culture change in itself.

2. The proposition that reflections on the strategy and the 'rules of the game' accepted within an organization should be a shared activity with maximum participation is also an intrinsically revolutionary concept for most companies, representing another big culture change in itself.

REALITY CHECK

BOEING CO.: VISION AND VALUES

In all our relationships we will demonstrate our steadfast commitment to:

Leadership: We will be a world-class leader in every aspect of our business – in developing our team leadership skills at every level; in our management performance; in the way we design, build and support our products; and in our financial results.

Integrity: We will always take the high road by practicing the highest ethical standards, and by honoring our commitments. We will take personal responsibility for our actions, and treat everyone fairly and with trust and respect.

Quality: We will strive for continuous quality improvement in all that we do, so that we will rank among the world's premier industrial firms in customer, employee and community satisfaction.

Customer satisfaction: Satisfied customers are essential to our success. We will achieve total customer satisfaction by understanding what the customer wants and delivering it flawlessly.

People working together: We recognize our strength and our competitive advantage is – and always will be – people. We will continually learn, and share ideas and knowledge. We will encourage cooperative efforts at every level and across all activities in our company.

A diverse and involved team: We value the skills, strengths, and perspectives of our diverse team. We will foster a participatory workplace that enables people to get involved in making decisions about their work that advance our common business objectives.

Good corporate citizenship: We will provide a safe workplace and protect the environment. We will promote the health and well-being of Boeing people and their families. We will work with our communities by volunteering and financially supporting education and other worthy causes.

Enhancing shareholder value: Our business must produce a profit, and we must generate superior returns on the assets entrusted to us by our shareholders. We will ensure our success by satisfying our customers and increasing shareholder value.

Source: http://www.boeing.com/companyoffices/aboutus/ethics/integst.htm (1998).

A GREAT INNOVATION: STRATEGIC REVITALIZATION CAN AND MUST BE PARTICIPATORY

The idea of involving as many stakeholders as possible in the design of a new culture may seem totally utopian but it is logically inescapable if you hope to create an environment based on MBV. MBV espouses values that recognize the potential of everyone to make a contribution based on their knowledge and experience, and that mutual learning is not constrained by notions of up, down or sideways, in a dynamic and open organization.

At the end of the 20th century, some business leaders are timidly beginning to consider a new organizational configuration for thinking and behaving at work: a new culture that breaks with the old arrogant supposition that only those at the top have 'the answers', have the knowledge, experience and energy to design and implement the strategies for survival and prosperity in the future. It is gradually being accepted that predictions and prescriptions by experts – even internal ones – are not as valid or effective as the creative visions shared by all. The stimulation of entrepreneurial initiative and behavior propounded by writers on 'excellent companies' is increasingly recognized as vitally important for competitiveness that few can muster convincing arguments against. What is really at issue is how to do it.

One central 'problem' is determining which people to involve and how to do it. Fortunately, this may resolve itself, for when the climate in an organization is ready for change people will often involve themselves, at lots of different levels and in different ways. The managers' task is then to identify those showing the most interest and commitment, and incorporate them into the change dialogue so that their contributions can be constructively considered. The question, 'Who should participate?' can be answered by another question, 'Who is committed to the organization?'

> **The manager's task is to identify those showing the most interest and commitment, and incorporating them into the change dialogue, so that their contributions can be constructively considered.**

The dialogue or internal debate from which the strategic revitalization will or should be produced needs three main characteristics:

1. It should generate new descriptions of realities for projection into the future.
2. There should be no constraints or preconceived notions in the analysis of the present; nothing should be put 'off-bounds.'
3. It is positive and useful to consider possible common values for the future by reflection on past experiences of successes and work well-done.

This dialogue is most meaningful when it comes to formulating operating values. But in practical and psychological respects, it is a function of the leadership to give expression and coherence to the consensus of final, fundamental ideas that emerge from the participation processes. In any case, participation in the process of strategic renewal, whether direct or indirect, is a decisive element for success. Its immediate effect is to reinforce the communication processes and to reduce resistance to change. Its long-term effect is to create a culture of participation where everyone is fully engaged and committed to the success of the organization and to one another.

FINAL VALUES INTEGRATED INTO THE VISION AND MISSION OF THE ORGANIZATION

In this section we aim to clarify the confusion between the terms 'vision' and 'mission' under MBV and to orient the action required with respect to each. To begin, it is helpful to briefly note how a company's approach to communicating shared values can vary greatly, as in the Reality Check on page 160.

The formulation of a collective vision can be defined as follows:

> The creation of a collective mental image of the values integrated in the vision of the future towards which the company wants to go, in the medium to long term (5–10 years), the decision to create the capability to reach this future, and the courage to believe in this future.

Inspiring the vision throughout the organization is a natural function of leadership, and above all, of transformational leadership. No one follows a leader who cannot clearly articulate a roadmap for the present and future where they, as collective members of a community, are going. A leader without this ability is only an administrator of a static collection of resources, not an inspirer of a dynamic organization. This is the essence of all true leadership. The vision statement is an expression of the organization's potential. A clear, compelling vision statement addresses the following:

- The type of enterprise the members wish to create and the business we are in.
- The type of role we wish to play in our chosen markets or sectors (market leader, most profitable company, innovator, highest standards of quality, most customer-friendly, lowest cost producer, etc.).
- The scale of operation intended, or even the general size of the organization and its operating components.

REALITY CHECK

National differences in companies' approaches to strategic thinking and the communication of values

	USA	France	Spain
Rituals: the collective events such as celebrations and meetings, public recognition of achievements, etc.	Very often	Sometimes	Rare
Symbols: logos, buildings, uniforms.	Very often	Very often	Very often
Company language and 'code': technical concepts, slogans, buzz words.	Very often	Sometimes	Sometimes
Transmission of company 'legends and myths': dramatic events and 'big' personalities from the company's history, particularly stories about the founder.	Sometimes	Sometimes	Very often
Rewards: communicating the systems of financial and non-financial reward for effort made towards fulfilling the company's essential values and goals	Very often	Rare	Rare
Vision statement	• Very often • Very explicit • Often delivered by the CEO	• Invariable • Not very explicit • Delivered by various units	• Normally, does not exist
Mission statement	• Very often • Very detailed • Emphasis on many objectives (social, economic, environment, employees, shareholders, etc.)	• Invariable • When stated, emphasis on social, economic and environmental objectives	• Explicit mission statement is normally absent. • Messages, however emphasizes economic objectives and past performance
Identifying most important stakeholders in the message	• Mix of stakeholders • Often	• Mostly to customers/clients	• Mostly to customers/clients

Source: Dolan, Garcia, Martin and Cuevas (1998). Used with authors' permission.

- The markets we want to participate in (i.e., geographical, sectors, degree of vertical integration or diversification).
- The level of risk we accept in our business activities.
- The image and kind of relationship we desire the company to have with its customers, suppliers, local community, public authorities, etc.
- The skills, professional abilities and personal qualities the members should be encouraged to develop (what kind of people do we want to be part of the organization).

A vision that simply represents the top managers' concern to preserve or extend their power is worth nothing. The vision needs the enthusiastic commitment of the maximum numbers of employees at all levels. The leader marks out the path ahead, and therefore has to be capable of generating a collective mental image of everyone's ambitions for the future of the company. The leader presents the vision as the inspiration to justify everyone's efforts to realize those ambitions. In the words of Seneca, *No wind is favorable for the sailor who does not know the course to steer.*

> **The vision needs to be sufficiently ambitious to excite enthusiasm, sufficiently comprehensive to embrace everyone, sufficiently consistent to be meaningful, yet sufficiently realistic to assure the shareholders that their investment will be profitable.**

The direction of the effort of change is the direction of the vision of the future. Without doubt, the preparation and consolidation of a clear and attractive vision of where the company is going constitutes an essential element to link the strategic business level with the psychology of the individual throughout the process of planned organization change. Organizations without a collective and explicitly formulated vision of the future are devitalized organizations lacking authentic leadership.

Among the specific purposes fulfilled by the vision are to:

- create a path to follow in the future;
- represent a target it is worth aiming for with enthusiasm;
- provide meaning to increase people's tolerance of ambiguity;
- transmit natural confidence in the leader;
- provide an idea of collective success; and
- be the point of departure (or better, the point of arrival) of the strategy of the company.

REALITY CHECK

VISION STATEMENTS THAT WORK!

'We know exactly where we want to go because our clients show us the road.'

(From AT&T vision statement)

'To manufacture, to distribute and to sell the best natural ice creams in the world with a wide variety of innovative flavors starting from fresh products of the region of Vermont.'

(From Ben & Jerry vision statement)

'To end up being a 125 billion dollar company in the year 2000'

(From Wal-Mart vision statement)

'To become the world's leading consumer company for automotive products and services.'

(From Ford Motor Company vision statement)

Sources: All quotes are sourced from the respective internet websites of these companies.

One much discussed subject is whether or not to publish the strategic vision of the company. The publication of the 'mission' or purpose of the company (such as 'Quality and health are our reasons for existing') and of the instrumental or operating values (i.e., 'honesty', 'creativity' etc.) is not usually regarded as representing any threat or loss of confidentiality. In fact, as we have demonstrated, it may be a useful part of the company's public relations. Nevertheless, there may be reluctance to make known to competitors how the company sees itself in the future, and what kind of trends it is basing its thinking on.

Taking into account the other risks of loss of confidentiality any company runs, such as a senior manager 'defecting' to a competitor, the publication of the vision would seem justified by the necessity to have it widely understood and assimilated by all the members of the organization, as well as by important customers and suppliers. If it is not widely known or kept behind locked boardroom doors, it might as well not exist. Martin Luther King's famous 'I have a dream' speech was a personal vision, but if he had not made the speech ...?

As Hammel and Prahalad (1995) state, 'The opportunities are there. They exist for many companies but not all have a vision of the future already formulated to take advantage of those opportunities, and not all can count on the human teams capable of taking advantage of them.'

ACTION/REFLECTION

For the purpose of facilitating the formulation of your organization's vision statement, we propose the following questions:

What type of leadership and what position would you like to occupy in your industry in the next 5–10 years (e.g., in terms of sales, profits, quality, innovation, etc.)?

_____

_____

_____

_____

Is there any company in your industry or other one to which you wish to emulate? Consider their vision statement as an example. What values do they express? What inspires you about their vision statement?

_____

_____

_____

_____

What size do you want to end up in reference to the company structure, geographical spread, personal and markets to enter? What levels of growth do you hope to achieve?

_____

_____

_____

_____

Who are the stakeholders that should be involved in crafting the vision statement?

_____

_____

_____

_____

THE RE-STATEMENT OF THE MISSION

Very close to, and complementary to the concept of the vision is the mission, or purpose of the organization. The mission is its reason for existing, the *raison d'être*. When you think about it, a company cannot have any kind of 'vision' unless it knows why it needs a vision! This 'why' comes from the organization's mission.

> A company cannot have any kind of 'vision' unless it knows *why* it needs a vision! This '*why*' comes from the organization's mission.

The formulation of the mission statement (and it must be a statement, without any conditions or reservations) calls for different qualities from the creative spark that inspires the vision. It requires an honest self-appraisal, based on a deep understanding of the motivations at work within the organization. It requires being explicit about fundamentals that may be taken for granted in one part of the organization, forgotten in another, and unknown in a third.

As shown in Table 7.1, the mission of every company has two distinct components, one economic and the other social. The latter depends definitively upon the former, so they cannot be separated, just given different emphases. Both components need to be expressed explicitly, and re-expressed according to the dynamic evolution of the organization. Naturally the economic mission refers to the profitability of the capital invested and the efficiency in the use of resources, depending on the nature of the organization and its ownership.

Success in terms of the financial mission makes possible the social reasons for existing, even though this may not have been made explicit in the

Table 7.1 Classification and examples of relative values pertaining to a company's mission

Two key components of a mission statement	Examples
Key Component I: economic values	Obtain benefits, efficiency, profit, generate wealth, satisfy shareholders, obtain a maximum return on investment
Key Component II: social values In reference to the entire organization	To generate employment, to develop professionals, to consume technology, to develop the wealth of the country, to increase the quality of life, to add value to the community
In reference to specific activity or sector	To entertain, to communicate, to develop the small and medium company, to cure, to empower employees, to restructure, to educate

past, and may not have been in the forefront of its owners' and managers' considerations. Organizations of all kinds may share some social mission values, such as the creation of certain kinds of employment, the effective use of the best technology, closeness to the users of the organization's products and services while other mission values may be specific to sectors of activity, such as to entertain and inform, to protect health and combat disease, to teach, to insure, to make cars, etc. The formulation and explicit communication of the mission is important for building a collective feeling of pride in belonging, for giving sense to the effort of doing one's job well, and to give confidence to the customers whose money is taken in exchange for the goods and services offered by the company. In all certainty, the companies that will be successful in the future will be those who can

---

REALITY CHECK
MISSION STATEMENTS THAT WORK!

SOUTHWEST AIRLINES

The Mission of Southwest Airlines
'The mission of Southwest Airlines is dedication to the highest quality of Customer Service delivered with a sense of warmth, friendliness, individual pride, and Company Spirit.'

To our Employees
'We are committed to provide our Employees a stable work environment with equal opportunity for learning and personal growth. Creativity and innovation are encouraged for improving the effectiveness of Southwest Airlines. Above all, Employees will be provided the same concern, respect, and caring attitude within the organization that they are expected to share externally with every Southwest Customer.'

∞   ∞   ∞   ∞

MERCK

Our Mission
'The mission of **Merck** is to provide society with superior products and services by developing innovations and solutions that improve the quality of life and satisfy customer needs, and to provide employees with meaningful work and advancement opportunities, and investors with a superior rate of return.'

Sources: www.southwest.com; www.merck.com.

express and communicate most incisively how their existence and activities contribute to people's quality of life.

There must, of course, be substantial differences in the way the mission is communicated internally and externally. In public relations communications, the mission is bound to appear generalized and somewhat removed from the actual daily work processes inside the organization. If it is to have real meaning for individual employees, then the mission statement must be closely tied to specific descriptions of the purposes for which particular operating units, departments and individual jobs exist. The line of logic and coherence of the mission statement must extend unbroken from the individual employee's mission to that of the entire, global organization.

The following questions and Action/Reflection will assist you in formulating the mission, or reason for existing, of your own organization:

1. Who are the owners of your company and what do they really expect from it, both in the short and long term (e.g., level of profitability, growth in underlying value, regular income, security of investment, efficiency in use of resources, respect for codes such as environmental protection, safety at work, non-abuse of monopoly, etc, 'blue-chip' prestige, etc.)?

2. What is it that your company knows how to do really well, distinctively, better than the rest, and what is it that your company really contributes to society (this list can cover virtually anything but should be short, selective, and realistic)?

3. What is it that your customers, and the users of your products and services, really need from your company, and will provide them with significant satisfaction (e.g., fun, health, safety, convenience, useful knowledge or information, status, sense of identity, etc.)?

4. What can your organization really and realistically provide for its employees (e.g., worthwhile careers, job satisfaction, collegiality, interest and new knowledge, pride of 'membership', a sense of purpose, financial reward, etc.)?

5. What do you provide for your other stakeholders?

ACTION/REFLECTION

With the help of the following matrix, attempt to identify the strong and weak points of the current values in your organization. This exercise will help you in crafting the mission statement.

Key Organizational Factors	Positive +	Negative −
Organization		
1. Agility of work processes	5...4...3...2...1...0...−1...−2...−3...−4...−5	
2. Training of the leadership team	5...4...3...2...1...0...−1...−2...−3...−4...−5	
3. Employee training	5...4...3...2...1...0...−1...−2...−3...−4...−5	
4. Motivation	5...4...3...2...1...0...−1...−2...−3...−4...−5	
5. Internal systems of communication	5...4...3...2...1...0...−1...−2...−3...−4...−5	
6. Strategic understanding throughout the organization	5...4...3...2...1...0...−1...−2...−3...−4...−5	
Products		
1. Quality (compared to market)	5...4...3...2...1...0...−1...−2...−3...−4...−5	
2. Price (compared to market)	5...4...3...2...1...0...−1...−2...−3...−4...−5	
3. Marketing	5...4...3...2...1...0...−1...−2...−3...−4...−5	
4. Market potential	5...4...3...2...1...0...−1...−2...−3...−4...−5	
5. Knowledge of the product/ service	5...4...3...2...1...0...−1...−2...−3...−4...−5	
6. Forecast evolution of the product	5...4...3...2...1...0...−1...−2...−3...−4...−5	
Technology		
1. Technology level throughout organization	5...4...3...2...1...0...−1...−2...−3...−4...−5	
2. Degree of technology updates	5...4...3...2...1...0...−1...−2...−3...−4...−5	
3. Degree of optimization of the technology	5...4...3...2...1...0...−1...−2...−3...−4...−5	
4. Level of development areas (i.e., R&D)	5...4...3...2...1...0...−1...−2...−3...−4...−5	
Finances		
1. Agility in collection from clients	5...4...3...2...1...0...−1...−2...−3...−4...−5	
2. Agility in payment system to suppliers	5...4...3...2...1...0...−1...−2...−3...−4...−5	
3. Level of knowledge and control of costs	5...4...3...2...1...0...−1...−2...−3...−4...−5	
4. Financial health (balance)	5...4...3...2...1...0...−1...−2...−3...−4...−5	
5. Financial planning	5...4...3...2...1...0...−1...−2...−3...−4...−5	
Image		
1. Demonstration of diversity and social responsibility	5...4...3...2...1...0...−1...−2...−3...−4...−5	
2. Knowledge of potential clients	5...4...3...2...1...0...−1...−2...−3...−4...−5	

3. Investment in corporate communication	5...4...3...2...1...0...−1...−2...−3...−4...−5
4. Level of employees' interest in the image of the company	5...4...3...2...1...0...−1...−2...−3...−4...−5
5. Usage of internet and intranet for projecting image	5...4...3...2...1...0...−1...−2...−3...−4...−5
Client Satisfaction	
1. Level of the employees' concern for the clients' satisfaction	5...4...3...2...1...0...−1...−2...−3...−4...−5
2. Agility in response to complaints	5...4...3...2...1...0...−1...−2...−3...−4...−5
3. Level of knowledge of client needs	5...4...3...2...1...0...−1...−2...−3...−4...−5
Production	
1. Capacity of production	5...4...3...2...1...0...−1...−2...−3...−4...−5
2. Guarantee of quality	5...4...3...2...1...0...−1...−2...−3...−4...−5
3. Quality of suppliers	5...4...3...2...1...0...−1...−2...−3...−4...−5
4. Policy of stocks control	5...4...3...2...1...0...−1...−2...−3...−4...−5
5. Innovation in production systems	5...4...3...2...1...0...−1...−2...−3...−4...−5

PARTICIPATION IN THE DIAGNOSIS OF YOUR 'CURRENT REALITY' USING THE SWOT METHOD

In essence, the SWOT approach means differentiating the stronger and weaker values from among an organization's existing set of core beliefs, and identifying those values in the external situation that represent opportunities and threats to the organization. Thus, it will be impossible to project any vision of the future of the company or formulate any statement of its mission without the basis of a certain diagnosis of the present reality. This means first looking inwards, at what the organization currently is and what the values are that underlie its current activities, people's current attitudes and the existing way of thinking and doing things; and second, looking outwards at the ruling values in the environment in which the organization functions, and assessing these in terms of the opportunities they offer to the company and the threats they pose. This now classic SWOT technique of situational analysis, proposed by Porter (1986) and now reduced to the initials SW (for strengths and weaknesses), has been used by many companies on the operational, marketing or technological levels. The way we propose that SWOT be used under

MBV for strategic situational analysis has two essential and innovatory aspects:

1. The SWOT analysis should be integrated into the participatory change process and carried out from within and with maximum participation. Very different views may be acquired of the same reality, whether external or internal, depending on the position of the observer (i.e., depending mainly on their role and place in the system of the company). If you doubt this, just remember the old Hindu fable about the group of blind people confronted for the first time by an elephant. The first touched the animal's tail and concluded it was a kind

ACTION/REFLECTION		
Core values presently operating throughout the company	**Strong points**	**Weak points**
Example: Hierarchical obedience	Saves time, avoids conflicts	Blocks employee creativity
_____ _____ _____ _____	_____ _____ _____	_____ _____ _____
Values regarding the social environment of the organization	**Threats**	**Opportunities**
Example: Importance of respect for the environment	Legal sanctions	Avoid sanctions; improve public image; contribute to the environment
_____ _____ _____ _____	_____ _____ _____	_____ _____ _____

of snake. The second touched the body and declared that it was obviously a hippopotamus. Whereas the third felt the legs and stated firmly that this was no animal at all, but a building on four columns.

In the same way, the perspectives on the company and its situation are bound to be different from the factory floor, from the sales office, from the warehouse or from the boardroom. But all perspectives, however, are needed to build a true picture of the organization. The detached view from outside provided by an experienced consultant can also usefully be incorporated (see absolute Action/Reflection below for another way to identify the operative values of the company).

2.   The second and equally important difference is that this SWOT analysis should consider not the product portfolio, nor the professional and technical skills of the personnel, nor the production facilities, but the values held and used by people in their decisions and activities concerning the company. Some of these values will be worth maintaining and strengthening, some will no longer be very relevant or useful, while others will be decidedly unhelpful or even damaging for the future, and so will need replacing or reversing.

WHAT NEW VALUES ARE NEEDED TO GENERATE AND TO SHARE TO ACHIEVE OUR VISION AND MISSION?

We need to be clear about the differences between the final values that are integrated into and sustain our vision of the future and our declared mission, the fundamental purpose for which our organization is in business and exists. The final values can be thought of as corporate goals that draw on shared values for their validity, while the operating values actually define the culture of the organization, define the ways of thinking and doing things in daily working activities. In terms of which is more important, or which comes first, there is not a clear or easy distinction possible, for we are dealing not with technicalities but the deeper feelings, beliefs and psychological interactions of employees in complex situations and environments where they are asked to employ their efforts and abilities. It is useful to consider operating or cultural values as being those that people regard as being the most instrumental, the most critical, for the achievement of the final values.

To return to the methodology of the change process, the cultural revitalization, we have now reached the stage where the vision and mission have been formulated, and the present situation has been analyzed, all with maximum participation. The next step is to establish the principles that are held in common and that will best guide the collective efforts to reach the desired future – the operating values that will be accepted as the basis of the new organizational culture. They are 'strategic' in the sense that they will orient the development and dynamics of the company. And they are 'operating' in the sense that they form the basis of the action objectives that all members of the company will put into practice in their work operations on the most practical level. In essence, the reflections offered by this book as a whole should help you to define what values should be adopted in order for the organization to fulfill its goals. However, real-life case studies demonstrate that most companies that formulate values do so without any clear ordering of priorities, and without appreciating the distinction explained above. Final and operating values tend to get mixed and muddled together, making it difficult for the company to get the full benefit from value-based change projects.

As a general guide, the limited set of operating values that a company needs to define should be taken from three orientations or view points as stated previously in the MBV model: (1) economic-pragmatic values; (2) ethical values; and (3) emotional-developmental values (see Table 7.2). This book cannot predict what particular values will emerge throughout the dialogues and from the processes in your particular organization, but in Table 7.2 we merely suggest some concrete examples of possible values a company may wish to adopt in each of these three areas, for illustrative purposes.

Table 7.2 **MBV taxonomy of values**

Economic-pragmatic values	Values necessary to maintain and bring together various organizational sub-systems. They include values relating to efficiency, performance standards and discipline. These values guide such activities as planning, quality assurance and accounting.
Ethical-social values	These are the values shared by the group members and those values that guide the way people behave in a group setting. Ethical values emerge from beliefs held about how people should conduct themselves in public, at work and in relationships. They are associated with social values such as honesty, congruence, respect, and loyalty. A person's ethical values will influence how they behave when living their personal economic-pragmatic values and their emotional-developmental values.
Emotional-developmental values	Values essential to create new opportunities for action. They are values related to trust, freedom and happiness. Examples of such values are creativity/ideation, life/self-actualization, self-assertion/directedness, and adaptability/flexibility.

Initially, in an overall formulation of a company's operating values, it is important to include at least one value from each of the above-discussed categories. The result of the 'distillation' process should be to pick the top ten values at most, perhaps the top five, these being the values no one has any doubts about being personally committed to. The fact that some employees argue strongly for additional values to be recognized as important does no harm at all, and the fact of omitting these from the core list does not prevent them from being practiced and promoted subsequently by those who have argued for them.

REALITY CHECK

A QUICK ETHICS TEST

Dallas-based **Texas Instruments** teaches its employees seven steps they can use to determine whether a decision is ethical. The result forms a 'quick test' and helps the employee see a decision more objectively – and ethically.

1: **Is the action legal**? 'If it's not legal then that's the end of the test,' says Glenn Coleman, manager of ethics communication and education. 'You just stop right there because we're not going to break the law here.'

2: **Does it comply with our values**? 'We have a very clearly stated set of company values. Sometimes an action just won't fit with them.'

3: **If you do it, will you feel bad**? 'Sometimes you make that decision that kind of hurts in the stomach. It wakes you up in the middle of the night, or it just gnaws on you. That's a warning flag that you may need to go back and revisit that decision.'

4: **How will it look in the newspapers**? 'If what you were thinking about doing this afternoon were going to appear in the newspaper tomorrow, would you still do it?'

5: **If you know it's wrong, don't do it**.

6: **If you're not sure, ask**.

7: **Keep asking until you get an answer**. 'If you think something's wrong, and you don't want to do it, go ask some questions. Ask your co-workers. Ask your company's legal department. Ask human resources. Call up the ethics office. Ask, ask, ask. Don't stand out there and feel like you have to carry all that pressure by yourself.'

Source: Flynn, G. (1995) 'Make Employee Ethics Your Business', *Personnel Journal* (now *Workforce*), June.

All stakeholders involved in this process should be made to clearly understand that they are selecting on the basis of priority of importance and relevance, from among a much larger set of possible and desirable values. The core set of values that results from the process is going to be used every day by every employee throughout the organization when they have to make decisions related to their work. All decisions are really choices between alternatives, and the important choices are usually between options each justified by different values (if we see a choice as between 'black' and 'white', we don't consider that a real decision, it's just obvious). This is why it is very important to rank the shared values by priority, so that hard choices can be made and justified by the higher value. The number one value in the core of essential operating values takes precedence over all the others when it comes to the most difficult work decisions. An example of how value priorities can be made actionable is noted below in the Texas Instruments Ethics Test.

If problems are encountered in prioritizing and differentiating between the core and the very desirable values, one useful technique to reach a consensus is for the working parties involved to specify the jobs, functions and activities for which each value is considered to be essential. The more people whose work is critically influenced by a certain value, the higher its priority. What is of primary importance for the success of MBV is that the identification and selection of these operating values is not a technical problem for which a solution is required by a certain date. The people participating – all the employees either directly or indirectly – are discussing the critical characteristics of the 'new' organization they want to belong to, and the process of discussion is as important as the 50 or 100 words of text in the final agreed document that emerges.

The participative discussion process is an organized series of dialogues, in which ideas and opinions are contributed, fundamental personal values are distilled and formulated, weighed against each other, and then constructed into a meaningful 'philosophy of work' with full consensus, enthusiasm and commitment. It is in fact the first real-life test of the proposition that change is really possible. The drivers and facilitators of change must tread very carefully: even if they are totally convinced of the need for certain new values to be accepted, their participation must be as equals, whose opinion is one among many. Managers must not expect their views to command support, just because of their position. They must be prepared to argue their case on its merits, as all other participants will be expected to do.

For the MBV to move forward to the next stages, this process must reach a clear conclusion on a new set of agreed values. Everyone must feel they have had the opportunity to participate and everyone must be happy with the result. A collective dialogue will have successfully begun the process of generating a new common spirit and a new sense of belonging to something worthwhile – an organization whose values are 'our values.'

Looking in more detail at the methodology, this is not something that can be performed by calling improvized mass meetings, with a show of hands at the end of set speeches. The process is similar to the drafting of a new constitution, with great care taken over the conditions under which groups of people come together for the discussions. The methods for organizing this dialogue require two basic focuses:

1. *Constructivism* – the proposition of the scientific approach known as 'constructivist', already discussed, is that what we consider as the truth is the consensus on a specific socially-constructed reality. Similarly, a good formulation of 'truthful' genuine values cannot be conducted by any instrument of diagnosis or 'positivist' scientific treatment: it must be the result of integrating, in a politically negotiated way, the perspectives of all the interested parties, of all the stakeholders in the organization.

2. *Investigation-action* – this second useful methodological focus involves the alternation between reflection and the contrast with reality. This approach avoids the two biases of the 'expert' focus (intelligence but detached from the reality) and the 'practical' focus (experience and skill, but incapable of conceptualizing actions).

Only a process of high-quality debate, with mutual respect instead of conflict, will produce the required 'unlearning' of old attitudes and behavior, and the construction of new shared ideas. A suitable scheme for organized dialogue to distill the operating values for the future consists of the following four steps:

1. Internal dialogue of the leader (e.g., what do I hope to achieve, what are my values, etc.).
2. Dialogue on the level of the management team.
3. Dialogue between all the stakeholders.
4. Distillation and communication of the 'core' set of agreed operating values.

Internal dialogue of the leader

To be credible as a leader, a person must begin by clarifying their own values and be capable of relating them to their collaborators. In fact, as we said at the beginning, leadership is a dialogue about values. When this happens on the individual level, it is the individual who clarifies their personal existing orientation, in effect by asking questions and providing satisfactory answers by way of an internal dialogue.

Dialogue on the level of the management team

All these reflections must be translated to specific working sessions of the management team, resolving possible dilemmas and confirming that there exists a common understanding of what the values they consider to be essential actually mean in practice.

Dialogue between all the stakeholders

The true development of the shared values in the company has to be a process of dialogue among all the stakeholders, not the 'selling' of a form of words composed at the top, to be 'bought' by those below (Cyrt and March, 1964; Johnson and Scholes, 1997). All companies can identify significant 'interest groups' who contribute in various ways to the operations of the organization: different functional units, professional groups, members of trades unions, people who work away from the base of the organization. There are also external groups linked to the organization, whose values can be significantly different from those working together day-to-day within the 'community' of the organization: shareholders, professional advisers and agents (e.g., legal, publicity, financial), suppliers, customers, and allied organizations. Although the involvement of all the internal groups is by far the more important, it can be valuable to find some synchronization with such outside groups, if possible. The best techniques for conducting the internal dialogues on operating values will depend very much on the characteristics of each organization, and external consultants should be able to help set up effective procedures. Some suggestions are:

- Semi-structured interviews in small groups, more 'in the presence of' rather than 'conducted by' one of the internal or external facilitators. The 'results' of which can be presented anonymously or aggregated with others, if the participants so wish.
- 'Cross' discussions, preferably again within a loose framework, between personnel from widely-different functional areas, people who generally have very little to do with each other in the normal course of their work.
- 'Nominal Group' or 'Delphi' exercises (rather like the application of the 'representative democratic process' of legislating on the national level, applied to the smaller world of the organization), as a final stage for ordering agreed beliefs and values according to a hierarchy of priority.

No one should be under the illusion that this stage of the process will be easy, or can be 'left' to happen provided a written explanation and a timetable are circulated. The degree of care and attention given to ensuring it functions well, on the part of the leaders, drivers and facilitators, must be greater than that given to the normal working of the organization. It must take place in a parallel and well-differentiated path from the normal work process. Many participants will be nervous or even apprehensive. It is important to convey the importance and intention of the initiative while also encouraging a sense of openness and even fun.

Distillation and definitive communication of the operating values

The process of organized dialogue about values should result in a distilled set of core principles and 'rules of behavior' that all are agreed on as essential for the kind of future they desire. These need to be drafted with great care and communicated throughout the organization. Depending on the size of the company, communication of the values will require a variety of media and techniques (booklets, posters, videos, internet and intranet, etc.) but above all by personal presentation. It is important that the leader initially conveys the outcome of this process. Other members of the leadership team can share in this endeavor but it must be very clear that the people who do make these presentations are doing so under the express delegation of the leader. What is being presented is not so much the results per se, but the results of a serious process of consultation and participation. The employees' commitment to the participative process that has just been carried out must be extended to embrace the results of that method.

IDEAL CHARACTERISTICS OF THE ESSENTIAL SHARED VALUES

The essential shared values must be distilled and put into practice by means of a careful and conscientious process. To use a gardening analogy, a good tree with strong roots and abundant foliage should be allowed to grow over the course of time, with plenty of water and fertilizer, not through 'miracle' hormone compounds and grotesque, forced grafts. Table 7.3 lists 12 characteristics to apply to the values your organization distills, and a scheme for evaluating them on a score ranging from 0 (very uncharacteristic) to 5 (very characteristic). In the remainder of this section we will elaborate a bit more on each.

- **Simple, few and easy to remember**. As recommended before, about six values seems to be an effective and reasonable number, this being the typical number of separate ideas most people can keep in their

Table 7.3 **Twelve characteristics of good operating values and their assessment**

Characteristics of good operating values	Evaluation
	0 (very uncharacteristic) to 5 (very characteristic)
1. Simple, few and easy to remember	0 -1 -2 -3 -4 -5
2. Associated with a brief definition	0 -1 -2 -3 -4 -5
3. Significant for the strategy of the company	0 -1 -2 -3 -4 -5
4. Chosen as a result of participatory process	0 -1 -2 -3 -4 -5
5. Significant values truly needed by all employees	0 -1 -2 -3 -4 -5
6. Transmitted by a specific process of communication and training	0 -1 -2 -3 -4 -5
7. Perceived as principles that are worthy of commitment	0 -1 -2 -3 -4 -5
8. People feel comfortable in participating in the rituals celebrating the values	0 -1 -2 -3 -4 -5
9. Consistency between theory and practice, at all levels	0 -1 -2 -3 -4 -5
10. Capable of conversion into measurable action objectives	0 -1 -2 -3 -4 -5
11. Periodical auditing of compliance, and linking to compensation system	0 -1 -2 -3 -4 -5
12. Periodical review and reformulation, as circumstances change	0 -1 -2 -3 -4 -5

mind simultaneously at any one time. It also helps if they are expressed in simple words that have a clear everyday meaning to people, words that are natural enough to be used in working situations – not pretentious phrases, and not clichés. An excellent example of brevity is seen in the values statement of the Mataró Hospital Consortium which includes: *agility, friendliness* and *professionalism*. Amway corporation includes six core values: *partnership, integrity, personal worth, achievement, personal responsibility* and *free enterprise*. In the case of Iberdrola, S.A., a large Spanish electricity company and a pioneer in the use of values in management, the following may be thought to be rather too lengthy but in their culture these might be perfectly effective: *honesty, respect, understanding, participation, responsibility, justice, solidarity, setting a good example, professionalism, improvement,* plus the concept that *the project of the company and the specific plans for its development are above the interests of any persons.*

- **Associated with a brief definition**. Values are words, and we all know that words have different meanings in different cultures and for different people. One of the basic purposes of the participative process is to ensure as much as possible that all members of the organization interpret the values being discussed in the same way. One important dimension of the concept of an 'organization culture' is that of having a common language, the development of which is a 'virtuous circle' of sharing values that will lead to a better understanding of the shared values.

For example, the simple one-word value 'respect' may be interpreted as respect for a person's position in the hierarchy, or respect for professional expertise and experience, respect as good manners in interpersonal dealings, or respect for every employee's right to personal satisfaction and development in their chosen job areas. All substantially different concepts! It is useful to review a case in point from one company that demonstrates its values in clear and concise language, and also provides definitions for each. Below are two examples from Danone's vision and values statement 1. Danone is a world leader in the food industry and has been listed as 'No. 1 worldwide in Fresh Dairy Products; No. 1 worldwide equally placed in Bottled Water (by volume) and No. 2 worldwide in Biscuits and Cereal Products' (www.danone.com). This type of communication leaves no mistake for misinterpretation of its vision and values.

DANONE

What makes Groupe **Danone** unique? How can we ensure that **Danone** remains unique? By developing a company vision and defending its core values:

Below are two of Danone's core values:

Openness – 'Diversity is a source of wealth and change a constant opportunity.'
  Curiosity: Characterizes an attitude of awareness and looking ahead, of being attuned to others, refusing to accept preconceived ideas and models, and imagination.
  Agility: Synonymous with vitality, energy, speed, flexibility and adaptability.
  Simplicity: Embodied in a management style that favors informality over formality and pragmatism over theory.

Humanism – 'The attention paid to individuals, whether they be consumers, employees or citizens, is at the heart of all our decisions.'
  Sharing: An approach that emphasizes dialogue, transparency and teamwork.
  Responsibility: Danone pays attention to the safety of people and products, acts pro-socially and is environmentally friendly.
  Respect of the other: Danone is sensitive to cultural differences, treats social and commercial partners with respect, and facilitates the development of its partners.

Source: www.danone.com

- **Significant for the strategy of the company.** The second of the above examples is a value which no one would reject but which, without the definition, might not easily understand its relevance to the strategy of the company or to the work processes of individual employees. The definition makes this relationship clear. Compare this with the five 'nuclear values' adopted by the tobacco company Philip Morris: 'the right of freedom of choice; to be 'winners'; initiative; promotion according to merit; and hard work and constant self-improvement.' The first and primary value relates very clearly to the special proposition that cigarette companies put to every consume: You must make your own decision regarding the 'trade-off' between the health damage and the pleasures of consuming this product. The second value clearly relates to the marketing environment of intense competition between brands, and the need to win this battle. Both values are seen as strategic imperatives.

- **Chosen by participation.** This is a critical factor under MBV, but it takes considerable effort and resources. Creating a participative process can be accomplished, however, and this is where an outside consultant can be very effective for their experience in various methodologies and for practical purposes such as time needed to create and coordinate this effort. Usually, when managers speak of having 'shared values', they nearly always mean that the employees (or rather the representatives of some of the employees) have been persuaded to accept a set of values issued by the top management. The concept of individual employees originating values that all, including those at the top, subsequently feel inspired to adopt, will create a true culture of shared purpose and meaning.

- **Significant values needed by all employees.** A company whose employees are referred to not only as 'human resources' but as people, creates a climate where members are effective because the values they hold as individuals are in tune with the strategic values of the organization and of which they feel they are members, will normally do well under MBV. McDonald's corporation, which has been in tune with the concept of MBV for many years, has decided to change the title of the senior vice-president responsible for human resources to: **Vice President of Individuality** (Dolan and Schuler, 1994). The essential operating values must represent the personal values that people need to have in order to work effectively as a cohesive and purposeful organization. This is the case of a Canadian steel company in Hamilton, Ontario, Dofasco, whose essential values are expressed as the following: 'vitality, responsibility and solidarity.' The slogan of the company is: 'Our product is Steel, our strength is our People' which emphasizes that the company recognizes the need of its employees to feel that their personal efforts are the main element in the success of the company.

Operating values that also happen to synchronize with predominant social values will also be more meaningful to employees, and will tend to secure higher levels of commitment. Many formulations of values are therefore likely to include respect for the natural environment, quality of life, health and safety. One flourishing American firm, AES Corporation, which produces electrical energy, includes 'enjoyment of our work' among its four essential values. By 'enjoyment of our work' they mean 'we want to create a working environment in which each person can flourish.'

- **Transmitted by a specific process of communication and training.** We have already mentioned that communications about a cultural change can never be effective without a long-term and consistent strategy. The multinational pharmaceutical company Boehringer Ingelheim has put into operation an impressive internal communications and training program in support of its corporate values aimed at significantly improving its position in the world market. 'Change as an opportunity, providing value as a competitive advantage, innovation in everything as a challenge, waste as the enemy' and 'our distinctive character is our strength.' The program includes lots of meetings, videos, open days, reflection sessions, specific booklets, and other effective and diverse communication vehicles.

- **Perceived as principles that are worthy of commitment.** If the values have not originated from the employees themselves, there is always the danger that, when they come to be committed to print all the employees will feel committed to do is to ridicule them or to treat them as a joke. Rather than representing a 'creed', the document stating the shared values freely acknowledged by employees as responsible and participating adult individuals will have the quality of a 'constitution' or 'Carta Magna.'

- **People feel comfortable in participating in the rituals celebrating the values.** An effective set of operating values will not merely be 'observed' like laws, but will actually be 'lived' by people as sources of inspiration, of pride of belonging, and of satisfaction and pleasure. This will imply their embodiment into the organization's rituals and symbols. From primitive times, rituals have had the power to influence collective behavior; the difference now is that our rituals are somewhat more sophisticated (so we like to think!). The written word is essential to give a concrete mental structure to an idea, but the image and ritual conduct derived from words are instrumental in turning the words into actions.

Examples of valuable rituals and celebrations may be the company 'Open Day', when the doors of the premises are opened to the families of employees who are invited to celebrate and recognize the significance and achievements of all the individuals who comprise the organization; the sales conferences when exceptional performance in the 'field of battle' that is the market, is rewarded publicly; the company newsletter spreading the happy news of employees' marriages, births of children, promotions, bright ideas, sports successes, civic duties performed, welcomes to new staff, and other important passages and milestones in life. Cynics may deride the 'warm glow' effect of such 'devices', but the cynics are a small minority, and most people instinctively know when such rituals are genuine and well-intentioned, even if they are a bit well-worn (but who says that old fashioned can't also be fun!). The attitude and involvement of the leader are important for helping people to interpret these rituals for what they really are. The leader can provide a framework of meaning without the heavy hand of corporate authority spoiling the spontaneity and human warmth of these events and symbols. The regular celebration of these healthy rituals is a good guide to the vitality of an organization's culture, and well-worth looking for before you accept that financially-interesting job offer!

- **Consistency between theory and practice, at all levels**. It is worth restating that a shared value is a commonly-held value by definition, and cannot therefore be considered to apply more to some members than to others. It would be a misinterpretation of MBV and culture change if the new values were thought to apply more to certain groups than others throughout the organization. However, it is a fact of life that the behavior of some groups or individuals is under greater public scrutiny than others. In any organization some members are inevitably taken as examples and followed or copied by the rest; this is the idea behind leadership. It is worth accepting this reality and taking special steps to ensure that such people realize the additional responsibility they carry – responsibility for setting a good example, and for evident consistency between their words and actions. If there is any doubt that a new value has this universal acceptability, or any doubt about the ability and willingness of a particular group to adopt the value, than it is better left off the list.

- **Capable of conversion into measurable action objectives**. The most rational way to convert values into actions that can be evaluated and rewarded is to make them into objectives, with some defined means of being achieved, either individually, or by the group or team, or by the organization as a whole. If, during the process of dialogue about desirable values, people are unsure how to go about putting them into practice, how to convert ideas into actions, then this may be another good reason for not including such values in the list.

- **Periodical auditing of compliance and linking to compensation system**. It is very typical that after all the hard work of dialogue and discussion to agree on the essential values, there is practically no management intervention to evaluate and compensate the efforts of people who work to achieve and to sustain them. Phases III and IV of the MBV project are intended to guide such interventions as part of the consolidation of the change.

- **Periodical review and reformulation, as circumstances change**. The force of a formulation of values is rooted in its vitality and capacity to attribute collective meaning and not in its static maintenance over the years. Although there will be some values whose relevance continues, there is no doubt that a periodical review and reordering of priorities gives new meaning to a set of values. Also, the natural rotation of personnel results in a gradual loss of those who participated most in the original formulation. Each year there will be fewer 'members of the constitution.' Such a review process should be undertaken at least every 10 years, and many organizations will feel the need to 'update' their culture perhaps every 5 years.

Phase II: we are actually changing! it's time to put the project teams to work

Whereas the activities of Phase I began changes in the way of thinking and doing things by the participative process of reformulating the essential operating values of the organization, this is the stage when changes of culture are translated into changes of working attitudes, work processes and work tasks. When an organization has an inspiring vision, a meaningful mission and a workable culture 'enshrined' in a good set of agreed operating values, then it is ready to define its principal lines of action in terms of a properly-thought out structure of long, medium and short term objectives. This activity is best organized through project teams.

CONVERSION OF THE ESSENTIAL VALUES INTO OBJECTIVES FOR ACTION

While the processes of formulating the final values of the vision and mission and the operating values of the new culture are undertaken in ways that ensure the individual employee can 'connect' immediately and directly with them, we are still left with the crucial process of giving all the values specific meaning in terms of the tasks and activities of employees in the course of performing their jobs. This is why an organized process of conversion of values into action objectives is required. Essentially we are moving into the area of Management by Objectives (MBO) and its procedures and techniques.

While MBV stipulates the conceptual logic of moving from values towards objectives for action, on the levels of the company as a whole, through the various group levels (departments, teams, etc.) and ultimately with every individual having a clear understanding of their own objectives for their job or professional position, we know from practical MBO experience that this stage offers valuable opportunities for dialogue, learning, motivation towards efficiency, and numerous other highly desirable activities, that will feed back to a better culture.

What are the characteristics of a 'good' objective? The list could be very long, but the champions of MBO research (Locke and Latham, 1990) conclude that the following 10 characteristics are the most important. The 'good' objective should be:

- Set with genuine participation
- Confirmed with clarity of expression/definition
- Specific, not general
- Realistic, in terms of degree of difficulty
- Measurable in quantitative terms
- Tied into the periodical monitoring of progress
- Limited to a defined time period
- Meaningful for people
- Meaningful for the company
- Associated with a specific reward for its achievement

Table 7.4 illustrates some examples of the conversion of the critical success factors that the essential values represent, into concrete action objectives. The first step is to propose indicators to measure the current situation of real development of the essential value. If there is no suitable indicator available, then one must be created. For example, 'team work' is a value that can only be measured by monitoring the behavior of the team members that should develop along certain lines in order for it to be considered effective as a unit. A practical way to do this is by the use of a survey or a questionnaire completed by each of the members to record the extent to which they listen to each other, the proportion of constructive to negative criticisms they make, and other key aspects of interpersonal processes.

One instrument that is especially effective in this regard, and is the first such instrument of its kind, is the Team Learning and Development Inventory (TLI; lingham, 2006). The TLI captures the team experience along four major spaces: Divergent (5 aspects), Convergent (3 aspects), Shared Leadership, and Openness. The TLI is a model and a method that extends both theory and practice to better understand the complexity of team experiences and to provide: (1) a method to measure and map these experiences in an easily understandable way; (2) a common language to

Table 7.4 **Sample of conversion of some of the essential values**

Essential values	Benchmarks and criteria	Current state	Desired state and objectives	
			Minimal	Maximal
Final values				
To be leaders in sales	Annual billing	Number 4 in ranking	Number 3	Number I
To be profitable	Fixed costs below the competition	Fixed costs at 20% above planned	10% below	20% below
Operating values				
Working in teams	Obtain baseline by using specific questionnaire	50% improvement in the team development in a certain area	75%	90%
Creativity	Number of new ideas presented and applied	It is not known (formal channel doesn't exist)	One per trimester	One per month
Enjoy work	To celebrate the achievement of significant objectives	Never or hardly ever	From time to time	Always
Honesty	Opinion in an evaluation session (questionnaire specific)	50% of desired	75%	100%
Client orientation	Number of clients complaints per trimester	5%	3%	1%
Agility	Response time for developing a new product	I year	6 months	3 months
Quality of working life	Questionnaire survey	Perceived low job autonomy and poor social support of supervisors and colleagues.	20% improvement within 6 months	50% improvement within 6 months

enhance member communication in order to relate to the complexity of team work; (3) immediate (or JIT feedback) of the team's present and desired future state (i.e., Real and Ideal conversational spaces); and (4) to generate knowledge and skills to foster team-directed learning and development (i.e., the identification of critical aspects that can be translated into concrete action steps to improve overall satisfaction and effectiveness). Measuring the performance of team processes will result in more motivated and autonomous workgroups since improvement is made visible and effectiveness can be rewarded. Members become empowered to create changes in their environment with data in hand to create the necessary action steps. Teams do not need to be torn apart by group conflict when they are focused on generating knowledge that will allow them to work better together. In this regard, the TLI is in alignment with MBV because of its focus on learning and development.

The search for the most suitable criteria usually brings up many opportunities for dialogue and learning. For example, if a company adopts the value 'agility' as one of its essential operating values, what reliable indicators can be used to measure the extent of the agility achieved across all the different functional areas of the company? Clearly, the first questions must be, 'What do we really mean by agility?' and 'In which of our activities is agility most important?' The answers may be that we really want to reduce time of response, from identifying a market need, to launching a new product, and that the key functional areas are marketing and R&D. Thus redefined, the search for indicators can focus, perhaps, on market research performance, laboratory procedures, or test marketing.

However, it must be recognized that the more a value depends on subjective variables, the more difficult it is to find ways to quantify compliance with it or to fix levels or degrees of compliance as objectives. It is not only difficult but, in many cases, does not make sense, since this quantification may hinder a behavior that only works by spontaneity. If compliance with the value is normally manifested in interpersonal relationships, then probably the best way to assess it is by an honest exchange of views among the persons concerned on a periodical basis to identify the trend toward improvement.

If, by means of the process of dialogue for the distillation of the essential values, people agree that something as fundamental to personality and behavior as 'honesty' should be adopted, it is not enough just to say so. Some more specific and detailed interpretation must also be agreed on how and why this value is of such relevance to this particular organization and these particular individuals. After all, who is going publicly to advocate 'dishonesty' as a shared value? This universal value must be given more meaning in the context of the organization's vision and mission, and this redefinition of the value should suggest some ways it can be measured in practice.

It is possible to devise sensible mechanisms to obtain the subjective opinions of certain groups of people that are of practical use in assessing progress in compliance with operating values, including mechanisms that involve people outside the organization. Outside consultants are better placed to advise on such mechanisms, and often to provide and operate them. Another word of caution about adopting universal values like 'honesty' without creating clear linkages to both context and practice; such values are characteristics describing both behavior and personality. Imagine the following scenario: (a) 'honesty' is agreed by all to be our company's number one essential operating value; (b) we all know that goods have been 'disappearing' from the warehouse; (c) do we conclude that our action objective is to ensure more honest behavior among warehouse personnel, or do we conclude that the warehouse manager is dishonest and should be investigated for theft? Further, should all the candidates for the vacant post of warehouse manager be given lie-detector tests? Or should everyone be expected to prove their honesty? If not, why not? There is a very descriptive name given to this sort of dilemma into which one can too easily fall by the over-simple application of MBV, namely 'a can of worms.'

FORMING AND PREPARING THE PROJECT TEAMS

Project teams are an ideal working structure for meeting complex objectives and for putting the shared essential values into practice in the short and medium term. The implementation of real changes at the level of structures, processes and policies in particular functional areas needs to be driven by the actions of a number of project teams. Each team should have a specified mission and be responsible for achieving the action objectives into which the new essential values can be converted. In effect, each team will convert a particular value into objectives and action plans, depending on the circumstances and needs of each situation. For example, one team might be responsible for all actions to improve 'orientation towards customer needs' throughout all the operations of the organization.

> Project teams are an ideal working structure for meeting complex objectives and for putting the shared essential values into practice in the short and medium term.

While the characteristics of these teams and their terms of reference will vary greatly depending on the organization and the values chosen to define its culture, the following guide may be useful:

1. Each team requires a coordinator with qualities of leadership, whose responsibilities will include maintaining close contact with the company's 'change management team' and with the operational management, particularly the leader and the most senior executives.
2. The team will work most effectively with between six and ten members, depending on the scope of its role.

3. Most of the members will be dedicated part-time to the team, continuing to fulfill all or most of their normal operating responsibilities. This point is critical and should be properly negotiated at all the relevant levels.
4. Team members should be drawn from a variety of different specialist areas, functions and levels in the structure.
5. Membership should be voluntary. A reluctant member can be more of a hindrance than a help.
6. Before it starts work, the team will require specific training in the techniques of working in a team (unless they have all clearly demonstrated this aptitude and skill).
7. Lastly, and most difficult to accept in many companies, the team should be rewarded, in financial and other terms, in accordance with effort and success.

However, it must again be emphasized that, even with project teams well-constituted, well-briefed and up-and-running, this still provides no guarantee that the change of culture will actually happen. It only means that some of the pre-conditions for success are in place.

Phase III: designing human resource policies based on values

The internal policies related to human resource policies (for example selection, training, promotion, incentives, evaluation, etc.) in most companies normally suffer from two basic characteristics:

1. They are not sufficiently coherent in their relationship to the strategy formally followed by the senior management.
2. They are not appropriately articulated nor integrated as a function of any type of model or strong ruling idea. As a result, they are developed in a fragmented way and thus lose their capacity to reinforce each other.

MBV is of great assistance in correcting these deficiencies in human resources management policies. Here we discuss the application of MBV to three areas of HR that are in much need of innovation and integrated development.

RECRUITMENT AND SELECTION BY VALUES

No matter how important the systems of training and incentives are, the touchstone for success of MBV – and for the basic functioning of any company in general – is the selection of people. When discussing the genesis of values in the company we proposed that it is very difficult to actually 'make' or persuade an individual to hold certain values, whether moral or of competence/ability in the work context (e.g., honesty, creativity, respect for others, intelligence, etc.) unless these have come to be incorporated in the individual's personality over the course of their life. Selection by values is a practice derived from MBV which contributes significantly to making a company culturally strong and 'in good condition.' In essence, it means that before bringing into the selection process the relative 'fit' between the candidates' paper qualifications and previous experience, and the functions of the position to be filled, those making the selection first assess the 'fit' between the candidates' personal values and those embodied in the organization culture, the essential operating values. This fit or match should be considered on the three key working levels of the individual job, the relevant group or team, and the organization as a whole (Bowen *et al.*, 1991). Logical and easy to specify, but extremely difficult to apply in practice, because each candidate must be given an equal opportunity to demonstrate that they best match the profile or specification for the position.

The more important a job position is for the strategic success of the organization, the more critical it is to apply selection by values. And it is increasingly evident that for jobs that are not specifically technical, such as management, supervision and consulting, specific academic profiles are less important than personal qualities and, above all, the willingness to learn and to develop new skills and abilities. For example, to manage a team of 50 people dedicated to distributing electronics products, what is more important: to be a qualified industrial engineer, to have a degree in economics or 'simply' to have demonstrated leadership and capacity for coordinating and motivating teams, and to demonstrate being in tune with the company's ways of thinking and doing things?

Even for jobs where a specific technical or professional qualification is essential (Finance, Medicine, Law, Engineering, Psychology, Human Resources Management), the differentiation between 'equal' candidates should tend to be on the basis of personal values. Part of the skill of recruitment and selection is to know which particular courses that lead to specific qualifications and degrees impart additional and desirable personal values and development. One candidate with an MBA is not equivalent to another candidate with an MBA. The institution and the teachers under which the MBA course was taken make a crucial difference. Major differences will be revealed in factors such as initiative, openness of mind, capacity for hard and intensive work, willingness to learn foreign languages, determination to overcome demanding admission requirements, enterprise in financing one's education, etc., in addition to variations in the technical content of courses.

One difficult area to adapt for selection by values is experience. From the values perspective there are 'good' and 'not so good' types of experience. The latter would be characterized by the mechanical repetition of a certain class of activities, while the former would incorporate the dimension of success achieved as a result of acquiring that experience; in other words, how the individual has actually employed that specific experience which is being offered as that candidate's advantage. Some kinds of experience can also be a strait-jacket on innovation, willingness to change and learn, and on tolerating mistakes made while others are learning.

A final point that is so obvious it may be overlooked: a recruiting organization must have a clear idea of the values it is seeking in candidates. Therefore it needs to have passed through a culture change process itself beforehand. It would be hypocritical (and often is) for recruiters and interviewers to expect candidates to demonstrate personal values and qualities that they themselves are not committed to. The three basic categories for grouping the values to be sought in job candidates are:

1. Values in tune with the vision and mission of the organization;
2. Personal values in tune with the operating culture; and
3. Personal qualities and technical/professional competencies for the specific job to be filled.

Having identified these values to be sought in candidates, those doing the selection have a basic decision to make in the event of not finding the 'perfect' candidate: to what extent is a candidate capable of acquiring or adopting new values, abilities and skills, once they are integrated into the organization and its culture? Some aspects to assess are individual competencies such as flexibility, adaptability, innovation, teamwork, and other related abilities needed by the organization. Critical incident interviews and case studies involving ethics can reveal one's values. Another way to approach a potential candidate is to simply ask them how they live their values. Today's HR specialists are well trained in many novel ways to assess an individuals organizational fit and it is strongly recommended, once again, to make certain that the person doing the initial recruiting is also a 'fit' with your new culture.

TRAINING AND DEVELOPMENT BY VALUES

Training and development is absolutely necessary to enable and sustain change. It is not a 'quick-fix' solution to an isolated or temporary deficiency, but rather a continuous improvement of the organization's most basic resource, with the aim of preventing deficiencies from occurring and promoting self-improvement.

However, in most companies training is carried out in a fragmented way, and not properly integrated with the overall business strategy. Of course, where a strategy has not been well-defined and communicated, it is only a matter of pure chance for such integration to be possible. But another part of the problem is that many managers do not really have confidence in training as a first-level tool that contributes to company success – too often they see the results of expensive training as 'walk out the door', when the trained employee quickly moves on to a 'better' job in another company, not infrequently a competitor. This does not have to happen.

> **An innovative way of increasing efficiency, coherence and company benefits from training is to integrate it into the planned development of the values newly-articulated in the culture through the process of MBV.**

An innovative way of increasing efficiency, coherence and company benefits from training is to integrate it into the planned development of the values newly articulated in the culture through the process of MBV. The value 'quality' has for some time now been integrated into the training activities of many competitive companies (in fact, 'quality' training is now an established mini-industry within the training industry). And quality has the advantage of being closely linked to many other desirable values, such as professionalism, team-work, customer satisfaction and service. Nevertheless, planned and continuous training is the key mechanism of action towards the implementation of the full set of values that everyone has agreed are critical for the success of the company.

To be able to design plans for 'training and development of values' there are two key questions that must be answered (Table 7.5):

1. What new beliefs must be learned, and old beliefs unlearned to be able to sustain and develop each one of the essential values of the company?
2. What knowledge and/or skills must be developed to be able to bring about behavior that is consistent with the essential values of the company?

A striking deficiency of many training programs typical of 'Total Quality' policies is that they neglect important OD concepts like 'quality of working life' and 'quality in personal work relationships.' Asking a training supplier for a 'management development course' is like ordering 'a computer' from an information systems supplier: it is a meaningless over-simplification. On the other hand, it is not at all easy to devise training interventions for specific groups of people at different stages of the culture change process. For a start, it means finding a training supplier who actually shares these values, as well as having the professional and technical competence to carry out the training.

Table 7.5 **Examples of objectives to be used in developing values**

Core values	Beliefs to be learned or unlearned	Skills and knowledge to be developed
Creativity	• Creativity is not only for 'geniuses'; it can be taught and encouraged	• Understanding the difference between creativity, innovation and change • Techniques for developing creativity (brainstorming, free spirited thinking, imaginary process, etc)
Teamwork	• Team development increases performance and improves quality of work and life • Working in teams produces good results only after initial periods of effort and large doses of communication	• Communication and interpersonal skills • Understanding and ability to diagnose the basic characteristic of an effective and cohesive team
Respect for the environment	• Projecting positive environmental image on behalf of the firm, yields good return in profits	• Implementing systems and techniques for cleaning toxic byproducts • Communicating publicly the firm's commitment to a clean and safe environment
Sincerity	• Sincerity is plausible and necessary for the economic success of the firm	• Knowledge of other cases (firms) who are known to be sincere and who succeed economically • Basic notions of company's ethics • Definition of the concept of sincerity applied to the work setting

To summarize, all the values formulated by the company as essential for its success should be strengthened by means of training interventions. How is it possible, for example, for any company to adopt a strategy of innovation without establishing a basic training program in techniques of creativity throughout all the functional areas of the organization? Probably, leaders of more than half the companies in any industry in any country would claim to be following a strategy of innovation, so this is by no means an unusual situation.

> **To be effective in modifying and strengthening personal values is one of the most interesting and rewarding training objectives one could aspire to.**

To be effective in modifying and strengthening personal values is one of the most interesting and rewarding training objectives one could aspire to. It is challenging on a professional level because it must be approached with exquisite respect for individual integrity and liberty of thought and expression. As Galileo said:

> A man cannot really be taught anything: he can only be helped to discover something for himself.

Logically, values are not modified by the transfer of data or techniques that takes place in most conventional training courses. What we are advocating is better described as training experiences in which the 'trainee' is guided through a process of self-directed change. Some innovatory training experiences and activities that may be considered are:

- Talks or learning venues (rather than lectures) by experts on intellectually and emotionally relevant subjects (ethics, social psychology, innovation), to open eyes and broaden minds.
- Creativity-stimulating sessions to free people's imaginations.
- More on-the-job training, integrated with more reflective sessions away from the workplace.
- Forums for the exchange of experiences.
- Development of supervised project teams.
- Mentoring.
- Training trips to the offices and plants of the company in other countries, followed by reporting and assessment of observations, differences and similarities, etc.
- Tutored project work.
- 'Cross-fertilization' sessions between departments or similar levels of the company.
- Group analysis of professional problems.
- Conference discussions under a guest-moderator.
- Debates.
- Open house lectures to spread ideas and experiences.
- Sessions specifically for learning from mistakes.
- Participative sessions with customers, suppliers, and other outside groups.
- Venture or out-door physical/mental training, to test abilities under demanding conditions, identify personal limits, and improve self-awareness and group interdependence.
- Exchange of ideas with colleagues from other sectors, other countries, with academic researchers, with community leaders, etc.

All these training possibilities are particularly important for implementing and sustaining MBV.

PERFORMANCE EVALUATION AND RECOGNITION OF EFFORT
ACCORDING TO COMPLIANCE WITH VALUES

Performance evaluation schemes suffer from the same problems as conventional MBO: they are usually excessively bureaucratic and end up being seen as an extension of the mechanism of hierarchical control. Their success depends only on the existence of good bosses who know their people well, with resources available to reward their

> **The most powerful factor for stimulating commitment to doing your job as well as possible in accordance with the values adopted in the company's culture, is the sense of being a co-owner of the company, in both the literal and psychological sense.**

efforts. Every company that is serious about improving the performance of its employees needs to be constantly perfecting new systems of variable salary, bonuses, flexible hours, and opportunities for development, career plans, and other meaningful rewards based on stakeholder needs. Equally important is the re-design of psycho-social work conditions: degrees of autonomy, job definition, feed-back, perceived importance, equity, and interpersonal support. It is also useful to give careful thought to new possibilities for acknowledging compliance with essential values by awarding people other limited resources in addition to money, such as free time, information, discretional extra training, supporting administrative staff, recognition of professional authority, access to consultants, work space, and information systems.

The collective sense of lack of recognition for effort is one of the most dramatic weak points that a company can have, from the point of view of its work force. This situation cannot co-exist with MBV. To encourage the essential values to be taken seriously, it is fundamental to reward consistently and fairly the efforts individuals make to translate the values into action. In fact, it can be stated that the day-to-day activity that takes place in a company is a function of which values are rewarded and which are not.

The most powerful factor for stimulating commitment to doing your job as well as possible in accordance with the values adopted in the company's culture, is the sense of being a co-owner of the company, in both the literal and psychological sense. For example, it is well-known that Bill Gates has become one of the richest men in the world, as the owner and leader of Microsoft. It is less well-known that a significant proportion of the ownership is in the hands of employees.

The focus of the performance evaluation, feedback and rewards, should not be focused exclusively on the individual employee. Because MBV stressed the importance of teams, efforts should be made to develop HR policies which will facilitate team work and cooperation. An example how this is done at Bell Helicopter Textron, is provided in the Reality Check below. Research also proposes the following practical guidelines for putting into practice HR compensation policies reinforcing a culture of team cooperation (Balkin *et al*, 1997):

- A reward and recognition taskforce should be developed, composed of both union and non-union members including some management employees. The goal of the taskforce is to develop a reward program that is conducive to both management and the union's needs. The taskforce is not part of the collective agreement or bargaining process but will operate separately from the contract. An individual should take the role of leader and facilitator of the reward and recognition taskforce. As the champion of the reward and recognition program, the facilitator should have some solid expertise in compensation, labour relations, total quality management and MBV.

REALITY CHECK

Bell Helicopter Textron Canada Limited (BHTCL), has adopted a participative management approach. In order to implement this approach, the production management system has been structured according to a model based on sectors of activity into which semi-autonomous teams are integrated.

The following results are expected from the production team:

- Improvement of the quality of working life;
- Manufacturing of a superior quality product;
- Cost reduction and schedule adherence.

Team work is the guideline at BHTC. Its main significant factors are team efficiency, synergy, cohesiveness and teambuilding. Several elements are required to build a team:

- a common goal;
- active involvement;
- sense of belonging;
- genuine interest for BHTC.

This approach enables more than 1200 BHTCL staff members to work in a modern management company. This method is flexible and can be readily adapted to serve the vitality of a constantly evolving environment.

Source: http://www.bellhelicopter.com/en/employment/montreal/work.cfm

- It is important to solicit customer feedback that includes internal customer feedback and external customer feedback in the performance metrics.
- The teams composed of employees should be empowered to self manage some of the personnel decisions such as selection and discipline of team members.
- The use of both monetary and non-monetary rewards should be used to support continuous improvements. Monetary rewards alone are not enough. Non-monetary rewards alone are not enough. Non-monetary rewards are useful to celebrate the success of teams and individuals in making quality improvements.
- For team awards and merit to coexist there must be integration between individual and team awards. Team members can receive individual incentives but these rewards would be given by other members of the team. Team members could nominate a fellow team member for outstanding contribution or effort to the team's outcome. This type of nomination process would not undermine team cohesiveness and synergy. In addition, there is also a reward mechanism for outstanding team effort that is given to all team members.

Phase IV: monitoring operational values via culture audits

The most frequent and regrettable error made is when company leaders think they have successfully reformulated the vision, mission and operating values of their company, is to publish them in an attractive format – and then do absolutely nothing to evaluate and reward employees' assimilation and compliance with the new culture. We have already discussed the importance of converting the shared values into action objectives that are directly relevant to everyday work processes and that, equally, are capable of measurement. This phase of auditing represents that function of measurement.

But beyond the successful adoption of a new culture, MBV also postulates the desirability of making that culture dynamic, with commitments by all employees to continuous learning, continuous improvement, periodical reviews of values, and the induction of new employees into the culture. This dynamic requires a process of auditing to monitor progress, and to ensure that everyone is actually doing what they have said they will do. This auditing process must be subject to the same conditions as the change process that generated the new culture that is being monitored. For one thing, it must be all-inclusive, with no levels and no areas excepted from scrutiny; it must be open; it must be undertaken professionally and sympathetically, not as a threat if deficiencies are revealed but as an opportunity for resolving misunderstandings, compensating for unexpected problems, for allocating more resources if underestimations were made.

Lewin, with his customary insight, stated: 'The best way to get to know an organization is to try to change it.' Organizations are highly complex and may not react in the ways expected to change, internal or external. Something similar happens to each of us if we travel to a new place we have not visited before: it calls for efforts of adaptation, but also shows us how adaptable we really are, and ways we can adapt better in the future to new situations. In addition, we may feel that all our available energies have been devoted to setting the process of change in motion, that we can put off thinking about the work involved in evaluating how it is all working out, or that others will automatically keep us informed. Sorry, but MBV is not really complete until you have checked how the outcomes measure up to the intention or purpose.

The notion of auditing is traditionally linked to the finance and accounting activity:

> The purpose of an audit is to verify the accuracy, integrity and authenticity of the financial statements, records and other administrative and accounting documents presented by the management, and to suggest any consequent administrative and accounting improvements.

However, the purpose of a 'management audit' or 'human resource audit' (Cashman and McElroy, 1991, Dolan *et al.*, 1998) is somewhat wider, and can be defined as: the review of the execution and implementation of systems, policies and procedures established by the management. Areas such as environmental protection, communication, quality or marketing are typically subjected to such commercial audits.

Any audit is the systematic examination of data concerning real behavior and activity, to compare them with theoretical principles, legal requirements or policies expressly formulated by the management of the company. However, for an audit of values or culture to be accepted as objective and valid by all the employees, it must be understood as being conducted not just for the management but on behalf of everyone who has subscribed to the values and culture being audited. It therefore needs to be transparent and the results need to be communicated to everyone. If the audit is seen as having connotations of control or sanctions, it will lose its universal validity, and the results will probably not be a true and fair picture of the state of the company culture.

An audit of values aims to measure objectively certain specified key areas of actual behavior and current practice, against the standards or ideals articulated in the vision, mission and operating values formulated (more or less) as we have recommended in this part of the book. In practical terms, it is inevitable that it will focus in large part, but not exclusively, on the way those members holding management responsibility actually use that responsibility. Much of the decision-making and exercise of responsibility by managers is tacit, not expressed or recorded formally like financial decisions. The values underlying this have to be inferred from behavior and results, from reactions and subjective opinions.

The values audit will examine a wide variety of sources, including:

- Managers' statements and views recorded in internal documents, memoranda, copies of correspondence, Internet and Intranet, etc. or specifically transcribed from conversations.
- Semi-structured interviews by the auditors with managers. Auditing as a word is derived from listening. Listening enables you to hear what people are saying and guess what they are thinking. To do it properly, you have to ask the right questions in the right way.
- Published material, such as publicity and public relations documents (now including web sites, of course), product and service support manuals, press coverage of company affairs, communications from customers, including but not primarily complaints, etc.
- Most important of all the specific documents that set out and amplify the vision, mission and operating culture, together with derived plans of strategy, objectives, targets, forecasts, and budgets.

One interesting technique that has some potential in this area of auditing is the computer scanning of information and documentation files actually to count the number of times particular words or phrases have been used. One such program available is called: NUDIST procedure (Non-Numerical Data Indexing, Searching and Theorizing). Needless to say, extreme care must be taken not to break confidentiality, not to invade individuals' privacy, not to interrogate or subject individuals to perceived intimidation or threats. The most sensitive parts of such audits, at least, require the work of experienced and trusted specialists.

Summary

- The essential architecture of a planned culture change rests on two pillars: one is the implementation of the change process (i.e., putting it into practice), and the other involves aspects of maintenance and sustainability through ongoing evaluation.
- The implementation of MBV requires five principal phases in the following sequence: Phase 0 – finding a legitimizing leader; Phase I – distilling

the shared essential values; Phase II – the work of project teams; Phase III – developing new practices and policies, and Phase IV – auditing the organization's commitment to its new values.

- MBV in three words means: alignment between **core values**, the organization's **mission** and its future **vision**.

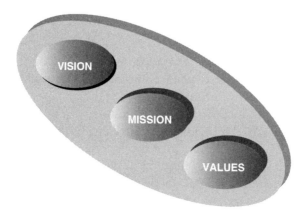

8 Putting MBV into Practice is Not Easy: 24 Likely Problem Areas, and Suggested Answers

In this last chapter we will provide some FAQs (frequently asked questions) and possible answers, on the difficulties of putting MBV into practice. We never said it was going to be easy! As we near the end of our book, we will highlight some of the problem areas, with the following selection of objections, worries and questions taken from practical experience.

1. **What if the existing 'leader' (President, CEO, MD, or whoever) needs to change, needs new values, and needs to be consistent between what he/she says and what he/she does? Who is going to tell him/her this?**

   The consultant is one possible candidate. We have already stated our belief that the absence of a transforming leader, with the qualities we have discussed, makes a change of culture practically impossible. However ... if the drivers of change are numerous enough, united enough and committed enough, they may succeed in convincing a reluctant or doubtful leader. And if they don't succeed, there are always other people, other authorities to whom any leader must pay attention; it is a case of convincing perhaps the majority shareholder, perhaps the retired founder or previous top person, perhaps the leader's wife/husband ...

2. **Should you push through a change as fast as possible, or in gradual steps?**

   It is perfectly logical and feasible, within a globally designed strategy for change in an extended organization, to do pilot experiments first to test the proposed procedures. But a significant change of culture involves changes in personal values of the deepest kind possible, and this cannot and should not be disguised, by talking of gradual, less perceptible changes. The timing of the process is much less important than getting it right, so better to avoid being tied into a rigid time schedule or a fixed deadline.

3. **People don't like change, because of inertia: they are too comfortable as they are.**

    This is true. Human inertia is a powerful force of resistance to change. If it were different, organizations would not need inspiring leaders, they would need armies of Personnel Managers to keep recruiting for the jobs that were being left every day! This inertia would not matter so much if we were living a few centuries back, when a major change in circumstances occurred once every generation: this now seems to happen once a week! However, inertia is not a constant. There are certain times, certain situations, certain persuasive people who can open up 'windows' in the 'walls' of inertia surrounding working people in their offices, factories, shops. This book is all about taking advantage of such 'windows of opportunity' for change.

4. **'This is the last time in my professional life that I am going to get excited by a project for change that then comes to nothing, leaving me even more frustrated than I was before. Never again!'**

    An understandable reaction, but not at all helpful. Such a cry from the heart, full of indignation and dashed hopes, should go straight to the deepest professional ethical values of both consultants and managers. In so many organizations, the climate for change is polluted by such disillusion, which only makes the work of successive management teams even more difficult (and challenging).

5. **Many successful companies owe their success to holding certain values constantly and consistently over their whole history, without much evident change and without shifts of strategy.**

    This is true, but only up to a certain point. For this reason, culture change must be approached very seriously, with due regard to the possible risks of breaking valuable continuities. Some companies do combine success and stability but often this only lasts for a generation, or until some major upheaval in their technology or their market occurs. But there are bound to be some fortunate organizations who inherit a healthy culture when there is a generational succession, and some leaders really are dynamic, inspiring and effective. If you feel that your company's existing culture is fine for the foreseeable future, then have it audited and confirm that your satisfaction is shared by all the employees.

6. **People systematically reject change, no matter what kind of change, because they are frightened they will have to work harder.**

    This is an observation we have found is frequently made in seminars and working sessions. Again, up to a certain point it is completely normal. It is unlikely that any business change has ever taken place with the goal of reducing employees' work while increasing their pay. What often happens is that the concept of 'change' raises irrational fantasies about what exactly will be different after the change. Doing anything new is usually viewed beforehand as more difficult than it turns out to be. Much better to counter this point with other questions: 'Why is it that people feel they are already working hard enough?' and 'Why is their particular work considered "hard", and presumably not satisfying or rewarding?' The underlying reason must be that the employees' values are 'out of tune' with the values of the company whose purposes the work serves.

There are three key arguments to deal with the 'knee-jerk' negative reaction to change. First, the change of culture must be understood and designed as a process of inter-change between each individual employee and the organization as a whole (of which the employee is, at least, a consenting, if not fully committed member); unless both 'sides' are satisfied, there is no deal. Second, the benefits from the change, which should justify each individual's satisfaction and acceptance, must be very clearly communicated. Thirdly, although 'new' things will be done (in the work processes) as a result of the change, 'old' things will cease to be done: the new work activities initiated by the new values incorporated into the culture, will be offset by old activities associated with old discarded values and attitudes that will no longer be done.

7. **The job of outside consultants is to tell the client what their strategy should be; it is the client's job to implement it.**

   This is a simplistic and short-sighted view on the part of both consultant and client, although it may represent a successful strategy for the consultant to charge a lot, for the achievement of very little. As regards implementation, the very minimum the outside consultant should do is to ensure their client organization has internal consultants capable of guiding the successful implementation of the change process.

8. **The vision of where the company is going should always be held in the mind, but I don't accept that it is so necessary to explain it and commit it to paper.**

   This belief is common in owner-managers of companies who continue to believe that they and their company are really one and the same person. It may well be that there is no true strategic vision for the future after they retire or sell up!

9. **When the Chinese manufacture silk ties for $1 – probably next week! – it will not be a question of changing, it will be time to close down and go home.**

   Exactly. The defeatists will give up: the realistic entrepreneurs will realize there is no time to lose in changing, and start now. Maybe this Western manufacturer of luxury clothing accessories should close down their factory and set up as the leading importer and distributor of silk ties Made in China – but designed in New York/Paris/Madrid/Milan ...

10. **The real problem is the middle managers: when the need for enthusiasm for the change gets down to their level, they don't respond. It even seems as if the ordinary employees at the bottom respond better.**

This phenomenon is sometimes referred to as the 'black hole' – the centre of the company structure into which ideas disappear, never to be seen again. It is typical of change projects designed exclusively by the upper echelon of the company, usually with the aid of external consultants following the 'expert' model, and then handed down as a *fait accompli* to the middle managers to be implemented. One has to sympathize with middle managers to a large extent, for they are subjected to pressures from both above and below – yet it is hard work to convince them that it is possible to change organization structures to eliminate a lot of the hierarchy problems. Middle managers are the natural victims of the corporate world, stressed, insecure, unmotivated, uninformed – and the first to go when a cut in overheads is called for. The interesting observation that the lowest levels among employees often respond more positively to new ideas is perhaps due to their relatively low expectations of participation, and perhaps also because they are more easily attracted by the novel and exciting aspects of change, optimistic about possible benefits but relatively unaware of potential problems and disadvantages.

11. **If the change were for the better, there would be no need to talk so much about 'managing the change'. What happens when the changes are for the worse?**

This is a very lucid reflection. To induce an employee to change from an office four square meters and badly ventilated, to a new one of 20 sq. meters with a view of the gardens does not call for great communication or persuasion skills and a 'change management team'. The real challenge for managers of change is to convince everyone that a dynamic organization has a better chance of survival and success than a stagnant one, that there will be costs and benefits for everyone from the kind of change we have been discussing, but that the benefits will substantially outweigh the costs, that there will be full and genuine participation, and that the organization will look after those members who really suffer the worst negative effects.

12. **Closing the company down and recovering the capital is much more convenient than all this complex and costly business of 'culture change'.**

Yes, free market capitalism does sometimes justify this view, but only as a very last resort. But the owners of the capital are just one of the stakeholders: the others should normally be capable of formulating an acceptable enough vision and mission to persuade the owners (or more likely the financial institutions that represent the true owners) that their capital stake will be worth more if left in a functioning enterprise with a potentially profitable future. If there is no entrepreneurial spirit left in the organization, no leaders, and no convincing economic purpose for keeping this particular set of resources together, then one must reluctantly conclude that the capital, the physical assets, and the employees would be better employed in some other enterprise.

13. **If we have to change our beliefs and values, is this because we are doing something wrong?**

    In a certain way, yes. But maybe the only thing you are doing wrong is not changing fast enough or in the correct ways to put your organization in the best condition for future survival and success. And those who don't recognize a need to change are likely to be living on borrowed time, with an organization culture that will soon be out of tune with its people's and its environment's evolving values.

14. **These days, it is not a question of 'desiring' a certain future vision for the company, it is the damned environment that forces a vision on you.**

    Precisely. Almost every organization suffers from the delusion that it has far more power over its own destiny than it really possess. And when this impotence becomes manifestly evident, it seems that the automatic reaction of most business leaders is to go for bigger and bigger mergers/takeovers/alliances and similar 'mega-deals'. What would the business world be like, one wonders, if all the efforts and resources devoted to these invariably futile mega-deals were put into MBV? Research and experience seem to be telling us that there is a severe limit on the size of an organizational unit that can be truly resilient – entrepreneurial, creative, responsive and accountable to its members while delivering job satisfaction, self-esteem, personal resilience (and fun). MBV is proposed as a logical and structured way to make organizational units of people more resilient, precisely because the future is so unpredictable, uncontrollable and, in many ways, frightening.

15. **Should leaders and managers always contract-in external consultants for change projects, or is it better to handle everything internally?**

    As we have argued in the book, we see a crucial role for 'facilitators' of change, experienced individuals skilled in interpersonal relationships and processes rather than concerned with the tasks and technicalities of the work activities. And we also differentiate this role from that of the inspiring 'leader' or the dynamic 'driver' of change. However, it really depends on the particular circumstances whether this role is filled externally or internally – the important thing is that it is fulfilled well. Some companies are accustomed to bring in external consultants for technological changes, new quality systems, marketing reorganizations, etc., so it would appear natural to all the employees if external consultants contributed to the most important change project an organization will ever undertake, the change of its fundamental culture. But often the real function of these detached experts is to give psychological support to decision-makers (and to take the blame for unpopular decisions). If an organization can already count on members who are capable of, say, conducting a SWOT analysis effectively, or preparing a good strategic plan, or implementing MBO, then there is no intrinsic reason why they should not organize the MBV project, perhaps after some specific outside training. Their advantage will lie in already having the shared 'mental representation' of the reality of the world of the organization. Human Resources professionals are often the best equipped to handle the 'facilitator' role in culture change (but sometimes they are the least well-equipped!).

16. **What happens when you generate people's enthusiasm for certain values and objectives, then they sell the company and put people onto the street?**

Yes, life is tough, but no one is guaranteed a job for life, nor should they be. Above all, don't feel guilty when events beyond your control hurt other people. It is natural and good to feel concern – and some responsibility if you have really exercised some responsibility for this situation and these people. All you can do is play your part to the best of your ability. Our specific answer (as against the foregoing generalities!) is that your past efforts towards MBV will be extremely valuable in giving such job-losers the extra personal resilience, self-confidence, and awareness of their own values and qualities, etc. that is the best basis for success in finding a new job, changing career, learning new skills, or any other plan of action these individuals formulate to 'deal' with the new situation. If you have done this, it is something to feel proud of, not guilty.

17. **All this stuff about MBV is very technical. The average businessman is only interested in buying cheap and selling high.**

Fair enough, but this average businessman you define is a trader, and this book is not written to help traders to trade better. But if this businessman claims to 'run' an organization to which he expects other people to be committed as productive and efficient employees (if he employs only members of his own family, this expectation often does not hold), then he will find plenty of useful ideas to think about in this book, even if he finds this 'MBV stuff' a bit technical. (Sorry, we've tried to keep it simple!).

18. **A lot is talked about change in the company, but what about the public administration?**

Until the public sector becomes more business-like, very little can be done. However, some units in some departments in some countries, are currently experimenting with MBV on a limited scale. We hope to provide more information about these experiments in the next edition of this book.

19. **Each time those at the top talk about change, no matter what the reason for it, my hair stands on end: another twist of the screw, more work and more stress. My wife has already had it up to here!**

In your case, those at the top clearly do not have sufficient professional training in the human aspects of governing change. If things go on like this, many companies will end up cooking the goose that lays the golden eggs. And their markets will be open to other competitor companies more sensitive to the need for their people to have balanced work schedules – amongst many other things.

20. **This emphasis on values will end up converting companies into a kind of religious sect.**

There are some companies with such a strongly-defined culture that it tends to generate a sense of obligation on the part of employees to adhere to company principles. To counter the risk of MBV leading to the coercion of people towards certain kinds of values and behavior, there are two specific recommendations, not necessarily easy to apply:

(1) It should always be legitimate for people to disagree with others or with the ruling culture, both in the initial phases of MBV and in periodical reviews. Indeed, it is important for the established conventional wisdom to be challenged. But differences of opinion need to be discussed reasonably and openly, not left to fester into problems, nor suppressed by brainwashing.

(2) Try to avoid people, at whatever level, being left with the feeling that they have no alternative but to stay in the organization and suffer its culture.

21. **The bigger a company is, the more difficult it is for MBV to function.**

Factors such as reaching consensus, communication, and monitoring compliance with values are more difficult in larger organizations. The roles of leader, driver and facilitator of change are more demanding in bigger organizations. But also the challenge of MBV is greater and the satisfactions and benefits from success are greater, too. However, there is a strong argument for creating smaller operating units out of larger organizations, for contracting out many specialist services, and for building functional networks that link operating units with each other, and with customers and suppliers.

22. **To think of a culture change program that lasts two or three years is impossible in practical terms ... it will have to be finished before the summer.**

   The change of culture is strategically important. The strategic mentality means thinking long-term. Also, if you think a culture change can ever be effectively 'finished' then you don't really understand what it is all about (Go back to the beginning of the book!).

23. **We tried this 'culture change' idea once, but it didn't work.**

   If your organization is successful the first time it tries to do anything significant, then it is unique. Sooner or later you will need to face up to a culture change, managed or enforced, so better try again. Anyway, true learning comes more from failures than successes: set up some reflection sessions on why it didn't work.

24. **Why is it that the managers who buy training for the change process send those immediately below them in the hierarchy to the courses or seminars?**

   One of the most common phrases heard on such courses is that 'all this will have to be explained to those at the top'. Of course, those at the top are considered to be responsible for everything in the organization – but this cannot be true in practical terms, and should not be used to justify defeatism or stagnation at all the lower levels. What actually happens is that those who have reached positions of responsibility believe that their success is due to a certain way of thinking and doing things, certain personal values, and that they cannot perceive the need to 'unlearn' some of these and change others in order to continue developing and improving in the future. They have arrived at their personal destination, and do not really want to go anywhere else. Another underlying motive for this reluctance to change is that they feel vulnerable because their achievement is really despite certain weaknesses or deficiencies that only they are aware of. The way to compensate for this vulnerability to criticism or competition or loss of status, is to project an image of unwavering self-confidence and conviction. Unfortunately, the stress of such powerful internal contradictions will soon put such a top manager into his nearest Intensive Care Unit after the inevitable heart attack, leaving his company with a hole at the top (but with at least an opportunity of changing for the better).

9 Postscript: An MBV Voyage – Past, Present and Future

'It is necessary to think about a new type of company with a new type of sensitive person in mind and about responsible freedom, that is to say, with maximum creative potential, because there is no creativity without freedom. And through this sensitivity, this type of person may feel the need to promote and firmly encourage moral, cultural, ethical and aesthetic values at a personal and social level, so that these values converge and do not diverge as has been the case until now, with the admirable material development of our time.'

(Pere Duran Farell, RIP, Former President of Natural Gas – Spain)

The birth of MBV: a synergy based on the authors' experiences and beliefs

MBV was born many years ago. In fact, MBV principles have been used ever since the first human attempts were made to organize work. Nonetheless, the articulation of MBV by us has been sequential and follows a series of internal debates and events based on the respective complementary experiences of the three authors.

Simon L. Dolan experienced a 'management reality shock' back in the 1970s which forced him to rethink the basic paradigms in managing people and managing organizations. He noticed the constant push of senior managers to increase firms' productivity with or without taking broader issues into consideration such as: why in fact do we work? What is the purpose of work organizations? Are money and benefits the supreme objective whereby any means justify ends? These fundamental reflections were derived following a marked experience he had while completing his doctoral studies in Minnesota. There, as a research assistant involved in studying patients at the Mayo Clinic who survived their first heart attack he discovered that over 90 per cent of these patients attributed their condition to stress at

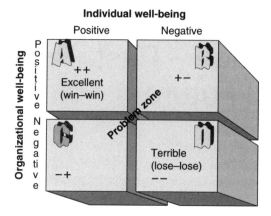

Figure 9.1 **A two-dimensional definition of well-being at work**

work. He thus realized that today we basically kill people at work, not with physical guns but rather with psychological ones such as: threats of losing ones job, pushing people to perform at a 'superman' level for prolonged periods, and so on. A new type of toxic agent comes to bear. One which has no color and no odor but causes suffering, illness and sometimes even death. The results of these experiences and observations led him to study occupational stress in a more scientific manner . . . the seeds of MBV were planted. In a book published in 1980 (*Stress Santé et Rendement au Travail*, Dolan and Arsenault, 1980), a new and rather simplistic model of corporate well-being was developed. This early MBV model defined two dimensions and is illustrated in Figure 9.1. In simple terms it was proposed that the concept of 'success' should be broadened to include both organizational and individual perspectives simultaneously. Only in quadrant A can one talk about true well-being (where people perform well while keeping their personal mental and physical health intact). Quadrant A represents a win–win situation. The most clearly problematic situation is quadrant D, where not only does the employee perform poorly, but health gets affected as well. Than there are quadrants B and C which are also problematic zones as either the individual health or the organizational health is affected.

The question that arose based on this simple bidimensional model of well-being was: can we create a culture whereby people's well-being will not be detrimented (or just minimally affected) and at the same time allow them to contribute to the organization's productivity? This is the foundation for MBV.

During his many visits to Spain, Simon Dolan had met a young physician who felt disillusion with practicing medicine and a passion for becoming an organizational consultant. The physician's name was Salvador Garcia (a co-author of this book). Intellectually, during many debates, both Dolan and Garcia realized that they had many common denominators, one of which was a chared desire to try and improve the workplace. Using medical paradigms, Garcia (consciously or unconsciously) talked about sick organizations vs healthy organizations (or sick units within the same organizations). Sick organizations were characterized by unhealthy cultures where values were not shared, where ambiguity often dominated, where people were uncooperative and where senior managers constantly use threats and manipulations to accomplish objectives. While the signs and symptoms of sick organizations were not always tangible and cannot always be easily detected, they resemble the list of symptoms that are used in medicine to diagnose sick patients.

Dolan and Garcia dreamed about creating a different culture in organizations and the result of their lengthy discussions led to the writing of a prototype book in Spanish, *Managing by Values* (Garcia and Dolan, 1997). Interesting enough, this book became an instant best-seller in McGraw-Hill's series on Management. Furthermore, CEOs of various organizations found the ideas expressed in the book intriguing, and the authors independently and jointly began a series of speeches and seminars around the world to promote the concept.

In 2002 the European Conference Board (a very prestigious thinktank of senior executives) met in Barcelona and for two days examined with the authors the concepts of MBV. This was an exhaustive and instrumental exercise which ultimately led to the conclusion that MBV seems to be a potentially sustainable and innovative management concept that will most likely be remembered as a fact and not a fad.

Bonnie Richley, our third co-author, an American-trained consultant in organizational development, came to Spain in 2004 aiming to complete a doctoral dissertation. She tried to better understand the unique experience of Mondragon (a large Spanish firm) in instilling values in their employees. Mondragon seems to be one of the most successful large-scale cooperative industrial empires in Europe and in spite of its enormous size, geographically spread locations and diverse product lines, is capable of maintaining a unique set of core values which translate into the 'Mondragon culture'. So, when Bonnie met Dolan and Garcia and learned about their MBV concept, instant interest was sparked to join the team, creating the synergy which has led to the writing of this book.

The dynamics and evolution of MBV

MBV is a dynamic concept. It grows and evolves based on the feedback of thousands of practitioners and academics who have had the opportunity to get to know its concepts. Since the first edition of an MBV book was published in 1997, numerous articles have been published and a new tri-axial concept of MBV has been developed (presented in Chapter 1). The shift from an initial bidimensional framework as explained above, into the current triaxial model, represent an important evolution. In the next couple of paragraphs we would like to share the details of this evolution into MBV's current triaxial model.

The starting point was Rockeach's (1973) theory of competence values which is characterized by distinguishing two different axes. We, on the other hand, believed that these two should be harmonized: (1) the axis of economic values (*praxis* values) or control values; and (2) the axis of emotional-creative values (*poetic* values) or development values.

Praxis means to work, to act, and also to transact, to negotiate, and from this Greek root come the terms 'prose' and 'pragmatism'. Values along this axis include for example size, technology, prestige, work effort, obedience, efficiency, and, of course, money. Due to these values, human beings have accomplished achievements as notable as the telephone, the washing machine, air conditioning and Internet, although these benefits are still not available to all. *Praxis* values are oriented towards controlling the system and people and are systematically inculcated and reinforced, like a new religion from the political, economic, and academic 'efficientist' perspective.

In contrast are *poiesis* and the *poietic* imperative. These terms come from *poieo*, an interesting verb which in Greek means to do, to make, to construct, but also to engender and to give birth to. The conjunction of the verb *poieo* can also mean to create or to innovate. The word *poíema* is derived from *poíeo* and it can mean anything from the creation of the spirit to poetry. Aristotle and Plato spoke of 'poetry' as creative activity in general. The main *poietic* competence values are imagination, freedom, tenderness, confidence, adventure, aesthetics, warmth, creativity, happiness, harmony, family, passion and mental openness. 'Autopoiesis' (Maturana, 1981) is the self-generating capacity of living systems. Hcmatopoiesis is the generative capacity of blood cells to manufacture themselves and multiply.

The generative or creative *poietic* states are associated with a special positive emotional disposition. Is it possible to have a new idea without expressing happiness? Can new ideas arise that positively transform things from depressive states? Can there be creativity in states of work-related, family or personal anxiety? Of course artistic creation can be associated with emotionally tense states or melancholic ones but we are concerned here with the relationship between positive emotional values (serenity, optimism, fantasy, etc.) and creativity in order to transform the things that surround us for the better. *Poietic* values are aimed at generating or developing and expressing more than controlling and measuring. They can also be called generative values. They refer to the health or 'emotional sustainability' of the company and together, with ethical values, correspond to a category of values of tremendous transformational potential.

The creation of companies – and of wealth – depends as much (or more) on development values than on control values. The birth and revitalisation of every business project depends on *poietic* values to generate new possibilities for action, such as imagination, freedom and enthusiasm.

Nevertheless, control values are essential for the effective and innovative application of new ideas, for the maintenance of the status quo and, in short, for the management of enterprise wealth (which is created through *poietic* values). An obsession over development by contrast, can easily turn into a poetic innocence that neglects the need to control and manage the resources within the system.

THE TRIAXIAL MODEL OF PRAXIS, ETHICAL AND POETIC VALUES

A typical error found in many companies' lists of corporate values is to name too many values, and especially to not classify them in a consistent theoretical manner (Garcia and Dolan, 1997 and 2003). Other authors dedicated to Management by Values, such as Blanchard and O'Connor (1997), do not mention this error nor do they propose a specific categorization of values.

By contrast, we propose in this book that by incorporating these values along three axes, the 'triaxial model', to try to completely systemize the different values: the praxic, poietic and ethical axes.

THE TRIPLE UTILITARIAN, INTRINSIC AND TRANSCENDENT MEANING OF WORK

The greater the value (or meaning) given by a person to the work they perform, the greater their commitment to giving the best of themselves, or by the same token, the more enthusiastically they will work. According to some authors, there are three possible levels of value or satisfaction regarding specific actions:

1. *Utilitarian or extrinsic value*: satisfaction for the person carrying out the action. This implies a reaction from one's environment which offers for example money or prestige.
2. *Intrinsic value*: satisfaction for the person carrying out the action (independently of the external effects of said action). This includes

characteristics such as learning, stimulus, fun or the opportunity of showing one's worth.

3. *Transcendent value*: satisfaction is produced in other people rather than in the person carrying out the action and as such is perceived as useful to others.

According to our concept, the completely motivating job has been triple defined as: utilitarian, intrinsic and transcendent. Being well-paid for what one does, enjoying work and feeling useful to others are a great satisfaction in life. Unfortunately, this satisfaction is seldom fully realised, though we should strive to attain it, both in terms of designing specific jobs as well as within our own mindset regarding what we want to achieve with our lives through our professional activities.

THE TRIAD OF PRAXIC, ETHICAL AND POIETIC VALUES

According to what we have termed a triaxial model (represented by three axes and being an axiological model referring to values) ethical values should be the central axis of an inverted triangle with two other important groups of values revolving on either side: praxic and poietic values. However, we recognise that the world does not revolve around the ethical imperative or creative or poietic emotional state, but rather around the pragmatic imperative of money, power and technologies which achieve efficiency.

Our experience in collecting data from many companies (in Spain, Brazil, Argentina, Canada, Holland, and more) shows that in most companies the ethical and poietic axes are generally atrophied in comparison to the praxic axis. An entirely different matter is what the majority of its members would like in terms of their own personal values or at least, what they say they would like. In practice, the values associated with knowing how to work tend to abusively outnumber the values associated with knowing how to live and even more so, to those associated with knowing how to share.

Figure 9.2 shows the typical difference found between the preferred personal values and the dominating work (day to day) values of a large telecommunication organization. The sample for this study includes over 800 senior executives.

The three groups of values are necessary, and a balance between them must be found in each organization in order to enhance the system's results for both organizational and individual well-being. The values should be aligned with the organization's mission and vision, developed in a participative manner (see Figure 9.3).

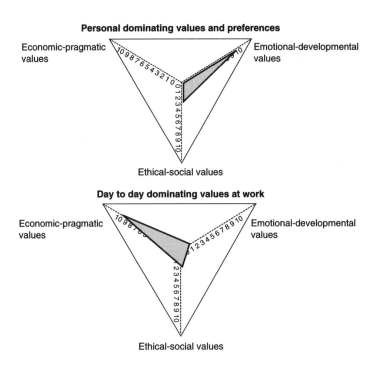

Figure 9.2 **Personal and work values**

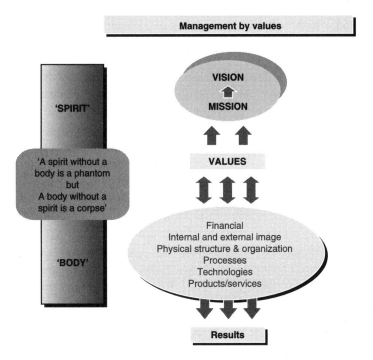

Figure 9.3 **Values, and an organization's mission and vision**

Culture, challenges and frontiers in MBV

THE POST-CONVENTIONAL MORALLY CONSCIOUS LEADER

> **An MBV classic as an impetus for culture change and synergy between the organization and the individuals:**
>
> *'A spirit without a body is a phantom',* but
>
> *'A body without a spirit is a corpse'*

On the subject of 'neurotic organizations', Kets de Vries and Miller (1984) observed that the neurotic defence mechanisms that leaders use to confront their own personal anxiety (such as negation, projection, compulsive working or paranoiac-type reactions resulting from distrust) have a cascading impact on the organization that they manage as a whole. The same phenomenon had been recently labelled by Dolan, Garcia and Diez Pinol (2005) as 'Low Corporate Self Esteem'.

By the same token, the level of evolution of leaders' moral conscience can have a significant impact on the axiological capital of the organizational system that they manage. The evolutionary psychologist Lorenz Kohlberg (1992) has proposed the existence of three sequential levels for the development of a mature moral conscience in the individual from childhood to adulthood, and these can be applied very conveniently to the notion of MBV leadership:

1. *Pre-conventional moral conscience.* The person judges what is or what is not correct from the perspective of his/her their immediate interests, of what suits or does not suit them in an egoistical and unsupportive manner. The right thing to do is seen as the option that does not lead to punishment, which follows the norms that have been laid down by authority figures and whatever brings immediate benefit. According to Kohlberg this is the moral reasoning of young children, although he affirms 'a good number of adolescents and adults still persist in using this way of thinking'.

2. *Conventional moral conscience.* When integrating into the educational system within the family and school – Business Schools included – people look at moral questions according to the rules, expectations and interests of the established social order, giving greater importance to being accepted by the reference group and believing that adapting to whatever their society considers as good to in fact be *good.*

    The clichéd manager with a conventional conscience is overwhelmed by his excessive daily commitments, and habitually thinks and acts conservatively, fearfully and authoritatively, adapting to the dominant line of thought within his/her circles of reference and social influence. In fact, he/she is not a leader exercising his/her own initiative properly speaking but a resource and values manager or administrator of the *status quo* that surrounds him/her. He/She is more of an 'order-taking leader' than an enterprising 'leader' or a visionary, transformer and creative leader at the service of an economic and socially significant project. Instead of improving his/her surroundings, he/she only dares to do what will merit general approval, instead of changing and transforming everything that reeks of corruption and endogamy; he/she directs his/her efforts to doing more of the same so that nothing actually changes.

In fact, many of the new and interesting *management* approaches these days (Codes of Ethics, ISO Standards, balance score cards, Six Sigma, and the like) are in essence no more than mere 'neo-Taylorisms'. Perhaps for that reason they are never able to transform the essence of the system, although they do go about perfecting it little by little. So little in fact, that we may be correct in thinking that both deep down and on the surface they have never really been interested in changing.

3. *Post-conventional moral conscience.* Starting from their basic cultural and educational map though going further, individuals can use their own criteria to distinguish between the norms of their surroundings and those ethical principles that may be considered universal and defensible, such as freedom, cooperation or happiness. Kohlberg affirms that this is less frequent, going on to mention examples, such as Socrates, Gandhi, or Martin Luther King. This is also related to the level of conscience associated with the most evolved democratic societies. A rare glimpse of such a leader is provided in the Reality Check box.

REALITY CHECK

Down With the King

King Jigme Singye Wangchuck of Bhutan, a tiny Himalayan kingdom, has introduced many rare innovations in his country, such as the use of a 'Gross National Happiness Index' to measure Bhutan's wealth. He is now urging his people to get rid of him; he believes that Monarchy is not the best form of government. Although he has ruled the country for 31 years, he cannot guarantee the quality of future kings and thus proposes a 34-point constitution and a two-party democratic party system.

Source: *Time*, 19 December 2005 p. 15.

Living, being alive and making a living: 'pendulum' and 'kaleidoscopic' perspectives of MBV

At present we are working on new developments in the evolution of the MBV model. These developments are proposed as a corporate guide to living, being alive and making a living in the 21st century. Because the concepts are still rudimentary they have not been addressed in detail in this book. Nonetheless, we wish to present the main thrust of the models in the following paragraphs.

In its simplest form, we may display the triaxial model in an interactive form where the instrumental praxis and poetic values swing around the axis of the ethical set. This movement is depicted in Figure 9.4. The inverted triangle symbolizes a foundation (made of ethical values) which forms the underlying structure for the system. Trust, as a value, is placed at the center of the triangle to represent a meta value.

A pendulum model of MBV can probably be labelled a utopian model. The idea here is to add the spiritual values to the ethical axis, which both swing downwards in the triangle, transforming it into a rotating pendulum in space. This represents a refinement of the model in that we have added spiritual elements (which are different from the emotional or creative ones). Trust remains paramount in the model, occupying a central role in holding the system together. Figure 9.5 depicts the ideas in this model.

Another type of model may be termed a kaleidoscopic model of MBV and takes a slightly different approach. The kaleidoscope (Greek origin: 'beautiful-form-to-see') is a contoured structure that through the use of mirrors and lenses set at different angles, creates a multiplicity of symmetrical patterns from fragments of various materials, illuminated by a source

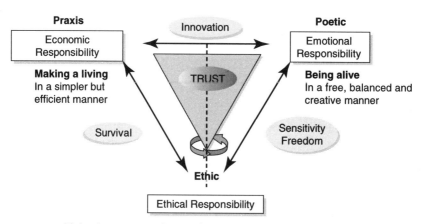

Living In a manner of respecting, sharing, generosity & equity

Figure 9.4 **An improved MBV model**

of light. The materials that produce the patterns are commonly shards or fragments of shattered stained glass. However, while these shards are the stuff of which the image is formed, the mirrors of the kaleidoscope are its heart. These mirrors or modes of reflection vary in quality, quantity and angles of placement. The better the quality of the mirror, the sharper and clearer the ultimate reflection; the greater the number of mirrors, the more diverse the shape of the image; and the narrower the angle of placement of the mirror, the greater the number of reflections produced. When directed toward an external entity and rotated, the object case, which contains the shards of various forms, colors, and densities, produces, in interaction with the mirrors, a 'beautiful form to see.' As a result, a mandala is created, a circular design of concentric forms, a 'sacred circle with a centerpoint' that is a universal image. . . .

By virtue of metaphor the idea is to place the triaxial triangular model suggested in this book in the center of the kaleidoscope. Rather that proposing an ideological model (as in Figure 9.5) where some axes of the triangle are more important than others, the relative centrality of the it will depend on the shared values of the members of the organizations and the external and internal circumstances which they experience. For example,

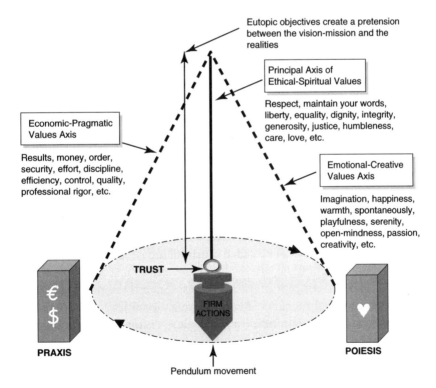

Figure 9.5 **Pendulum model of MBV**

during harsh economic times, the base of the triangle might be survival (i.e. making a living) but without neglecting the other two axes. In contrast, if the organization has an unethical leader and long-term survival in jeopardy, the principal (but not the exclusive) axis that can be viewed via the horizontal line of the kaleidoscope will be the ethical axis.

Taking a kaleidoscopic perspective on organizational transformation requires examining how changing contexts call for different kinds of collaborations which pursue new visions of institutional distinctions.

A final word to the reader

Business organizations can represent what in physics and mathematics are designated as 'chaotic' systems. In the 21st century it becomes imperative to view organizations as complex systems. Only such a view will reinforce organizational leaders to fine-tune their managerial philosophies in order to provide orderly management within a culture of organized chaos. It is on the boundary of chaos that the greatest creativity occurs (Dolan *et al.*, 2003).

In the 21st century, companies will no longer be effectively managed by rigid objectives or instructions. Their capacity for *self-organization* will be derived from how their members accept a shared set of *values*. Complexity theory deals with systems that show complex structures in time or space, often hiding simple deterministic rules. This theory holds that once these rules are found, it is possible to make effective predictions. The state of chaos that self-organizes thanks to the appearance of a 'strange attractor', leads to creativity and innovation. In this self-organized state of chaos members are not confined to narrow roles and develop their capacity for differentiation, growing toward their maximum potential contribution to the organization.

The turbulence of the international financial and labour markets, the stunning leaps made by technology and the troubling cases of terrorist and political instability are all factors that contribute to chaos and make it practically impossible to engage in clear-line planning. All that a firm can do to survive is to construct so called self-fulfilling prophecies in the arena of organizational values; the latter will channel activity and decision-making towards a heuristic concept of future success. Such is the principal task of the transformational manager. Many organizational leaders have articulated this concept by communicating a clear vision statement to their stakeholders.

If in the past an organizational consultant were to state in their final report 'Your entire corporation is in utter chaos', this would have called for a strenuous rebuilding. Today, in light of the above arguments, it would imply that this firm has an opportunity for transformation. The modern consultant who has detected the state of chaos, who has perceived the presence of transformational leadership and who senses an articulation of shared values should encourage the organization to begin this journey.

In this way, values act as organizers or 'attractors' of disorder. In a culture that cultivates or shares values of autonomy, responsibility, independence, innovation, creativity and proaction, the risk of short-term chaos is mitigated by an overall long-term sense of direction (Dolan *et al.*, 2003). A more suitable approach to manage the complexities that organizations are currently confronting is to alter their dominant culture under the principles of Management by Values (MBV). The 21st century is the MBV era.

Driving your high-performance MBV organization to success

Instilling MBV in your organization is like fitting the most modern – and safest – **wheels** on an automobile. There are of course four required in order to achieve control, stability and speed, plus a very important 'spare'. As with a car's wheels, if any one fails, the whole machine, however sophisticated, is immobilized.

FIRST WHEEL: LEGITIMIZING LEADERSHIP

- There must be leadership with the capacity to provide values and with unquestioned authority. These must be delivered consistently with the promises made, no matter what difficulties might arise.
- This leadership must be personified in one person of outstanding qualities with a global vision and the skill of developing similar qualities in their collaborators. The leader's criterion of success will be the successes achieved by his collaborators and followers throughout the organization.
- This leadership needs to have the will and skill to communicate values persuasively and from the different perspectives of the different parts of the organization, not just from the top.

SECOND WHEEL: REWARDS COMMENSURATE WITH EFFORTS

- The efforts individual employees make to comply with and sustain the operating values of the organization should be assessed and reflected inexplicit and differentiated rewards, not just financial but in personal recognition, publicly celebrated. Without the fulfillment of this justified expectation, calls for commitment are just hollow words.

THIRD WHEEL: SPECIFIC AND RELEVANT TRAINING

- Committed employees want to learn the new skills, the new knowledge and the new behaviors required to put into practice the essential values of the organization. Whatever their job, Director or office custodian, the individual employees and the organization as a whole can and will perform better.

FOURTH WHEEL: PARTICIPATION

- The finest, most worthy of values cannot be used for managing an organization unless people believe in them and apply them in their work activities and decisions. This will not happen unless people have actually participated in formulating them, and continue participating in checking how well they and the rest of the organization measure up to these values over the course of time.

THE SPARE WHEEL: HONESTY AND COURAGE

- If you have followed our arguments this far then it should hardly be necessary to re-state our belief that the most fundamental of all values are vital for the success of MBV, of culture change, of business management, of joint endeavor, in fact of anything that is worth the effort of working on.

MBV is in no way just another fancy management gadget. Managing by values is integral to entrepreneurial spirit and business leadership at the most essential level. Today, no-one can claim there is an over-supply of true entrepreneurs and true leaders among our business organizations. MBV is a conceptual tool which secures the maximum added value in the management of people and their work within companies. It addresses real human needs, it has real meaning, and it makes sense on both the individual and organizational level. It may not be the last word, because there is no such thing, but it comes pretty close.

Appendices

On-line instrument for auditing and measuring value gaps and benchmarking in your organization (the MBVsuite – www.mbvsuite.com)[1]

Ask yourself: What kind of values would you rather share with the most important people in your life? Would you prefer to control or to trust people in key relationships?

Ask yourself: To what extent are your personal values and preferences consistent with your organization, team or other reference group? What is the source of these congruencies or incongruencies? How are these gaps connected to the MBV triaxial model discussed in this book?

The MBVsuite (on-line software) is specially developed to get an instant assessment on your own personal values as well as a comparison to the values of your organization or other benchmarks (your team, your unit, etc.). MBVsuite is an essential tool (when used collectively) to transform your organization into a better place to work.

If you would like to take the on-line assessment, contact the webpage at the following address to get a free access code:

http://www.mbvsuite.com/Form.aspx

You will be asked to fill in the Account and your (valid) e-mail details before clicking on the Apply button. An e-mail containing your access code will be sent to you

| Account | TRIAL |
| Your e-mail | |

---

[1] The MBVsuite™ is a registered trademark of Gestion MDS Inc. (Montreal, Canada). The software was developed jointly by Gestion MDS Inc. (Canada) and Octrium B.V. (Holland) under a special arrangement with Simon L. Dolan, co-author of this book.

instantly. You can then proceed to do the value audit. A report and analysis of your value gaps and a short interpretation of their meaning will be sent to you.

MBVSUITE

Remember: The MBVsuite is a step-by-step procedure to assess personal values compared to selected benchmark and to generate reports. It runs on the internet (browser independent) and is provided free of charge to readers of this MBV book. We hope that you will find the evaluation instrumental.

Instrument for measuring leadership readiness for championing culture change[2]

This annex appears at the end of this book as a way of highlighting the crucial importance that the existence of legitimizing leadership has for pushing ahead the philosophy of MBV.

After you have read the book, place yourself in a position of evaluating an individual in your organization who can assume the position of this transformational leader. This can apply to a head unit, a section head, a department head or the CEO of the organization. The latter can be of utmost importance in playing one or multiple roles such as:

- A change agent (a manager working in the middle or upper level echelon of the organization).
- A change promoter (professional who advocates change from his/her own level).
- Technical agent of change (professional who has to put some level of change into practice).
- Recipient of change (members of the organisation who have to change how they think and do things).
- Facilitator or consultant who is attempting to implement change.

So, kindly circle the number that best defines your personal opinion regarding the leader you have in mind (i.e. this can include yourself if you wish to self-assess your own readiness) **who has to render legitimacy or validate change, i.e. the 'champion' or 'sponsor' of change.** When circling each of the criteria below, think about a particular person/leader in your organization that has sufficient power and authority to change the culture of the organization.

---

[2] This measure was originally developed and validated in Spanish by Salvador Garcia (© 1995). Since then it has been modified and adopted by the authors of this book.

1. Consistency and personal credibility

1 2 3 4	5 6 7 8	9 10
It is believed within the company that he/she has never shown consistency between what he/she thinks and what is really done.	There is no defined criterion in the company regarding his/her consistent and personal credibility.	It is believed within the company that his/her ideas and conduct are extremely consistent and followed by actions.

2. Readiness to question deep-seated beliefs and values held by the company

1 2 3 4	5 6 7 8	9 10
He/she is not at all prepared to put into question beliefs and values that have sustained the success of the organisation in the past.	He/she is not totally convinced about readdressing beliefs and values that the company has 'always upheld'.	He/she is wholeheart-edly in favour of unlearning beliefs and values that have sustained the success of the organisation in the past.

3. Readiness to change own beliefs and values

1 2 3 4	5 6 7 8	9 10
He/she does not beli-eve that changing how the company thinks and does things should include himself/ herself in any way.	He/she is not completely convinced that he/she should be the one to change.	He/she is fully willing to accept that change in his/her ways of thinking and doing things should begin with himself/ herself.

4. Emotional satisfaction with the current status quo

1 2 3 4	5 6 7 8	9 10
He/she is completely satisfied with the current status quo.	He/she is not completely satisfied with the current status quo.	He/she is completely dissatisfied with the current status quo.

5. Belief in own leadership ability to direct change

1 2 3 4	5 6 7 8	9 10
He/she has no faith at all in himself/herself as a leader of change.	He/she doubts in his/her ability as a leader of change.	He/she firmly believes in his/her ability as a leader of change.

6.   Level of trust in promoters of change

1 2 3 4	5 6 7 8	9 10
He/she deeply distrusts those who advocate change	He/she doesn't completely trust professionals who push for change.	He/she has enormous trust in those who advocate change

7.   Reasons for change

1 2 3 4	5 6 7 8	9 10
He/she doesn't have a clearly defined nor assimilated idea concerning the motives behind change.	He/she has a slight idea of the motives behind change but still hasn't completely assimilated them.	He/she puts forward the reasons why change is necessary clearly and passionately.

8.   Knowledge of what is to be changed

1 2 3 4	5 6 7 8	9 10
He/she has no idea of what should be changed.	He/she has a slight idea of what should be changed.	He/she is perfectly aware that certain ways of thinking and doing things have to change.

9.   Competence in the psychological aspects of change

1 2 3 4	5 6 7 8	9 10
He/she is neither aware of nor interested in assuming any responsibility in the psychological aspects of change.	He/she is unsure as to what extent his/her own competence and involvement in the psychological aspects of change are important.	He/she is convinced that successful change depends on his/her personal capacity and involvement in addressing the psychological aspects of change.

10.   Readiness to assign resources necessary for change

1 2 3 4	5 6 7 8	9 10
He/she does not believe that the change project really deserves specific personnel, time or funding resources.	He/she would like to but is unable to assign all the resources necessary for pushing the change (training, communication, consultancy, etc.).	He/she can and intends to commit to assigning all the personnel, time and funding resources that may be required for the project of change.

11. Public commitment to the project of change

1 2 3 4	5 6 7 8	9 10
He/she is unable and unwilling to show the necessary public support to firmly back the project of change.	He/she will approve the project of change but prefers to show little public support for it.	He/she is able and willing to publicly show that the project of change is among his/her professional priorities.

12. Private commitment to the project of change

1 2 3 4	5 6 7 8	9 10
He/she is unable or unwilling to comment on the importance of the project with key people and groups in private.	He/she will occasionally discuss the project but is unable or unwilling to get involved in private.	He/she is able and willing to privately meet with all the key people and groups to secure a strong commitment to change.

13. Role as motivator of change

1 2 3 4	5 6 7 8	9 10
He/she is unable or unwilling to use managerial functions to support the implementation of the programme.	He/she would prefer to facilitate the process but will not use a system of incentives and pressure.	He/she is able and unwilling to compensate whoever facilitates the process and reprimand or sanction whoever does not.

14. The follow-up of the project of change

1 2 3 4	5 6 7 8	9 10
He/she is reluctant to think that there is a need to ask for formal or informal reports on progress and problems related to the project.	He/she thinks that there is a need to ask for reports from time to time but is unwilling to establish a specific monitoring process.	He/she is convinced that there is a need to ensure that there is an accurate follow-up of all the aspects related to the project of change.

15. Awareness of personal sacrifice associated to change

1 2 3 4	5 6 7 8	9 10
He/she does not think that he/she has to make any type of sacrifice to	He/she only favors and is aware of the need for personal sacrifices to	He/she is fully aware that an enormous amount of personal

1	2	3	4	5	6	7	8	9	10
secure the success of the project of change, neither in terms of his/her personal energy nor of the risk of losing status.				comply with his/her role as leader of change.				energy has to be dedicated and that he/she may have to even risk his positioning order to champion change.	

16. Support

1	2	3	4	5	6	7	8	9	10
He/she does not get any kind of support from above (i.e. superiors or members of his/her board of directors).				He/she is only supported from above (i.e. superiors or members of the board) when changes prove successful.				He/she gets a lot of support from above (i.e. superiors or members of the board), regardless of the results of the change efforts.	

17. Capacity to "unlearn"

1	2	3	4	5	6	7	8	9	10
He/she is very rigid when it comes to listening, 'unlearning' and changing.				He/she shows a moderate capacity for 'unlearning'.				He/she shows an enormous capacity for listening, 'unlearning' and changing.	

CALCULATING YOUR SCORE AND INTERPRETATION

1st step: Add up all the scores.
2nd step: Divide by 17.
3rd step: Multiply the result by 10.

Calculate and place your final score here

Recommendations and interpretation based on your score:

If you score between 0 and 35:   Do not continue with the MBV project until another more reliable source of legitimisation is available. Your organization does not seem to be ready for the implementation of change, and an ambitious project such as MBV can only create confusion and perhaps frustration.

If you score between 36 and 75:   Move on to the initial phases in the MBV project, develop the source of legitimisation, create alliances and political support, and perhaps attempt the implementation of MBV as a pilot project (i.e. small-scale). If you gain success, broaden the legitimacy and move to a large scale MBV implementation.

Between 76 and 100:   Roll up your sleeves and get to work. Your organization seems to have a legitimizing and courageous leader who can champion the implementation of MBV. Although there's a lot of work to be done, the chances of success are high! Good luck and enjoy the process.

References

1 Managing by Values (MBV)

Argyris, C. (1971) *Management and Organizational Development*. New York: McGraw-Hill.

Dolan, S.L. and Garcia, S. (2002) 'Managing by values: cultural redesign for strategic organizational change at the dawn of the 21st century', *Journal of Management Development*, vol. 21(2), pp. 101–17.

Hirschman, A.O. (1970) *Exit, Voice and Loyalty: Responses to Decline in Firms, Organizations and States*. Cambridge Mass.: Harvard University Press.

Mintzberg, H. (1988) *Mintzberg on Management: Inside our Strange World of Organizations*. New York: Free Press.

Savater, F. (1991) *Etica para Amador*. Barcelona: Ariel.

Soto, E. Dolan, S.L. and Johansen, O. (2005) *Decisiones en contextos de incertidumbre*. ESADE-Duesto Series on Managing People. Barcelona: Deusto (Grupo Planeta).

2 Values: But What Actually Are They?

Allport, F.H. (1924) *Social Psychology*. New York: Houghton Mifflin.

Auerbach, A. and Dolan S.L. (1997) *Fundamentals of Organizational Behavior*. Scarborough: ITP Nelson.

Batstone, D. (2003) *Saving the Corporate Soul and (Who Knows?) Maybe Your Own*. San Francisco: CA: Jossey-Bass.

Dolan, S.L. (1995) 'Individual, Organizational and Social Determinants of Managerial Burnout: Theoretical and Empirical Update', in P. Perrewe (ed.), *Occupational Stress: A Handbook*. New York: Taylor & Francis, pp. 223–38.

Dolan, S.L. (2006) *Stress, Self Esteem, Health and Work*. Basingstoke: Palgrave-Macmillan.

Drucker, P.E. (1993) *Post-Capitalist Society*. New York: HarperCollins Publishers, Inc.

European Commission Communication No. 143 (1994) *Una mejor gestion mediante el analisis de valor*. Innovation Series. Luxemburg. Publication Office of the European Community.

Freeman, R.H. (1990) 'Ethics in the workplace: recent scholarship', in C. Cooper, and I. T. Robertson (eds), *International Review of Industrial and Organizational Psychology*. Chichester: J. Wiley & Sons.

Oshry, B. (1977) *Power and Position*. Boston: Power and Systems Training Inc.

Porter, M.E. (1985) *Competitive Advantage: Creating and Sustaining Superior Performance*. New York: Free Press.

Richley, B. (2006) *A Study of Mondragon Corporacion Cooperativa and its Influence as an Exemplary Business/Social Model: An Inquiry into The Diffusion of Values-Based Innovation*, unpublished doctoral dissertation, Case Western Reserve University, Cleveland, OH.

Rockeach, M. (1973) *The Nature of Human Values*. New York: Palgrave-Macmillan.

Rockeach, M. (1976) *Beliefs, Attitudes and Values: A Theory of Organization and Change*. San Francisco: Jossey-Bass.

Schein, E.H. (1988) *La cultura empresarial y el liderazgo*. Barcelona: Plaza & Janes.

Turner, R.H. and Killian, L.M. (1987) *Collective Behavior*. Englewood Cliffs: Prentice-Hall.

Zander, V. (1965) *Sociology*. New York: Roland Press.

3 Renew or Die

Dolan, S.L. and Garcia, S. (2002) 'Managing by values: cultural redesign for strategic organizational change at the dawn of the 21st century', *Journal of Management Development*, vol. 21(2), pp. 101–17.

Nadler, D., Michael Tushman, and N. Hatvany (1980) *Approaches to Managing Organizational Behavior: Models, Cases and Readings*. Boston: Little, Brown & Company, Inc.

Schein, E. (1985) *Organizational Culture and Leadership*. San Francisco: Jossey-Bass.

Schein, E. (1999) *The Corporate Culture Survival Guide: Sense and Nonsense about Culture Change*. San Francisco: Jossey-Bass.

Siegel, I. H. (2001) 'From symbols, stories and social artifacts to social architecture and individual agency: the discourse of learning and the decline of "Organizational Culture" in the "New Work Order"', AERC Proceedings (http://www.edst.educ.ubc.ca/aerc/2001/2001siegel.htm).

Watzlawick, P. (1989) *Cambio*. Barcelona: Herder.

4 The Logic of Two Different Cultures

Auerbach, A. and Dolan, S.L. (1997) *Fundamentals of Organizational Behaviour*. Scarborough, Ont: ITP Nelson.

Bennis, W. (1970) *Toward a Truly Scientific Management: The Concept of Organizational Health*. General Systems Yearbook, 7.

Dolan, S.L. and Schuler R.S. (1994) *Human Resource Management: The Canadian Dynamic*. 2nd edn. Scarborough, Ont.: ITP Nelson.

Dolan, S.L., Lamoureux, G. and Gosselin, E. (1996) *Psychologie du travail et des organisations*, 2nd edn. Montreal: Gaetan Morin.

Fayol, H. (1949) *General and Industrial Management*. London: Pitman.

Goldsmith, W. and Clutterbuck, D. (1985) *The Winning Streak*. London: Penguin.

Lewin, K. (1951) *Field Theory in Social Science: Selected Theoretical Papers*, D. Cartwright (ed.), New York: Harper & Row.

Likert, R., (1967) *The Human Organization*. New York: McGraw-Hill.

Maslow, A.H. (1943) 'A theory of human motivation', *Psychological Review*, 50, pp. 370–96.

Mayo, E. (1933) *The Human Problems of Industrial Civilization*. Cambridge, MA: Harvard University Press.

McGregor, D.M. (1957) 'The human side of enterprise: adventure in thought and action', in *Proceedings of the Fifth Anniversary Convocation of the School of Industrial Management*. Cambridge, MA: MIT Press.

Nevis, E. (1983) 'Cultural assumptions and productivity: the United States and China', *Sloan Management Review*, Spring, 24(3), pp. 17–29.

Roethlisberger, F.J. and Dickson, W.J. (1930) *Management and the Worker*. Cambridge, MA: Harvard University Press.

Savater, T. (1991) *Etica para Amador*. Barcelona: Arriel.

Taylor, F.W. (1911) *The Principles of Scientific Management*. New York: Harper.

Trist, E. (1978) 'Adapting to a changing world', in G.F. Sanderson (ed.), *Readings in Quality of Working Life*. Ottawa: Labour Canada.

Weber, M. (1946) 'Bureacracy', in H. Gerth and C.W. Mills (eds), *Max Weber: Essays in Sociology*. New York: Oxford University Press.

Weisbord, M.R. (1989) *Productive Workplaces*. San Francisco. Jossey-Bass.

5 The Relationships Between OD and MBV

Argyris, C. and Schon, D. (1978) *Organizational Learning: A Theory of Action Perspective*, Reading, Mass: Addison-Wesley.

Balkin, D., Dolan, S.L. and Forgue, K. (1997) 'Rewards for team contributions to quality', *Journal of Compensation and Benefits*, July–August.

Bennis, W. (1970) *Toward a Truly Scientific Management: The Concept of Organizational Health*. General Systems Yearbook, 7.

Cummings, T.G. and Huse, E.F. (1989) *Organization Development and Change*. Minneapolis, MN: West Publishing.

Dolan, S.L., Lamoureux, G. and Gosselin, E. (1996) *Psychologie du travail et des organisations*. Montreal: Gaetan Morin.

Dolan, S. and Schuler, R.S. (1994) *Human Resource Management: The Canadian Perspective*. Toronto: ITP Nelson.

Fayol, H. (1949) *General and Industrial Management*. London: Pitman.

Goldsmith, W. and Clutterbuck, D. (1985) *The Winning Streak*. London: Penguin.

Hackman, J.R. (1990) *Groups that Work (and Those that Don't): Creating Conditions for Effective Teamwork*. San Francisco: Jossey-Bass.

Hammer, M. and Champy, J. (1993) *Reengineering the Corporation: A Manifesto for Business Revolution*. New York: Harper Business.

Katzenbach, J.R. and Smith D.K. (1993) *The Wisdom of Teams: Creating the High Performance Organization*. Cambridge: Harvard Business Press.

Likert, R. (1967) *The Human Organization*. New York: McGraw-Hill.

Lingham, T. (2004) 'Developing a measure of conversational learning spaces in teams', doctoral dissertation, Department of Organizational Behavior, Case Western Reserve University.

Maslow, A. H. (1954) *Motivation and Personality*. New York: Harper.

Maslow, A.H. (1943) 'A theory of human motivation', *Psychological Review*, 50, pp. 370–96.

Mayo, E. (1933) *The Human Problems of Industrial Civilization*. Cambridge: Harvard University Press.

McGregor, D.M. (1957) *The Human Side of Enterprise*, Proceedings of the Fifth Anniversary Convocation of the School of Industrial Management. Cambridge, MA: MIT Press.

Mohrman, S.A., Cohen, S.G. and Mohrman, A.M. (1995) *Designing Team-Based Organizations*. San Francisco: Jossey-Bass.

Oshry, B. (1977) *Power and Position*. Power & Systems Training, Inc.

Pedler, M. (1997) *Action Learning in Practice*. Aldershot, Hampshire, England, and Brookfield, Vt., USA: Gower.

Roethlisberger, F.J. and Dickson, W.J. (1930) *Management and the Worker*. Cambridge: Harvard University Press.

Savater, T. (1991) *Etica para Amador*. Barcelona: Arriel.

Taylor, F.W. (1911) *The Principles of Scientific Management*. New York: Harper & Row.

Trist, E. (1978) 'Adapting to a changing world', in G.F. Sanderson (ed.), *Readings in Quality of Working Life*. Ottawa: Labour Canada.

Weber, M. (1946) 'Bureaucracy', in H. Gerth and C.W. Mills (eds), *Max Weber: Essays in Sociology*. New York: Oxford University Press.

Weisbord, M.R. (1989) *Productive Workplaces*. San Francisco: Jossey-Bass.

6   Creating a Culture Shift

Aprix, R.D' (1996) *Communication for Change*. San Francisco: Jossey-Bass.

Bennis, W. (1989) *On Becoming a Leader*. Reading, MA: Addison-Wesley.

Burke, W.W. (1994) *Organization Development: A Process of Learning and Changing*. Readings, Mass.: Addison-Wesley.

Burnes, T. and Stalker, G.M. (1961) *The Management of Innovation*. London: The Tavistock Institute.

Dolan, S.L. and Arsenault, A. (1980) *Stress, santé et rendement au travail*. Monograph no. 5, Université de Montreal.

Dolan, S.L. and Schuler, R.S. (1994) *Human Resource Management: The Canadian Dynamics*. Scarborough, Ont.: ITP Nelson.

Dolan, S.L., Lamoureux, G. and Gosslin, E. (1996) *Psychologie du travail et des organisations*. Montreal: Gaetan Morin.

Dolan, S.L., Garcia, S. and Diez-Pinol, M. (2005) *Estrés, autoestima y trabajo*. Madrid: McGraw-Hill.

Ford, J.F. and Ford, L.W. (1995) 'The role of conversations in producing intentional change in organizations', *Academy of Management Review*, vol. 2(3), pp. 541–70.

House, R.J. (1971) 'A path goal theory of leadership effectiveness', *Administrative Science Quarterly*, September, pp. 321–52.

Karlof, B. and Ostblom, S. (1993) *Benchmarking*. Chichister, UK: John Wiley & Sons.

Kobasa, S.C., Maddi, S.R. and Kahn, S. (1982) 'Hardiness and health: a prospective study', *Journal of Personality and Social Psychology*, 42(1), pp. 168–77.

Lingham, T., Richley, B.A. and Soler, C. (2005) 'Experiencing organizational change: types of change across levels and its critical context', ESADE Business School Working Paper Series, Barcelona, Spain. Presented at the Academy of Management Annual Conference, Managerial Education and Development Division. Honolulu, Hawaii, August 2005.

Rusbult, C.E. (1988) 'Commitment in close relationships: the investment model', in L.A. Peplau, D.O. Sears, S.E. Taylor and J.L. Friedman (eds), *Readings in Social Psychology*. Englewood Cliffs, NJ: Prentice-Hall.

Schein, E. (1987) *Process Consultation*. Reading Mass.: Addison-Wesley.

7   A Step-by-Step Approach

Balkin, D., Dolan, S.L. and Forgue, K. (1997) 'Rewards for team contributions to quality', *Journal of Compensation and Benefits*, July–August.

Cashman, E.M. and McElroy, J.C. (1991) 'Evaluating the HR function', *HR Magazine*, January, pp. 70–3.

Dolan, S.L., Belout, A. and Valle, R. (1998) 'Stakeholder approach to measure human resource effectiveness: an assessment and commentary', *Proceedings of the 6th International Conference on Human Resource Management*, Paderborn, Germany.

Dolan, S.L., Garcia, S., Martin, A. and Cuevas, J.M. (1998) 'Communicating corporate values: what can we learn from the corporate web pages?', paper presented at the 6th International Conference on Work Values and Behavior. Istambul, Turkey, 12–15 July.

Dolan, S.L. and Schuler, R.S. (1994) *Human Resource Management: The Canadian Dynamics*. Scarborough, Ont.: ITP Nelson.

Hamel, G. and Prahalad, C.K. (1995) *Compititiendo por el futuro*. Barcelona: Arriel.

Lingham, T. (2006) 'Beyond the individual: team development and change through measuring and mapping real and ideal interaction and task processes', unpublished manuscript.

Locke, E.A. and Latham, G.P. (1990) *Theory of Goal Setting and Task Performance*. Englewood Cliffs. NJ: Prentice-Hall.

Porter, M.E. (1986) *Competition in Global Industries*. Boston: Harvard Business School Press.

9   Postscript

Blanchard, K. and O'Connor, M. (1997) *Managing by Values*. San Francisco, CA: Berrett-Koehler.

Dolan, S.L. and Arsenault, A. (1980) *Stress, santé et rendement au travail.* Monographie no. 5. Montreal: Ecole de relations industrielles, Université de Montreal.

Dolan, S.L., Garcia, S. and Auerbach, A. (2003) 'Understanding and managing chaos in organizations', *International Journal of Management*, 20(1), pp. 23–36.

Dolan, S.L., Garcia, S. and Diez-Pinol, M. (2005) *Estrés, auto-estima y trabajo.* Madrid: McGraw-Hill.

Garcia, S. and Dolan, S.L. (1997) *La direccion por valores.* Madrid: McGraw-Hill.

Garcia, S. and Dolan S.L. (2003) *La direccion por valores.* 2nd edn. Madrid: McGraw-Hill.

Kets de Vries, M. and Miller, D. (1984) *The Neurotic Organization.* San Francisco: Jossey-Bass.

Kohlberg, L. (1992) *Psicologia del desarrollo moral.* Bilbao: Desclée de Brouwer.

Maturana, H.R. (1981) 'Autopoiesis', in M. Zeleny (ed.), *Autopoiesis: A Theory of the Living Organization.* North Holland: New York, pp. 21–33.

Rockeach, M. (1973) *The Nature of Human Values.* New York: Palgrave Macmillan.

Index